for Quentin Skinner
with best wishes,

Mark Phillips

D1486020

MARK PHILLIPS is a member of the Department of History at Carleton University

Francesco Guicciardini: the historian's craft is an essay in the art of reading history, designed to make the works of one of Italy's greatest historians more accessible to the modern reader. It is based on the assumption that historical writing is a literary genre and that histories are essentially narratives, an assumption natural to the Renaissance intellectuals of Guicciardini's time. Focusing on the texts themselves, particularly the *Ricordi* and the *Storia d'Italia*, the author examines the structure, language, and themes in these writings, demonstrating Guicciardini's mastery of his craft and tracing the various stages of his intellectual development. As the first full-scale examination of Guicciardini and his works, this book makes a significant contribution to Renaissance literary and historical studies.

Portrait of Francesco Guicciardini

Giuliano Bugiardini
Yale University Art Gallery
The Rabinowitz Collection, Gift of Hannah Rabinowitz

Francesco Guicciardini: The Historian's Craft

MARK PHILLIPS

University of Toronto Press
Toronto and Buffalo

Library of Congress Cataloging in Publication Data

Phillips, Mark, 1946-
Francesco Guicciardini : the historian's craft.

Bibliography: p.
1. Guicciardini, Francesco, 1483-1540. 2. Italy –
Historiography.
DG465.7.G84P48   945'.06'0924   76-056341
ISBN 0-8020-5371-8

This book has been published during the
Sesquicentennial year of the University of Toronto

To my parents,

first and best teachers

Contents

Preface

The purpose of this study is to make the works of Francesco Guicciardini more accessible to the modern reader. Through a close reading of his most important writings, the *Ricordi* and the *Storia d'Italia*, I have called attention to some of his principal preoccupations and have tried to demonstrate how his craft as a historian was shaped by these concerns. Since writing was his life-long avocation, some consideration of his minor works is a necessity; and when these are examined alongside his major achievements, a coherent pattern of development emerges which is, I believe, more satisfying than any we have had until now. This book is not, however, intended as a comprehensive study of Guicciardini's historiography, much less of his intellectual biography. Rather I have attempted to cut a slice through his works in order to stimulate further reading and fresh views.

The biographical introductions which precede the readings are intended primarily as a service to the reader who is not familiar with Guicciardini's life; in part too, they are included because biography itself is a kind of explanation, especially for a writer who was only rarely disengaged from an active public career. I have also arranged the readings in chronological sequence and lingered over minor works longer than the specialist might like in order to confirm themes found elsewhere. In all this, however, my principal concern has been with what might be called the practical criticism of historical writing, and my first purpose has been to assist the reader's entry into works which by their massiveness (in the case of the *Storia d'Italia*) or their apparent fragmentation (the *Ricordi*) may at first dismay or confuse.

My own interest in Guicciardini is that of a historian who seeks a fuller understanding of his discipline through close study of a past master. More than most historians, Guicciardini submitted himself to the discipline of narration; in writing about him I have worked on the assumption that historical writing is a literary genre and that histories, whatever else they may be, are essentially narratives. This assumption is as uncongenial to most modern historians as it was natural to Renaissance intellectuals. Thus where we talk of reading history, they wrote of reading histories; and where we are most concerned with methods of research, they stressed the means of expression. It is not surprising, therefore, that modern studies of historical thought provide few models for the student of historical narratives, while literary scholars seem largely to have avoided the special problems posed by narratives which are non-fictional. Fortunately in the case of Guicciardini we have much assistance of another sort: excellent editions, a scrupulous biography, and a masterly general study of the political and historical thought of his generation. With all these as aids, we can afford to concentrate on the texts and attempt to make ourselves attentive readers of Italy's greatest historian.

An approach that so emphasizes the reader as against the researcher has clear limitations; but I have chosen not to risk broadening the base of my enquiry at the cost of blunting its point. Without question there is still much to be learned about Guicciardini in the archives – though we should be wary of the common prejudice that unconsciously equates the difficulty of retrieving information with its historical value. More will be learned, too, from a systematic study of the historian's sources, and such a study has been promised by the most recent editor of the *Storia d'Italia*. But any method must be chosen and judged by its fruitfulness. The art of reading history has been neglected, and though few historians, Renaissance or modern, will repay such single-minded attention, those who do are our classics.

This study owes a great deal to the help of friends and teachers. To my wife Ruth, Charles Wittenberg, and John LaGrand I owe the continual stimulus of their companionship. At various stages of the work I have benefitted from the advice and encouragement of William Bouwsma, Natalie Davis, Werner Gundersheimer, John Hale, James McConica, Brady Polka, and Donald Wilcox. My scholarly debt to Felix Gilbert should be evident on every page; but I have a far deeper personal debt to him for the wisdom, patient criticism, and extraordinary generosity that he has always shown me and which I am most grateful to have an opportunity to acknowledge.

Finally, I wish to thank the Canada Council for its generous support of my studies. The book has been published with the help of a grant from the Humanities Research Council of Canada, using funds provided by the Canada Council, and with the help of the Publications Fund of University of Toronto Press.

A Note on Texts and Translations

All of Guicciardini's works, except the *Cose fiorentine, Carteggi,* and *Ricordi* which have been edited and published separately, have been cited in the standard Laterza editions (see the Selected Bibliography).

Wherever possible I have used the available English versions of these works in giving translations. This should enable the reader who cannot read the originals to locate these passages and read further. Inevitably there are times when the English does not fully render the sense or nuance of the Italian; but to have altered the standard translations in order to bring the wording closer to my own reading would have been a risky procedure, and I have preferred to let the reader decide for himself whether the interpretation is sustained.

I wish to thank the following for permission to quote their texts, complete bibliographical details of which are given in the Selected Bibliography: Casa Editrice G.C. Sansoni (*Ricordi edizione critica*); Casa Editrice Leo S. Olschki (*Cose fiorentine*); Gius. Laterza & Figli (*Dialogo e discorsi del reggimento di Firenze, Scritti politici e ricordi, Storia d'Italia,* and *Storie fiorentine*); Harper & Row, Publishers (*The History of Florence* and *Maxims and Reflections of a Renaissance Statesman*); Istituto Storico Italiano Per L'Età Moderna E Contemporanea (*Carteggi*); Macmillan Publishing Co., Inc. (*History of Italy*); Oxford University Press (*Selected Writings*), Princeton University Press (*Machiavelli and Guicciardini*); Washington Square Press (*The History of Italy* and *The History of Florence*); and Yale University Art Gallery (portrait of Guicciardini).

PART ONE

The Minor Works and the *Ricordi*

Introduction

He was a perfect representative of his class, his generation, and his profession.[1] By birth Guicciardini belonged to the small circle of leading Florentine families that made up the Medici oligarchy, and his family had long played a leading role in the political life of the city. But he was an oligarch who grew to maturity in a time when republican virtues and institutions were re-emphasized and his own view of politics would long be instinctively patrician, opposed equally to the 'tyranny' of the one and of the many. Legal training, too, smoothed his path to office in a city in which lawyers increasingly acquired important political influence.[2] Thus from his early manhood, Guicciardini was anxious for the political career that

1 The biographical material in this and in later chapters has been drawn from Roberto Ridolfi's excellent work, *The Life of Francesco Guicciardini*, trans. Cecil Grayson (New York: Knopf 1968). This replaces the earlier biography by André Otetea, *François Guichardin, sa vie publique et sa pensée politique* (Paris: Librarie Picard 1926). It seems superfluous, then, for me to cite Ridolfi at every turn, especially as my intention here is not to rewrite Guicciardini's life but only to provide a framework for the critical reading of the texts. Where I have sometimes gone further than the authority of Ridolfi's scrupulous biography is in the attempt to make some contextual connections between the texts, biography, and the wider political movements of the times.
2 On Guicciardini as a lawyer see Gino Masi, 'Il Guicciardini e la giurisprudenza del suo tempo,' in *Francesco Guicciardini nel IV centenario della morte*, Supplement No. 1 to *Rinascita* (Florence: Centro Nazionale di Studi sul Rinascimento 1940), and Paolo Rossi, *Guicciardini criminalista* (Milan: Fratelli Bocca 1943). More generally, Lauro Martines has emphasized the role of lawyers in Florentine statecraft in his *Lawyers and Statecraft in Renaissance Florence* (Princeton N.J.: Princeton University Press 1968). William Bouwsma, in a recent wide-ranging article, cites Guicciardini as an example of the influence of jurisprudence on Renaissance thought: 'Lawyers and Early Modern Culture,' *AHR* 78, 2 (April 1973), pp. 303–27.

seemed to be his by training and by birthright. Unlike his father who shied away from public responsibilities this ambitious young lawyer and patrician republican seems always to have wanted the risks and opportunities of the public life traditional to members of his class in Florence.

Guicciardini's first opportunity for office came not in the republic but in the Church. A benefice that had been held by a near relative was vacated, but Francesco's father had taken seriously the message of Savonarola and he refused to allow his son an ecclesiastical career entered into for worldly motives. Law was a better bet for a bright youth and Guicciardini was sent to study at Florence, then Ferrara, and later because Ferrara did not satisfy him, to Padua. When he came back to Florence in 1505 he was a doctor of laws and entitled to be called Messer Francesco. He began a busy practice and sought to establish his reputation in the city. And he was soon teaching law as well. Meanwhile he waited until at age thirty he would be allowed by Florentine custom to enter active political life. There were two things he could do in preparation: marry well and write. His marriage with a daughter of Alamanno Salviati linked Guicciardini to an extremely powerful political family. At the same time this marriage cemented his oligarchical allegiances because Salviati was the leader of the patrician opposition to the regime of Piero Soderini and his populist policies.

Writing too was a preparation. In a single year, 1508, Guicciardini began to compose in his notebooks three separate pieces. Perhaps the first chronologically was his family memoir, the *Memorie di famiglia*. With this work, so much in the tradition of merchant chroniclers, he began his career as an historian. The *Memorie* takes the form of seriatim biographies of prominent members of the Guicciardini family, with indications of the roles that they had played in Florence's history. Like so many family chroniclers before him, he intended his work to be read only by his family, present and future, and he instructs them not to let it be seen by strangers. His purpose, he writes, is to exalt the city and his family:

> *I want two things in this world more than any other: one is the perpetual exaltation of this city and of her liberty, and the other is the glory of our house not only in my lifetime but forever. May it please God to preserve and increase both.*[3]

---

3 Francesco Guicciardini, *Memorie di famiglia, Scritti autobiografici e rari*, ed. Roberto Palmarocchi, IX: *Opere* (Bari: Laterza 1936), p. 3: 'Desidero due cose al mondo più che alcuna altra: l'una la esaltazione perpetua di questa città e della libertà sua; l'altra la gloria di casa nostra, non solo vivendo io, ma in perpetuo. A Dio piaccia conservare e accrescere l'una e l'altra.'

These sentiments, fine, eager, traditional, aptly characterize not only the *Memorie* but the early writings as a whole. The most important among these is Guicciardini's first full-scale history, the *Storie fiorentine*, a work closely related to the family memoir.[4] For both works Guicciardini drew on the same sources, largely those he found in the family archive. In the *Memorie* Guicciardini writes that he has read 'ricordi' and especially letters, 'which have been like a mirror allowing me to know not only the things they did, but even their qualities and habits.'[5] The methods (and message) of the *Storie* would remain much the same as those of the 'Memorie,' as can be seen in numerous overlapping passages. The spirit of family pride suffuses the history too, but naturally enough less weight is now given to the family and more to the equally cherished city. There were political reasons too, in this period of revived republicanism, for not overstressing the prominence of the Guicciardini in the front ranks of the Medici oligarchy. But certainly, and for us this is the important point, it is clear that at this time Guicciardini was aware of no conflict or even disjunction between his two proclaimed loves – for Florence and her liberty and for his family. Indeed his desire to serve the Republic seemed guaranteed by his family position, just as his first history grew out of the family memoir.

The third of the works begun in 1508 is the *Ricordanze*, a rudimentary personal chronicle of transactions, obligations, and important occasions. Guicciardini begins by a summarizing his life up to 1508 and the spirit in which he records events indicates something of his mentality in this period. Of his desire to inherit the benefices of his uncle, the archdeacon of Florence and Bishop of Cortona, he writes:

> *I wanted them, not to fatten on great revenues as most other priests do, but I thought because I was young and had some letters that it might be the way to become great in the Church, and I might one day hope to become cardinal.*

But his father, as we have seen, refused:

> *because he thought the affairs of the Church were decadent. He preferred to lose great present profits and the chance of making one of his sons a great man, rather than have it on his conscience that he had made*

4 Nicolai Rubinstein, 'The *Storie fiorentine* and the *Memorie di famiglia* by Francesco Guicciardini,' *Rinascimento*, Anno Quarto, 2 (1953).
5 Guicciardini, *Memorie*, p. 3: 'le quali mi sono state specchio a conoscere non solo le cose fate da loro, ma *etiam* le qualità ed e' costumi loro.'

*one of his sons a priest out of greed for wealth or a great position.
This was his real reason and I had to accept it with as good grace as
possible.*[6]

We have the sense of a man both ambitious and matter-of-fact. He is clear
about his motives and hides nothing of his high hopes. The same tone is
struck again when he talks of his marriage, but here we see something else
as well, that reverence for his father which is apparent in several of Guicciardini's writings:

> *And yet I could then have had a much larger dowry and girls of noble
> families, and this connexion gave little pleasure to Piero my father for a
> number of reasons: Alamanno and Iacopo di Giovanni Salviati, his
> cousin, were the enemies of Piero Soderini, at that time gonfalonier for
> life, and as they were prominent in interfering in the affairs of the city,
> he feared their eventual ruin. Further, he wished me to have a larger
> dowry ... Further, as these Salviati were very rich and lived sumptu-
> ously, he feared lest their daughters were brought up in too much lux-
> ury and great style. Nevertheless I determined to take her, because at
> that time Alamanno and Iacopo were far greater in family connexions,
> wealth, reputation, and popularity than any other private citizens in
> Florence. I set great store by such things and therefore wanted their
> alliance at all costs. I also felt that five or six hundred ducats more
> would not radically alter my position ... Please God it may be for the
> health of my body and soul, and may He forgive me if I tried Piero too
> hard. Although up to now I have been glad that I made the alliance, I
> cannot help but have some doubt or scruple that I may have offended
> God, especially having such a father as mine.*[7]

6 Trans. by Margaret Grayson in Cecil Grayson ed., *Francesco Guicciardini:
   Selected Writings* (London: Oxford University Press 1965) p. 132. 'Io desideran-
   dolo non per poltroneggiarmi colla entrata grande come fanno la piú parte degli
   altri preti, ma perché mi pareva, sendo io giovane e con qualche lettera, che fussi
   uno fondamento da farmi grande nella Chiesa, e da poterne sperare di essere un
   dí cardinale.' [But his father refused] 'Parendogli che le cose della Chiesa fussino
   molto transcorse; e volle piú tosto perdere la utilità grande che era presente e la
   speranza di fare uno figliuolo gran maestro, che maculare la conscienzia sua di
   fare un figliuolo prete per cupidità di roba o di grandezza: e questa fu la vera
   cagione che lo mosse, ed io ne fui contento el meglio che io potetti.' Francesco
   Guicciardini, *Ricordanze, Scritti autobiografici e rari*, ed. Roberto Palmarocchi,
   IX: *Opere* (Bari: Laterza 1936), pp. 55-6.
7 *Selected Writings*, pp. 134-5. 'E benché io trovassi allora molto maggiore dote e
   fanciulle di nobile case, e che questo parentado non satisfacessi molto a Piero mio
   padre per piú ragione: perché detto Alamanno ed Iacopo di Giovanni Salviati suo

Young Guicciardini had great respect for his father-in-law as well, though nothing to match the piety with which he speaks of his own father. When Alamanno Salviati dies, Guicciardini expands on Salviati's public service and the public loss, but he does not fail to recognize the loss to his own fortunes as well. 'It grieved me beyond measure so that in all my life I had felt nothing to compare with it, having lost so great a father-in-law of whom I had been going to make so much capital.'[8]

Guicciardini's first political assignment was his election as the Republic's ambassador to Spain. He records that he had doubts about accepting a task that would bring little profit, disrupt his law practice, and take him away from the city. But his father persuaded him, pointing to the prestige of the court to which he was posted and the honour of having been chosen at so young an age. Having set off on his mission, Guicciardini at first sent back enthusiastic letters in which his only real complaint is the lack of communication with Florence. Above all he is full of praise for the generosity and 'umanità' of King Ferdinand who makes himself as easy to talk to as a private man.[9] Guicciardini never did lose his admiration for this clever monarch, though he soon came to see him less naively, and as his embassy dragged on and things settled into a dull routine, he still felt that it was

cugino erano inimici di Piero Soderini gonfaloniere allora a vita, e faccendosi loro innanzi e travagliandosi assai delle cose della città, dubitava che uno dí non capitassino male; e perché ancora desiderava che io avessi piú dota ... e perché ancora sendo detti Salviati molto ricchi e vivendo suntuosamente, dubitava dette fanciulle non fussino allevate con troppa pompa e suntuosità; nondimeno io mi dirizzai a volerla torre, perché allora Alamanno ed Iacopo di parentadi, ricchezza, benivolenzia e riputazione avanzavano ogni cittadino privato che fussi in Firenze ed io ero volto a queste cose assai, e per questi rispetti gli volevo a ogni modo per parenti; parendomi ancora che l'avere uno cinquecento o seicento ducati piú di dota non avessi a essere lo stato mio ... A Dio piaccia sia stata la salute dell'anima mia e del corpo, e mi perdoni se ne feci troppa importunità a Piero; che benché insino a qui io mi satisfaccia di aver fatto el parentado, pure non posso fare non abbia qualche scrupulo e dubio di non avere offeso Dio, e massime avendo uno padre della qualità che io ho.' *Ricordanze*, p. 58.
8 *Selected Writings*, p. 144. 'A me dolse incomparabilmente e tanto che a' mia dí non avevo sentito piú dolore simile a questo, avendo perduto uno tanto suocero di chi avevo da fare capitale grandissimo.' *Ricordanze*, p. 68.
9 Letter of 22 August 1512, *Carteggi*, ed. Roberto Palmarocchi, I ('Fonti per la Storia d'Italia'; Rome: Istituto Storico Italiano 1938), p. 91: 'Nè mi dispiace per altro questa legazione, se non per tanta incommodità di avere e mandare lettere, che per ogni altro conto mi piacerebbe, massime per la umanità grande di questa Re e la facilità delle audienzie, che si hanno da lui a ogni ora che l'uomo le vuole, e con tanta commodità di tempo, che non sarebbe maggiore a parlare con un uomo privato.'

only the 'umanità' of the king that made it bearable.[10] This was a chance
to learn, too, and he writes home that he is glad to have been in Spain at a
time of war when he could observe Spanish military methods and estimate
their strength.[11] Back in Italy, French power collapsed, and with it the
popular government of Soderini, and Guicciardini had to suffer the indig-
nity of hearing the news first from the triumphant Spanish king rather
than from his own government. The new Medici regime was pro-Spanish,
but Guicciardini was wise enough now to warn the Florentines against ally-
ing themselves too closely with Spain. The king, he says, will only have less
regard for you, and your display of loyalty will not bring help when you
need it except where it is required by his own simple self-interest. Here
they follow their own interests and nothing else: 'qui si va sola drieto allo
utile sansa respetto di cosa alcuna.'[12] He was learning to distrust the calculated gestures of Ferdinand and warned his father to observe the things the
king does in Italy rather than the words he says in Spain, because here one
can't trust anything but the day-to-day realities, the 'effetti che si veggono
giorno per giorno.'[13] Clearly Guicciardini was learning some lessons in political realism at the court of Spain. And in his later writings Ferdinand will
often be cited as the model of the art of political deceit, which testifies,
given the unusually wide choice of examples available, to the lasting impression the Spanish embassy left on Guicciardini.[14]

Before we leave the subject of these letters, two further observations
seem appropriate. First, it is striking, I think, how much alike his public
and private letters are in their concentrated concern with politics. His
thirst for political news from home and his assumption that his brothers
and father wanted the same kind of news from abroad speak to his own

---

10 See letter of 9 January 1513, *Carteggi* I, p. 139.
11 Letter of 14-17 December 1512, *Carteggi* I, p. 91: 'Pure ho caro di esserci stato
   in questi tempi di guerra, e avere viste le preparazioni che gli hanno fatte, el modo
   della milizia loro; che si è veduto tanto, che si può fare a dipresso giudicio quanta
   sia la potenzia di questi regni, e in modo che si potrà ragionarne.'
12 Letter of 14 December 1512 to Piero Guicciardini, *Carteggi* I, p. 133: 'Saratene
   da lui e dalli altri stimati meno, nè fate conto che il mostrare amore o fede abbi
   ne' bisogni vostri a farvi valere di lui, se non quanto lo conducessi lo interesse suo
   schietto; e chi facessi el conto altrimenti, potrebbe travarsene ingannato, perché
   qui si va sola drieto allo utile sanza respetto di cosa alcuna.'
13 Letter of 17 September 1512, *Carteggi* I, p. 102: 'È da porre mente più alle opere
   che se ne faranno di cosà, che alle parole che si dichino di qua, perché ci si vive in
   modo che non si può dare fede se non alli effetti che si veggono giorno per giorno.'
14 For Guicciardini's view of Ferdinand and of the Spanish generally see Vincent
   Luciani, 'Il Guicciardini e la Spagna,' *PMLA* LVI (1941), pp. 991-1006.

intensely political character as well as that of his family and the patriciate in general. By way of obvious contrast, nothing is said of his wife and new born child. Secondly, there is a sense of *italianità* in these letters which may relate to the experience of being abroad. The common lot of the Italians, their common abuse by the foreigners competing to dominate Italy, seem to be taken for granted. Spanish manoeuvres over the succession in Milan, for instance, evoke the protest that Spanish control there will displease everyone in Italy 'because they will not have acquired the liberty of Italy but only changed masters.'[15] Thus, 'Italy' is an important fact and a daily point of reference in these letters well in advance of the expression of an equivalent consciousness in Guicciardini's more formal writings.

Three new writings came out of the period of Guicciardini's Spanish embassy (1512-13): The *Relazione di Spagna*, the *Discorso di Logrogno*, and the first collection of *Ricordi*. The *Relazione* is a description of Spain and the Spanish. It is an ambassador's report, related to the whole class of diplomatic writings of which the *relazioni* of the Venetian ambassadors are the most famous example. In such writings ambassadors closely described the background to politics in their host countries; not only did they bring together a great deal of political, military, economic and topographical information, but they also were encouraged to provide dispassionate analyses of interests, motives, and personalities. Thus, though Guicciardini was an historian before he was ever a diplomat, there can be no doubt that the daily practice of political observation trained him for history, just as it trained Machiavelli and a generation of others to the discovery and use of a more exact and analytic language of politics.

The *Discorso di Logrogno* represents another side of Guicciardini's self-education as politician, diplomat, and historian. In this early treatise the young ambassador far from Florence occupied the enforced leisure of his embassy by analysing the best form of a constitution for the republic. The solution he adopted here, a mixed constitution with the patricians holding the balance, set the lines along which his future political ideas would continue to develop. In practical terms, what Guicciardini wanted was a senate to balance the power of the Gonfaloniere and the people. And practical terms were exactly the basis on which Guicciardini chose to support his ideas for a constitution. Disregarding theory in favour of tra-

15 Letter of 17 September 1512, *Carteggi* I, p. 102-103: 'E massime quando si intendessi che oltre al Papa, la dispiacessi a qualcuno altro di Italia, come ragionevolmente doverebbe dispiacere a tutti, perché non si sarebbe acquistata la libertà di Italia, ma arebbe mutato padrone.'

ditions specific to Florence, he states that there is no point in disputing whether government by the few or the many is better. Liberty is natural to the city and Florentines have always lived with it.[16]

The third of the works begun in this period, the *Ricordi*, would only be perfected in Guicciardini's middle years. Then these reflections would change colours, mature, and acquire an immensely larger significance. But as yet there is little in this first collection of maxims to hint at the paradoxical brilliance and ironic observation later versions would develop. What we find instead is direct statement and idealistic utterance and an absorption, almost naive, in civic and republican ideals. It is the citizen who stands at the centre of these aphorisms as later the diplomat and politician would:

> *Citizens who seek reputation in their city are praise-worthy and useful provided they seek it not by faction or usurpation but by striving to be considered good and prudent and by doing some good works for the public. Would to God that republics were full of such ambition!*[17]

The rationalization of his own ambitiousness is clear, but equally clear is the sincerity of his beliefs. He was still, quite obviously, a young man wanting to seem wise rather than an older man who really was so. His experience and his loyalties were still so simple, so local, that he seems not to speak for himself but for his class. 'Great defects and failings are inherent in popular government. Nevertheless,' he asserts with a great show of sagacity, 'wise and good citizens prefer it as a lesser evil.'[18]

16 Francesco Guicciardini, 'Dialogo di Logrogno,' *Dialogo e Discorsi del Reggimento di Firenze*, ed. Roberto Palmarocchi, VII: *Opere* (Bari: Laterza 1932), p. 223: 'Nè accade disputare quale sia migliore amministrazione o di uno o di pochi o di molti, perché la libertà è propria e naturale della città nostra. In quella sono vivuti e' passati nostri, in quella siamo nutriti noi ...' See Felix Gilbert, *Machiavelli and Guicciardini* (Princeton: 1965), p. 83ff.

17 Mario Domandi, trans. Francesco Guicciardini, *Maxims and Reflections of a Renaissance Statesman ('Ricordi')* (New York: Harper and Row 1965), p. 142. 'Quelli cittadini che appetiscono riputazione nella città, pure che non la cerchino per via di sette o di usurpazione, ma collo ingegnarsi di essere tenuti buoni e prudenti e fare qualche buona opera pel publico, sono laudabili e utili alla città: e dio volessi che le republiche fussino piene di questa ambizione.' Francesco Guicciardini, *Ricordi*, ed. Raffaele Spongano ('Autori Classici e Documenti di Lingua Pubblicati dall' Accademia della Crusca'; Florence: Sansoni 1951) Q-2, no. 2, p. 37.

18 *Maxims*, p. 143. 'Grandi difetti e disordini sono in uno vivere populare. E nondimeno e savi e buoni cittadini lo appruovono per meno male.' (*Ricordi*, Q-2, no. 5, p. 237.)

These maxims, civic, prudential, moral, are closely related to the personal record Guicciardini kept in the *Ricordanze*. But most of the flourishing tribe of notebook scribblers that Florence above all other cities seems to have nurtured would not have maintained this strict separation between record keeping and aphorism. This is a point to be noted, for the clear separation of his various early works into distinct genres may be the first indication that there is something individual and portentous in the writings of this young patrician. One has only to look back over the range of writings we have surveyed – family memoir, civic history, diplomatic report, constitutional proposal, personal chronicle, and collected maxims – to feel how rooted Guicciardini is in the traditions of his class. Scramble these works and recombine them in varying proportions and you have the *Ricordi* of Morelli, the *Zibaldone* of Giovanni Rucellai, or the *Istorie* of Cambi. But Guicciardini from the beginning has a sense of genre, of what is private and personal and what is public and political. By the time Guicciardini was thirty, then, he had tried his hand at the full range of traditional Florentine political and mercantile writings, and in the future each would enrich his work. But even now when he wrote history he did it with a clear sense of its own special requirements, an indicator of the maturity of his generation but also an early sign of his own great future.

Guicciardini was still the Florentine ambassador in Spain when at home the Soderini regime collapsed in irresolution and the Medici once more installed themselves in Florence. The new rulers were in no hurry to replace Guicciardini and so his embassy dragged on, frustrating his ambition to get home and get started. Even before leaving Spain, Guicciardini sent a flattering letter to the young Lorenzo de' Medici in an obvious attempt to ensure his own position among the new ruling group. But as he travelled home through northern Italy in the last days of 1513, having been away from Florence for twenty-three months, he found himself in unexpected mourning for his father. The young Guicciardini obviously loved and admired his father for his upright character, even while chiding him for his habit of retiring from political responsibility. Guicciardini writes:

> *His death grieved me more than I can say, just when I was returning home with a great desire to see him again, and thinking how I would enjoy his company even more than in the past, and then his death came upon me suddenly which I had never expected or thought of. I loved him more dearly than men commonly love their fathers, and I thought his age and constitution such as to allow him to live several years more. Still it pleased God to have it so, and we must accept it*

and it ought to be easier when one thinks how virtuous my father's
living and dying were, and that truly and in the opinion of all he was
such a man that we must be very proud to have been the sons of such
a father.[19]

Guicciardini's return to a politically remade Florence, the death of his
father, the attaining of political majority, and the beginning of his association with the Medici all more or less coincided, and they mark Guicciardini's political coming of age. Florence too entered a new phase, not only
because of the reinstitution of autocratic rule, but because the election
shortly thereafter of Cardinal Giovanni de' Medici as Pope Leo X tied the
politics of the city to the fortunes of an ambitious pope. For the next two
decades the history of Florence tends to merge with the history of Rome,
and Guicciardini would later come to see this connection as injurious to
his native city. In the early days of Leo's papacy, however, it must have
seemed to many Florentines that the gates of ambition had opened unex-
pectedly wide. For Guicciardini himself, here in another form was the
chance of that career in the Church that his father's scruples had denied
him; here was the widest scope in Italy, if not Europe, for a diplomat; and
here too was the possibility of exercising real power as an administrator in
the States of the Church.

All these opportunities were Guicciardini's in the next two decades and
his rise was reasonably smooth and rapid. Once back in Florence after his
Spanish embassy, Guicciardini resumed his legal work, to which he soon
added the prestige of public office. His father, Piero, had been a man
above faction, so the return of the Medici no more changed his position in
the city than their expulsion had done almost twenty years earlier. Piero
had been appointed to a place on an important commission consisting of
the principal citizens of the new regime but he did not live to enjoy it and
Francesco, his third son, took his place. This choice of a successor to the
neutral and well-liked Piero (a choice which annoyed the eldest of the
brothers, Luigi) indicates the respect Francesco Guicciardini already had in

19 *Selected Writings*, pp. 149-50. 'A me dolse tanto che io non lo potrei dire, tor-
nando io con uno desiderio grandissimo di vederlo, e mi pareva averlo a godere e
gustare più ora che mai pel passato, quando mi sopragiunse adosso la morte, fuora
di ogni mia opinione o sospetto. Amavolo piú ardentemente che non sogliono
essere amati e' padri da' figliuoli, e mi pareva ancora di età e di complessione da
vivere qualche anno; pure a Dio è piaciuto così, ed a noi è necessità accommo-
darci, e ci doverebbe essere meno difficile considerando con quanto bontà e' sia
vivuto e morto, e che in verità e secondo la opinione di tutti gli uomini e' sia
stato di qualità che noi abbiamo da gloriarci assai di essere suti figliuoli di uno tale
padre.' *Ricordanze*, pp. 72-4.

Florence. In the following year, 1515, Guicciardini was made one of the
Signori, the highest of the traditional offices of the commune. 'He had
thus reached the pinnacle of ambition,' Ridolfi comments, 'although the
Medici had meantime blunted and lowered it a good deal.'[20] The next year
Guicciardini's career advanced by a giant step: he was made Governor of
Modena by the pope and later Reggio was placed under his charge too.
Under the second Medici pope, Clement VII, Guicciardini had still higher
office as President of the Romagna and Lieutenant General of the papal
armies. He was now among the inner circle of Clement's advisors, a powerful administrator within the secular government of the States of the
Church charged with a large budget, a considerable staff of retainers, and
wide responsibilities. And these honors were also financially rewarding.
Though Guicciardini retained an interest in the family silk firm and was
even able to increase his investment from the profits of office, it is important to recognize that his considerable fortune was the reward of personal
service. Thus Francesco Guicciardini's economic position was qualitatively
different from that of his father or his brothers, though his younger brothers reaped some of the benefits since Francesco sometimes farmed out to
them the less pressing of his commissions and the eldest, Luigi, also pursued the profits of office.[21] Without perhaps being fully aware of it, Guicciardini was participating in the economic transformation of the Florentine
patriciate from a class that had been politically and financially independent
to one that owed many of its resources as well as its privileges to princely
authority. Though Guicciardini deplored this transformation, at least in
its political aspect, he recognized fully his personal economic stake in the
Medici. Unlike Francesco Vettori, for instance, Guicciardini was not
wholly dependent on the salaries of political office, but his economic position does clearly distinguish him from other patricians, even within his
own family, who could support the overthrow of the Medici in 1527 with
more enthusiasm. Thus Iacopo Guicciardini, a staunch republican and a
merchant, though less wealthy than his famous brother, clearly could afford to be more independent politically. Francesco Guicciardini had to
admit (with a grim honesty that has unfailingly been held against him) that
despite his hatred of the luxurious clergy, 'the positions I have held under

20 Ridolfi, *Life*, p. 49.
21 For the economic position of Guicciardini and his family, see Richard Goldthwaite, *Private Wealth in Renaissance Florence* (Princeton, N.J.: Princeton
   University Press 1968). Randolf Starn has studied the family context in 'Francesco Guicciardini and his Brothers,' in Anthony Molho and John Tedeschi, eds.
   Renaissance Studies in Honor of Hans Baron (Dekalb, Ill.: Northern Illinois
   University Press 1971).

several popes have forced me, for my own good, to further their interests.'
But serving Medici popes must have been politically uncomfortable as well
as rewarding. Guicciardini was not only anti-clerical but a patrician republican and the glamour of his own advancement could not have hidden from
him the truth that the patriciate was losing power and independence because of Medici rule.

Guicciardini's career reached its highest point just as papal fortunes
were about to fall to their lowest. And in part he himself was responsible.
He was one of those who urged on Pope Clement the anti-Imperial alliance
known as the League of Cognac. Perhaps the policy was the right one but
by a series of mistakes the inept commanders of the League's armies
opened the way for the Imperial troops to sack Rome. This was the great
symbolic shock of the age, and the memory of the looting and sacrilege of
the Imperial troops long remained the symbol of Italy's catastrophies.

The Medici had tied Florence to Rome and the disaster at Rome signalled rebellion in Florence. With this second expulsion of the Medici,
Guicciardini sought a cautious retirement in his villa. Honour and ties of
personal service to Clement, whom Guicciardini seems to have respected as
an individual though he could not admire him as a leader, forbade Guicciardini to take any part in the new regime. In any case, the republicans
must have looked on this man, prominently identified with the Medici,
with suspicion. Guicciardini had thrown aside the caution of his father and
now found himself, like Machiavelli under parallel but politically reversed
circumstances fifteen years earlier, reduced to the role of an interested observer. His loyalty to Florence, however, certainly ruled out any active
opposition to the new government and he was, in fact, sympathetic. The
regime was, at least at first, a predominantly oligarchical republic – Guicciardini's youthful ideal – and one in which many of his class, including his
own brothers, took a part. Ultimately, however, the possibility of a choice
disappeared. Under increasing external pressure from the pope and emperor, now reconciled, the Republic moved leftward. It cast aside its early
leader, Niccolò Capponi, a friend of Guicciardini and a moderate patrician,
and increased its own pressure on internal enemies. For Guicciardini personally this meant exile and confiscation. Of his brothers only Iacopo
remained with the republicans and he could do nothing for Francesco except buy back his books at public auction.

Guicciardini, like Machiavelli, filled his enforced leisure with writing.
The works of his middle life (the later redactions of the *Ricordi*, the *Cose
fiorentine*, and the 'Considerations on the *Discourses* of Machiavelli')
belong to this period, and they show, perhaps for the first time, his special

talent. In these writings, as we shall see, Guicciardini develops a position on historical knowledge that directly prepares the way for the *Storia d'Italia*. Here his style matures, acquiring characteristic weight and compression. And most of all, he develops a shrewd analytic insight into political behaviour that feeds on his mood of dejected irony.

Against the background of the late 1520s – unexpected disaster, estrangement, and then exile – it is hardly surprising that Guicciardini's personal writings are filled with self-accusation. We have already cited his accusation of self-interest in one of the bitterest, most ironic, and most misinterpreted of the *Ricordi*, and a similar mood dominates the other personal writings of this disjointed period. In three short exercises, the *Consolatoria*, the *Oratio Accusatoria*, and the *Oratio Defensoria*, he examines his present position and past actions. In the first of these he notes the collapse of his fortunes, but finds consolation in the fact that even in more fortunate days he did not regard his honours and riches as more than transitory. He is aware of the hatred of his compatriots and the accusations of corruption made against him, but since these are false he feels he can bear them undisturbed. Most bitter of all perhaps is the charge that he is responsible for the war which brought such disaster, but he consoles himself by saying that he is a counsellor not an astrologer or prophet and that his advice was reasonable at the time. Like another Florentine historian in the same period, Francesco Vettori, Guicciardini took refuge in a divorce between motive and event.[22] But these consolations do not appear to have been enough and Guicciardini repeated his self-examination in the *Accusatoria* and *Defensoria*. He was fond in any case of paired argument, pro and con, as a means of analysing an issue (perhaps the habit derived from his legal training) and now he imagined himself before a court. There is a curious mixture of enjoyment and misery in these twin rhetorical exercises, the one complete and the other, written in self-defence, just a fragment. The accusations of pride, pomp, and disloyalty are far too rhetorical to be taken literally and yet the exercise itself must be taken seriously, the more so as Guicciardini may actually have expected such a trial. But once again the most ringing denunciation concerns Guicciardini's real or imagined responsibility for the war: 'Because of you Rome was so cruelly sacked, with so much damage to so many of our citizens: because of you heretics control the holy places, because of you they have thrown the relics

22 Francesco Vettori, 'Sommario della storia d'Italia dal 1511 al 1527,' in *Scritti storici e politici*, ed. E. Niccolini (Bari: Laterza 1972), p. 242. 'E sebbene le azioni de' Principi non debbono essere dannate o commendate secondo li effetti sortiscono, ma secondo sono cominciate e ordinate con ragione o no ...'

to the dogs.'[23] 'You are,' he concludes modestly, 'the plague, the ruin, the
fire of the whole world ... enemy of God and of man, enemy of the
"patria" ...' Guicciardini obviously delights in the rhetoric of self-excoria-
tion and we might speculate that he left the defence (relatively) speechless
because here the matter was more sober, and ill suited the consolation he
derived from this peculiar intellectual game. And yet we must not be blind
to the misery of a man who sits down, as Guicciardini does in the 'Accusation,' to write his own biography as seen through the malign eyes of a pro-
secuting attorney. Nor should we forget, as Guicciardini's later accusers
have done (with no less rhetoric than the imaginary one) that the writings
of these years are the fruit of a particular crisis in his life. Thus the moral
judgments of De Sanctis and Symonds focus on the foreground of the
Ricordi, eliminating in a background haze the disturbances of these years.[24]
But Guicciardini's thoughts during this disjointed interregnum have a somewhat desperate character which we have no right to assume *a priori* stayed
with him when the crisis was over.

Guicciardini's active career resumed with the fall of the last Florentine
Republic in 1530. Even Guicciardini, as he makes clear in the *Ricordi*,
could admire the heroic resistance of the besieged Florentines who carried
on their battle against the combined forces of pope and emperor for almost
a year. The Republic was obstinate, but it had too many enemies and the
killing siege ended Florentine republics forever. Guicciardini himself returned to a not very attractive role as one of the chief enforcers of the new
order and incurred the lasting bitterness of the exiled republicans. As
Governor of Bologna, the chief town of the Papal State, he again exercised
great power on behalf of Clement, but he was never again so close to the
centre as in the disastrous days of the League of Cognac. With the death of
Clement in 1534, the point at which he later concludes his history, Guicciardini's gradual retirement began. The new ruler of Florence was Alessandro de' Medici who, not distracted by duties elsewhere, ruled Florence
in person and preferred other advisors perhaps less sober and more com-
pliant. The assassination in 1537 of the dissolute Alessandro by his cousin
Lorenzo (known to history and literature as Lorenzaccio, a pejorative suf-
fix earned by his one good deed) threw the Medici party into crisis. Lorenzo

23 (My trans.) *Oratio Accusatoria*, in *Scritti Autobiografici e Rari*, ed. Roberto
   Palmarocchi, IX: *Opere* (Bari: Laterza 1936), p. 242: 'Per te è andata Roma a
   sacco con tanta crudeltà, con tanta ruina universale e particulare di tanti nostri
   cittadini; per te gli eretici dominano e' luoghi santi; per te hanno gittate a' cani le
   reliquie.'
24 See Chapter II note 1.

had committed tyrannicide, or so he would explain in a humanist justification written in the illusory safety of Venice, but he failed to notify any of the partisans of liberty of this fact before he fled. As the body of Alessandro rotted in his palace, the men of the regime met in considerable panic and Guicciardini was prominent among those who ensured an orderly succession by conferring power on Cosimo. A few years earlier he had analysed in the *Ricordi* the invidious position of the king-maker. Now, contradicting what he had already written, perhaps short-sighted or just stoical in performing a necessary duty to a traditional ideal, Guicciardini attempted to impose conditions that would limit the new ruler's power. This last conservative gesture towards the fading idea of a mixed constitution was futile. The patricians, including Guicciardini himself, had given their power to the Medici. Above all, everyone was anxious for order. The real force in Italy now was with the Hapsburgs, and Cosimo made excellent use of this fact to promote himself to Grand Duke of Tuscany.

1/Within the Florentine Tradition: The *Storie Fiorentine* and the *Dialogo del Reggimento*

There is a perverse cheer in the ordinary beginnings of extraordinary talents. Although by the standard of its own times the *Storie fiorentine* is already a solid and sophisticated work, Guicciardini's first history is little more than a promise. And despite the scattered brilliance of certain passages, what is promised is still far from clear. Guicciardini was a precocious observer of the catastrophe of his times, but no one in 1510 could possibly comprehend the full impact of the invasions or foresee their outcome.[1] Nor had Guicciardini yet developed the historical ideas and scruples that distinguish his middle years. In short, he was still working within traditions that he would later revolutionize; but for us this is precisely the value of the *Storie fiorentine*. Not a work strong enough to establish its own criteria, nor one that fits precisely the program of either the humanist or *volgare* historiographical traditions, the *Storie fiorentine* is the essential link between Guicciardini's mature work and Florentine tradition. Like Machiavelli's *Florentine History*, though more imperfectly, it makes a bridge between history and chronicle, between humanist chancellors and merchant diarists; by marking precisely Guicciardini's point of departure, this history measures for us not only the height of his own achievement but the solidity of the base on which it was built. Thus it is worth reminding ourselves that by the time Guicciardini wrote, narrative history had long been a well-established and highly valued genre in his city and among members of his class and that, though its greatness is lonely and idiosyncratic, the *Storia d'Italia* represents the perfection of an old art rather than the naive beginnings of a new one.

---

1   For the Italian reaction to the invasions, see Felix Gilbert, *Machiavelli and Guicciardini*, esp. pp. 255ff.

The *Storie fiorentine* nevertheless remains a work whose quality lies in its phrases or in an occasional extended passage and is not sustained. Because the young historian had no clear sense of the historical unity of his period, the events are seen in themselves and not as an unfolding.[2] There is little creativity, skill, or subtlety in the forms of the narrative and, lacking a disciplined drill pattern, its movements are mustered without speed or authority. The author himself seems parochial and unselfconscious. And yet this naivety has its value: it allows him to be swift in his phrasing, judging and condemning by virtue of unquestioned criteria of class politics and austere morality, and permits him to express all this in direct and often colloquial speech. Twenty-five years later he will write in a way far removed from the spoken language and, just as now his quick phrases add up to a slow and sometimes clumsy narrative, he will then construct a swift and precise narrative out of elaborate, almost laboured phrases.

This young Guicciardini, parochial in outlook, is also naive about his craft. He freely and frequently admits to large gaps in his knowledge and thus impairs his credibility as a narrator. Of course, we can choose to see these 'lapses' as honest and charming, a refreshing change from the authoritativeness of the more practised historian. Too often, however, he seems ruled by his information rather than ruling it. Thus the description of a siege in the interminable struggle against Pisa may take up five or six pages, yet the attack on another minor *castello* or *fortezza*, presumably no more or less critical than the first, is passed over with apology because the historian lacks information.[3] At times, too, we may feel that the apprentice historian lacks a sophisticated sense of the difficulties inherent in historical knowledge. Summing up the life and character of Lorenzo the Magnificent, for instance, Guicciardini declares that although Lorenzo died when the

2 Nonetheless I find totally unacceptable the argument that Guicciardini's work progresses from politics to history made by Vittorio de Caprariis, *Francesco Guicciardini: dalla politica alla storia* ('Istituto Italiano per gli Studi Storici,' Bari: Laterza 1950). De Caprariis was the first to attempt to trace the full development of Guicciardini's political and historical ideas, but the value of the work, I believe, is severely limited by the inadequacies of his thesis. In order to establish this evolution from political thinker to historian which is the overriding theme of his book, De Caprariis discounts the historiographical character of the *Storie Fiorentine* and argues that it was simply a political treatise.
3 See for example Francesco Guicciardini, *Storie fiorentine dal 1378 al 1509*, ed. Roberto Palmarocchi, VI: *Opere* (Bari: Laterza 1931), p. 163: 'E così e' viniziani sendo ingrossati in quello di Pisa, si fece a Santo Regolo uno fatto di arme, e' particulari del quale non narro perché non sono in mia notizia. Lo effetto fu che e' nostri furono rotti ...'

author was just a young boy and his information could not therefore be gathered at first hand ('per quanto n'abbi ritratto non da esperienza') nevertheless he has it 'from authentic sources and from people worthy of faith; so that, unless I am deceived, what I am about to write is the pure truth.'[4] It seems doubtful that the mature Guicciardini, whose distinctive quality is his sceptical attitude towards historical truth, could ever have made such a claim to 'la pura verità.' Closer at first glance to the scrupulousness of the mature historian is Guicciardini's final judgement on Savonarola:

> For my part I am in doubt, and have no firm opinion in the matter.
> I shall reserve my judgement for a future time, if I live that long; for
> time clears up everything. But I do believe this: if he was good, we have
> seen a great prophet in our time; if he was bad, we have seen a great
> man.[5]

Leaving aside the strangeness of the justification which follows (that any man who could dissimulate prophecy for so long and fool so many people would be a great man anyway!) it is clear that Guicciardini's suspension of judgement arises out of reverence for the friar rather than respect for the opacities of history. If the 'pure truth' could be known about Lorenzo, in time it would also be revealed for Savonarola: the works of a tyrant are known immediately, but with a prophet it takes a little longer.

I do not want to paint the picture of Guicciardini's early talent too negatively. There are moments, of course, when he already shows himself to be a prudent historian careful not to judge too quickly or without evidence. He comments cautiously, for example, about a rumour that the Duke of Milan had conspired at someone's death:

> Nevertheless, I cannot vouch for the truth of that, and anyone who
> makes such a judgement does so through conjecture, not through evi-
> dence. For if such an agreement did take place, we may well believe

4 Mario Domandi, trans., Francesco Guicciardini, *The History of Florence* (New York: Harper and Row 1970), p. 70. 'Da persone e luoghi auttentichi e degni di fede, e di natura che, se io non mi inganno, ciò che io ne scriverrò sarà la pura verità.' *Storie fiorentine*, p. 73.
5 *History of Florence*, p. 148. 'Io ne sono dubio e non ci ho opinione risoluta in parte alcuna, e mi riservo, se viverò tanto, al tempo che chiarirà el tutto; ma bene conchiuggo questo, che se lui fu buono, abbiàno veduto a' tempi nostri uno grande profeta; se fu cattivo, uno uomo grandissimo.' *Storie fiorentine*, p. 159.

*that it was shrouded in secrecy. Besides, conjecture is often mislead-
ing ... Now, it may well be true; but for my part I will pass no judgement on it.*[6]

This is certainly judicious, yet such prudent doubting fails to carry authority. Having nothing to offer but his apologies, the author gives us neither
an alternative explanation for events nor a penetrating narrative, itself a
kind of explanation.

If the young historian was unsure of aspects of his craft, he could at
least feel sure of his audience. He often speaks without self-consciousness
or elaboration of 'us' or 'the city.' Naturally the young patrician did not
mean to include all the residents of Florence; he spoke of and to those
who counted. In a work in which, as in the chronicles, the mere recording
of the names of officeholders retains some importance, a list of priors vot-
ing for and against a critical measure dismisses two lower class representa-
tives as 'one of the artisans ... the other artisan.'[7] He seems entirely bound
by his *campanilismo* and his class; and it is a class both so fervently political that Guicciardini can write that when things were bad in the city the
good people were almost tired of life, and so thoroughly mercantile that
he can say axiomatically that it is in the city's interests to protect the
wealthy.[8] In short, Guicciardini lacks distance from himself and his city.
He exemplifies his subject as much as he portrays it.

Florence is always at the centre. Events elsewhere are given sudden relevance (one almost wants to say reality) by a reference to how they were
seen in the city. Italy too is present, but it is an occasional, fitful presence,
insubstantial by the standards of the later history. Even at this early stage,
Guicciardini is fully aware of how critical peace is to Italy. He is pained by

6 *History of Florence*, p. 15. 'Nondimeno a me non è manifesta la verità, e chi fa
   questo giudicio, lo fa per conietture e non per certezza, perchè se una tale cosa fu,
   è da credere si trattassi segretissimamente, e nelle conietture è molto facile lo in-
   gannarsi ... ed io per me non ne fo giudicio in parte alcuna.' *Storie fiorentine*,
   pp. 14-15.
7 *Storie fiorentine*, p. 142.
8 *Storie fiorentine*, p. 240: 'Questi modi dispiacevano tanto a' cittadini savi e che
   solevano avere autorità, che erano quasi stracchi del vivere; perché e' vedevano
   la città rovinare ed andarne alla 'ngiù cento miglia per ora.' And p. 194 (commenting on a proposal for a severe tax): 'questo modo così proposto, benché
   fussi ingiustissimo e di danno al publico, perché gli è utilità della città mante-
   nere le ricchezze, pure pensando ognuno alle commodità sua, aveva favore assai.'
   The fall of the Medici and loss of Pisa brings a similar response, p. 99: 'La mutazione dello stato nostro e la ribellione di Pisa; le più principali cose si potessino
   alterare nello essere nostro.'

the domination of the 'barbarians' and feels the cultural differences that distinguish Italians.⁹ And yet when he writes of the fall of Milan and the displeasure that people felt on seeing Italy dismembered and the Venetians strengthened, it is not clear which of the two hurts him more. But the flickering image of Italy in this history is not simply a sign of parochialism; it is also the effect of deficiencies in the narrative. The young Guicciardini lacks the skills to keep several stories alive, the very quality that gives dramatic tension to the *Storia d'Italia*. At times he tries to overcome this problem by recapitulating, 'più da alto' as he says, but there is not always time or energy for this. The result is that events of the greatest impact may be introduced inconsequentially. Thus the entry of the Spanish into the greedy business of dividing up Italian spoils, a moment of terrible importance, is mentioned obscurely, without emphasis or preparation.¹⁰

The substantial ties between the *Storie fiorentine* and Guicciardini's family chronicle, the *Memorie di famiglia*, have already been mentioned. They indicate clearly that the historian's early outlook is strongly conditioned by familial as well as communal loyalties. This was not only a matter of family pride (though no one would say that the role of the author's family is neglected in this history) but it reflects as well the chief resource available to the apprentice historian, his family archives. Since the ingredients of both works came from the same larder, it is no surprise that, despite the difference in menus, much of the food ends up tasting the same. And yet the differences in form in the end outweigh the similarities of content because the history is intended for a different audience.

The *Storie fiorentine*, it is true, begins somewhat strangely with the Ciompi rebellion. One must suspect that the true reason for this was that a Guicciardini was then *gonfaloniere*, which allows the historian to begin with this oddly undramatic first sentence: 'In the year 1378, while Luigi Guicciardini was Gonfalonier of Justice, the Ciompi rebellion took place ...'¹¹ But the author's more serious intentions reveal themselves a few pages later when he announces that he will now commence the narra-

9 *Storie fiorentine*, p. 195: 'E' milanesi che sommamente aveveno desiderata la ruina del duca Lodovico, avevano mutato volontà; e con tutto che e' modi de' franzesi non fussino stati disonesti in verso loro e non gli avessino oppressati ed in effetto non si potessino dolere della signoria loro, nondimeno sendo di natura e sangui diversi, ed inoltre non si potendo assettare a mancare di quegli piaceri ed ornamenti dava la corte, ne erano tanto infastiditi che non gli potevano comportare ...'
10 *Storie fiorentine*, pp. 214-15.
11 *History of Florence*, p. 1: 'Nel 1378 sendo gonfaloniere di giustizia Luigi di messer Piero Guicciardini successe la novità de' Ciompi.' *Storie fiorentine*, p. 1.

tive proper. From this point, he says, he will tell the story in greater depth because no one had yet written about this period.[12] What is indicated here is that Guicciardini obviously saw himself in the succession of the chancellor-historians of Florence, men like Bruni and Poggio, for whom history was a public function and a civic ornament. They had not brought the history of Florence beyond the Peace of Lodi and there Guicciardini intended to take over. Like his predecessors he saw his history as a civic monument and his own role as additive.

Such a history sites itself in the piazza and assumes a public function: to record, to celebrate, and to instruct. It provides examples, both good and bad, conserves tradition, and fosters civic pride. In all this Guicciardini is still close to the humanist school and, like Machiavelli, departs from it more in vocabulary than in intention. Nowhere is this clearer than in his account of the Pazzi plot. Guicciardini narrates the story of this conspiracy, which is also the first fully rounded event in the history, in vigorous and often colloquial language. And when reaction follows rebellion, the losers are listed, then dispatched, with swift effectiveness. Thus, in the description of the death of Montesecco the abrupt finality of the last phrase catches the cold surprise of the axe:

> *Giovan Battista da Montesecco was held prisoner for quite a few days. Upon intensive examination, he confessed that he had come to Florence on orders from his master the count, and that he had taken on the assignment of murdering Lorenzo. Nevertheless, when he heard that it was to be done in Santa Reparata, he was horrified and refused to do it. This proved to be Lorenzo's salvation, for if a man so skillful, brave, and experienced had done the job, he would surely have killed Lorenzo. His head was cut off.*[13]

But the real merit of this narrative lies, as I have indicated, in its quality of roundedness. The event is seen whole and it is as a whole that it has meaning for the author. This tumult, says Guicciardini with irony, though it nearly cost Lorenzo his life as well as his state, could be considered very

12 *Storie fiorentine*, p. 8: 'Le quale cose secondo la mia notizia narrerò più particularmente, perché da quello tempo in qua non ci è ancora chi abbi scritto istorie.'

13 *History of Florence*, p. 35. 'Giovan Batista da Montesecco fu tenuto parecchi giorni preso; esaminato diligentemente, confessò essere venuto a Firenze per commandamento del conte suo padrone ed avere preso el carico di amazzare Lorenzo; e nondimeno quando si prese lo ordine per in Santa Liperata, essergli venuto orrore rispetto al luogo, e ricusato farlo; di che nacque la salute di Lorenzo, perché se lui pigliava la cura, sendo uomo valente animoso ed esercitato, lo amazzava; fugli tagliato el capo.' *Storie fiorentine*, p. 37.

fortunate for him. The death of his brother eliminated a possible political
rival and meant that he would not have to divide his wealth. His enemies
were defeated and the populace roused itself in his cause. And as a result
of the attack he was given the extraordinary privilege of a permanent
armed guard. In effect, Lorenzo had become something very like the 'signore' of Florence and his power which hitherto had been great but suspect
now became greater still and secure. The moral is clear:

> That is the way civil discord and strife end: the one side is extermi-
> nated, the head of the other becomes lord of the city. His supporters
> and adherents, once companions, become almost subjects; the people
> and the multitude become slaves; power is passed on by inheritance,
> and very often it passes from a wise man to a madman who then
> plunges the city into the abyss.[14]

The strict logic of this passage takes us in a series of stages from the specific narrative to wider and more abstract judgements on its effects. First
we have the event and its immediate consequences. This is followed by a
judgement on its significance. Next comes a more general statement about
the type (or class) of event it is and a generalization about the effects that
may be expected from such cases. Finally we are left with an obvious hint
about the future which completes the process of abstraction, future contingencies being the furthest removed of all from past facts.

The account of the Pazzi conspiracy is effective because of both the
vigour of the telling and the lesson it teaches. This lesson gives the events
meaning and focus; retrospectively it shapes the narrative and leaves in the
mind's eye a sharper after-image. But this approach to historical writing,
which Guicciardini shares with Bruni and Machiavelli, can only work if the
narrative appears strong enough to bear the added weight of the didactic
coda. It is essential that the lesson appear intrinsic to the story and combine explanation and judgement in proper balance. If judgement over-
whelms explanation, the narrative itself loses consequence and the lesson
appears an arbitrary intervention of the historian rather than the shaping
conclusion of the event itself. Guicciardini does not always prove capable
of such clarity and balance and his immaturity as an historian is revealed in
other narratives that lack the straight lines and compelling logic of this
Pazzi episode. In the case that follows, for instance, the event seems con-

14 *History of Florence*, p. 36. 'E questo è el fine delle divisione e discordie civile: lo
   esterminio di una parte; el capo dell' altra diventa signore della citta; e' fautori ed
   aderenti sua, di compagni quasi sudditi; el popolo e lo universale ne rimane schi-
   avo; vanne lo stato per eredità e spesse volte di uno savio viene in uno pazzo, che
   poi dà l'ultimo tuffo alla città.' *Storie fiorentine*, p. 38.

trived in order to provide the appropriate model. In short, in his hurry to judge, the historian seems to have forgotten his obligation to explain.

The story takes place against the background of the revived Republic under the leadership of the Gonfaloniere, Piero Soderini, a man whose 'democratic' politics Guicciardini deplored. As a result of the rebellion of Pisa in 1494 and the mismanagement of her affairs, Florence appeared to be losing her grip on her territories. A prime chance to recover Arezzo, also in revolt, was lost, though all that was needed was to send in some troops. Guicciardini's explanation is an odd one because it includes no secular causality: 'But it was not done, either because God ordained it that way for some good purpose, or because fortune wanted to have some fun with our affairs, and have us to be considered mad and worthless.'[15] This is followed by a narrative which, logically, must be read as a fulfilment of a pattern set by providence or Fortune. Soderini proposes to send troops but is opposed by others who, 'in the usual fashion of worthless and ignorant men,' suspect oligarchical trickery and refuse.[16] Guicciardini principally blames a man named Puccini, 'an artisan who hated the leading citizens and who was a very reckless, headstrong man, with a tongue longer than his body.'[17] The young historian here as so often is a frank spokesman for his class and the same spirit of faction governs his conclusion:

> The city lost the chance to retake Arezzo easily and inexpensively.
> Now it became evident – not to everyone, but to the wise – what a
> great error Piero Soderini had committed when, out of ambition, he
> had put the entire weight of the city on the shoulders of the Colleges.[18]

Here judgement and explanation are mixed and confused. We are finally given a secular analysis of the events in an explicitly explanatory form (i.e. this happened because that happened) but we are left with the insoluble problem of connecting this condemnation of Soderini's policy with the

15 *History of Florence*, p. 206. 'Ma non si fece, o perché così fussi a qualche buono fine ordinazione di Dio, o perché la fortuna volessi ancora giuoco de' fatti nostri, e farci con nostro danno tenere pazzi e da pochi.' *Storie fiorentine*, p. 225.

16 *History of Florence*, p. 206. 'come fanno gli uomini da pochi ed ignoranti ...' *Storie fiorentine*, p. 225.

17 *History of Florence*, p. 207. 'Artefice, uomo ardito, caparbio, e che aveva più lingua che persona, ed inimico capitale de' cittadini principali.' *Storie fiorentine*, p. 226.

18 *History of Florence*, p. 207. 'E cosi si perdè la occasione di ricuperare Arezzo facilmente e con poca spesa, per cagione, come è detto, de' collegi, e si vedde non per ognuno, ma pe' più savi, quanto fussi stato lo errore di Piero Soderini in avere per ambizione messo adosso a loro tutto el pondo della città.' *Storie fiorentine*, p. 226.

previous explanation in terms of God and Fortune, from which it has been awkwardly separated by a page of narrative.

It is not the invocation of Fortune itself that catches an eye used to the assured habits of the older historian. Indeed, the role of Fortune is much expanded in the later history. (On the other hand, God is never invoked as an explanation in the later work.) But what is really unsatisfactory here is the scattering of the elements, the seeming inability of the historian to sort out the various levels of his story and to keep them bound within a logical framework. In the *Storia d'Italia* Guicciardini would have offered us Fortune and politics as alternative explanations and tied them together in a single statement. 'Either because of fortune or the ignorance of the multitude,' he might have written, 'nothing was done.' By contrast these two strands are not wound together in the early work, and when belatedly the secular motive is offered it is enmeshed in the historian's partisan condemnation of his political enemies. Thus we do not have, as in the case of the Pazzi plot, the sense that here is a satisfying pattern that clarifies the events. Rather we are made aware that all along the author has been erecting a target on which he now scores too easily. The whole point of the narrative was to provide an occasion for this condemnation. Both Guicciardini's politics and his historiographical inheritance demand that the narrative be given shape as much by the lesson it teaches as by the analysis of events that it offers. In this case the lesson is the condemnation of Soderini, but we are still left wondering about the role of providence and Fortune. Perhaps the answer is that the judgement on the Gonfaloniere had to be clouded because Soderini did after all request that troops be sent – just as the historian wished. In any case, the picture is obscured still further when, a few pages later, Arezzo falls once again into Florentine hands, and God, not Soderini, is thanked: 'But God, who has helped us several times in our extremity, did not want to allow the city to perish.'[19] And then a page later it is fate or luck that takes up the Florentine cause: 'but, as the fate of the city would have it, they chose an excellent Signoria.'[20] Little sense can be made of this kaleidoscope which both separates and confuses motive, explanation and judgement. We are left uncertain and unsatisfied, and feel that we are in the hands of an opportunistic guide.

When he wrote the *Storie fiorentine* Guicciardini had not yet given himself the long schooling in political analysis that is embodied in the political

---

19 *History of Florence*, p. 211. 'Ma quello Dio che ci ha piú volte aiutato nelle estremità, non volle lasciare perire la città.' *Storie fiorentine*, p. 230.
20 *History of Florence*, p. 211. 'Ma come volle la sorte della città, fece una signoria ottima.' *Storie fiorentine*, p. 231.

dialogues and the *Ricordi*. In the latter work especially he learned to express acute perceptions in a pin-point style and he later made good use of
this ability in the *Storia d'Italia*. If we follow a single motif from the early
history through the maxims to the late history we can see this growth concretely. In 1494 the appearance of hostile French armies on Florence's
doorstep sent Piero de' Medici rushing out to meet the French king. The
parallel with Lorenzo the Magnificent's heroic summitry at Naples a quarter
of a century earlier was not apparently lost on either the historian or Piero
himself. Unfortunately the young Medici's effort was as miserable a failure
as his father's had been a brilliant success. Guicciardini comments, 'Following the example of his father's trip to Naples – though this time the circumstances were different and the trip made little sense ...'[21] Here he is
already hinting at a whole chain of understanding which, as we shall see,
will be at the heart of his mature historicism, but it is in the *Ricordi* that
the thought foreshadowed in the *Storie fiorentine* first acquires an analytic
frame. There he issues a very stiff warning against judging by example because two cases must be alike in every little particular or the judgement
will be false.[22] The same maxim is then restated even more powerfully in
the *Storia d'Italia* and once again the occasion is the foolishness of Piero,
who, in his fear, decided precipitously to seek safety in the arms of his
enemies when he no longer hoped for it from his friends:

> *But governing oneself by examples is undoubtedly very dangerous if
> similar circumstances do not correspond, not only in general but in all
> particulars, and if things are not managed with similar judgement, and
> if, aside from all other fundamentals, one does not have similar good
> fortune on one's side.*[23]

With the inclusion here of prudence and Fortune the warning has become
more explicit and even less hopeful. Who, after all, can be so sure of his
fortune? Thus, a simple commonsense judgement, part of a wider unfavour-
able characterization, has grown into an independent maxim, only to be
transplanted again into the historical soil where it first took root.

---

21 *History of Florence*, pp. 90-1. 'E seguitando adunche, benché in diversi termini e
   poco a proposito, l'esemplo del padre ...' *Storie fiorentine*, p. 95.
22 *Ricordi*, C117.
23 *The History of Italy*, ed. and trans. Sidney Alexander (New York: Macmillan
   1969), p. 57. 'Ma è senza dubbio molto pericoloso il governarsi con gli esempli se
   non concorrono, non solo in generale ma in tutti i particolari, le medesime ragioni,
   se le cose non sono regolate con la medesima prudenza, e se, oltre a tutti gli altri
   fondamenti, non v'ha la parte sua la medesima fortuna.' Francesco Guicciardini,
   Storia d'Italia, ed. Costantino Panigada, I: *Opere* (Bari: Laterza 1929), pp. 83-4.

Guicciardini's analytic failures are related to his inability at this stage to shape the narrative as a whole. The disproportion of the text is obvious. The four decades from the Peace of Lodi to the death of Lorenzo are subjected to a rapid summary, despite the author's stated intention to narrate these events more closely. These quick pages are then followed by an outsize portrait of Lorenzo. This graceful set-piece has won much praise for the author's style. But that should not be allowed to hide the fact that the portrait by its excessive length overshadows and divides the narrative. Finally, from 1494 to 1509 – where the text ends uncompleted – the pace slows as events are described extensively. It is only at this point that Guicciardini adopts the annalistic convention of classical historians. The use of this convention by any modern historian is often condemned out of hand, though it would surely be more reasonable to evaluate its use in terms of its function. From this point of view, Guicciardini sins in this work not because he uses the annalistic device, but because he fails to use it enough. Had he applied it consistently, the disproportions of his text would have been corrected. But perhaps our attention is drawn to the annalistic pattern because the work lacks any more significant design. The dramatic events of 1494 (the invasion of Italy and the fall of the Medici) are not, as we might have expected, used to focus the history. One thing follows another but without any sense of filling out a larger story. Perhaps this should not surprise us, given the moment of composition and Guicciardini's choice of a starting point for his history. In a work that lacks an end or a significant beginning we can hardly expect a pregnant middle.

At the end of the first decade of the sixteenth century it had not yet become clear that Italy had been plunged into a new world. Thus the sense is missing in this early work of that irrevocable discontinuity with the past which gives unity to the *Storia d'Italia* and allows Guicciardini to see each incident in his long history as a moment in a terribly important story. Change, fundamental, comprehensive, and irrevocable, marks the later history. The initial entry of the French into Italy, for instance, is rightly described with awe and grave rhetoric not because of the immediate consequences of that event, which are soon undone, but because this is the first glimpse of a huge new design. Taken all together, the invasions are conceived of as a truly enormous event, incomparably the greatest of recent history; but nothing like this realization binds together the far more manageable *Storie fiorentine*.[24] Here the great crisis of the 1490s splits the

24 Guicciardini's sense of the changes the invasions brought is much more restricted in the earlier than in the later history. The *Storia d'Italia* proclaims that the invasion brought change in everything, extending beyond politics to include customs, manners, dress, and even new diseases; The *Storie fiorentine* on the other hand

book rather than launches it, and Florence rather than Italy is the subject. Within this narrower scope, Guicciardini, had he been more of a populist, might have chosen to see the re-establishment of the republic as the focus of his work. As it was, though a republican, he was in opposition to Soderini and the Great Council. Machiavelli, Soderini's henchman, might have done much better with the story of these decades. He, at least, would have expressed the tremendous importance of this experiment in civic renewal and seen 1494 as the hinge of great political changes.

It may seem as though we have been collecting evidence against Guicciardini. In a sense this is so: wanting to know how far he will travel in the next three decades, we need to fix the point at which he began. But it should not be made to seem that all the journeying was done after 1508. Already in the *Storie fiorentine* there are those moments of brilliance to which I have referred. Guicciardini's first account of the initial impact of the French invasion, for instance, though it is inferior to the later tableau in dramatic power and historical insight, is clearly pictured in the same eye. Only later would the historian have firmly in mind both the culprits and the lesson of the disaster: the cupidity of the Italian princes and the instability of all human affairs. Only later could he work out the several stages of the deepening crisis and see that the initial shock had permanently destroyed the 'instruments of peace.' And yet even in 1510 most of the motifs of the later work are already present: the disruption of equilibrium, the new methods of war, the terrifying impact of the artillery, the selfishness of rulers unregarding of the fate of their neighbours, the overthrow of regimes.

> *The French invasion, like a sudden storm, turned everything topsy turvy. The unity of Italy was broken and shattered, and gone were the care and consideration that each state used to give to common affairs. Seeing cities, duchies, and kingdoms attacked and conquered, everyone sat tight and attended only to his own affairs. No one moved, for fear that a nearby conflagration or the destruction of some nearby place might lead to the burning and destruction of one's own state.*[25]

refers only to changes in regimes and methods of warfare. Of course it must be remembered that in the early work he was very close to the subject; indeed, by the end of the book he was chronicling contemporary events.

25 *History of Florence*, p. 89. 'Ora per questa passata de' franciosi, come per una subita tempesta rivoltatasi sottosopra ogni cosa, si roppe e squarciò la unione di Italia ed el pensiero e cura che ciascuno aveva alle cose communi ... ciascuno stando sospeso comminciò attendere le sue cose proprie, né si muovere per dubitare che uno incendio vicino, una ruina di uno luogo prossimo avessi a ardere e ruinare lo stato suo.' *Storie fiorentine*, p. 93.

The explanation, with its emphasis on the common concerns of Italians, is more sentimental than analytical. Guicciardini clearly assumes here that the norm of antebellum politics was unity, 'la unione di Italia'; but when these thoughts are reformulated in the *Storia d'Italia* this idealistic notion of unity is replaced by the idea of the balance of contrary interests. The balance of power may itself be an idealization of Quattrocento politics, but even so it is clearly a more precise and analytical version of the vaguer concept of a community of interest. And yet here, as elsewhere, Guicciardini's comparatively superficial view allows him an expressiveness lost in the more ponderous and thoughtful prose of the late history. The text continues without any change of tone, but far more impressively:

> *Now wars were sudden and violent; entire kingdoms were conquered and captured in less time than it used to take to conquer a village. Sieges were successfully carried out not in months, but in days or hours. Battles were fierce and bloody. And finally, states were maintained, ruined, given, and taken away not by plans drawn up in a study, as used to be the case, but in the field, by force of arms.*[26]

Nothing that Guicciardini later wrote equals this for the clear sensation it conveys of nostalgia for more orderly times, of the shock of sudden loss of mastery that came over Italy like an attack of vertigo. Here is Guicciardini's first recognition, still dazzled, of the new era in politics. From now on the rules would be different, politics would come from the barrel of a gun, energy would prevail over reason, success would be everything. And, if I am not mistaken, Guicciardini seems to face these changes with the naive exhilaration of a young man off to war.

Guicciardini's freshness in this early history is also evident in his characterization. He often proves capable of fixing a character or situation in a few bright phrases. His description of Bernardo Rucellai, for instance, is quick and sharp. His nature, says Guicciardini, was such that he would sooner break than bend.[27] The real show-piece of character description in the *Storie fiorentine* is the extended portrait of Lorenzo the Magnificent. For purposes of comparison I have reserved discussion of this famous text

26 *History of Florence*, p. 89. 'Nacquono le guerre subite e violentissime, spacciando ed acquistando in meno tempo uno regno che prima non si faceva una villa; le espugnazione delle città velocissime e condotte a fine non in mesi ma in dì ed ore; e' fatti d'arme fierissimi e sanguinosissimi. Ed in effetto gli stati si cominciorono a conservare, a rovinare, a dare ed a torre non co' disegni e nello scrittoio come pel passato, ma alla campagna e colle arme in mano.' *Storie fiorentine*, p. 93.
27 *Storie fiorentine*, p. 85: 'di natura più tosto da rompersi che piegarsi.'

until later, but for the moment let me cite just one sentence from that rather glossy passage:

> In fact, we must conclude that under him the city was not free, even though it could not have had a better tyrant or a more pleasant one. His natural inclinations and goodness gave birth to an infinite number of good results; the exigencies of tyranny brought with them several evils ...[28]

One can only admire the balance and conciseness of this formula which in fact summarizes ten pages.

These fragments of character study display the talent of their author, but let me end this brief reading of the *Storie fiorentine* with a passage that I think more than any other exhibits Guicciardini's already distinctive touch. In a premature obituary of the Medici, Guicciardini writes that Piero's foolishness in giving up Pisa has more than cancelled out any benefits that the city has received from the Medici house. Men wondered, he says, which was the greater event, the recovery of liberty or the loss of Pisa. But the historian himself had no hesitation in choosing:

> I should like to say that the former is far more important than the latter; for it is more natural that men should seek their own freedom first, rather than dominion over others. Besides, speaking truthfully, one who is not free cannot be said to have dominion over others.[29]

Here is the path to the *Ricordi* and through them to the *Storia d'Italia* itself. This compression and stern refusal to mistake the apparent for the real we may more easily or more often identify with the older man; but here in the *Storie fiorentine* the irony is not yet cynical and the realism is still illuminated by republican idealism. These are virtues that Guicciardini would later lose.

We have seen that in 1508 when Guicciardini was writing the *Storie fiorentine* he demonstrated a range of literary activity quite typical of the traditions of Florence's merchant class. But Guicciardini, like other members

---

28 *History of Florence*, p. 76. 'Ed insomma bisogna conchiudere che sotto lui la città non fussi in libertà, nondimeno che sarebbe impossibile avessi avuto un tiranno migliore e piú piacevole; dal quale uscirono per inclinazione e bontà naturale infiniti beni, per necessità della tirannide alcuni mali ...' *Storie fiorentine*, p. 80.

29 *History of Florence*, p. 95. 'Voglio conchiudere aversi tanto piú da stimare l'una cosa che l'altra, quanto egli è piú naturale agli uomini cercare prima avere libertà in se proprio, che imperio in altri; massime che, parlando veramente, non si può dire avere imperio in altri chi non ha libertà in sè.' *Storie fiorentine*, p. 100.

of his generation, was soon subjected to political experiences which led
him away from the familial and communal interests of his earlier writings.
As the research of Felix Gilbert has made clear, the double crisis of foreign
invasion and constitutional turmoil, though its impact was somewhat delayed, turned Florentines to a self-consciously pragmatic view of politics
which centred on the question of the constitution. Guicciardini's most important political work, the *Dialogo del Reggimento* of 1521, is no exception. Guicciardini had already accumulated considerable diplomatic and
administrative experience. Adding this personal maturation to that of his
generation, he now took a more technical interest in politics and a more
political interest in history. Thus by comparison with the earlier *Discorso
di Logrogno* his constitutional discussion has become more elaborate and
more hard-headed, and in contrast to the *Storie fiorentine*, history now is
put to strictly political uses.

The *Dialogo* consists of three parts, each of which holds a different
kind of interest.[30] In the 'Proemio' Guicciardini explains his reasons for
writing a republican constitution while in the service of the Medici; this is
followed by a first book, in which the participants discuss the relative
merits of Medici government before 1494 and the popular regime that succeeded it, and decide against the popular regime; finally, the second book
takes up the question of the best form of government for Florence. Let us
examine these in reverse order. Book II is Guicciardini's major statement
of his constitutional ideas, but from the point of view of our interest in
his historiographical development it has less specific relevance than the
first half of the *Dialogo*. It should be sufficient, I think, to note that
Guicciardini here reaffirms his loyalty to the idea of the mixed constitution which he had articulated a decade earlier in the 'Discorso di Logrogno.' The fundamental institution of his proposed government was to
be a Great Council similar to that which the republic of Soderini and
Savonarola had adopted from the Venetians – and he even strengthened
the Council somewhat as compared to his earlier proposal.[31] And there was
also to be a powerful Senate, representing the aristocratic principle in government. Beyond these constitutional ideas, the second book is notable
for its pragmatic insistence on outlining ideas that suit the specific situation of Florence, rather than searching for an imaginary government such
as, he says, might exist in books like Plato's, but not in practice.[32] And, in

30 *Dialogo del reggimento di Firenze*, in *Dialogo e discorsi del reggimento di
    Firenze*, ed. R. Palmarocchi, VII: *Opere* (Bari: Laterza 1932).
31 See Gilbert, *Machiavelli and Guicciardini*, pp. 100 and 117.
32 *Dialogo*, p. 99: 'Ma io non so se a noi è a proposito el procedere così, perchè non
    parliamo per ostentazione e vanamente, ma con speranza che el parlare nostro

a related attack on idealist notions, Guicciardini's spokesman openly acknowledges the divorce between politics and morality. In speaking of certain harsh measures against the Pisans, he admits that he has not spoken as
a Christian but according to the reason of state: 'secondo la ragione e uso
degli stati.' You cannot, he says, live according to the world and not offend God, but he admonishes the other interlocutors not to speak of these
things in less select company.[33]

Turning back now to the first book of the *Dialogo*, we find Guicciardini
operating in a mode that is more familiar to us in Machiavelli, that is, he is
putting history at the service of politics. More specifically, he conducts an
historical investigation which contrasts the good and bad points of the
Medici regime and the popular government in order to prepare the ground
for the discussions of Book II. The *Dialogo* pretends to be a report of real
conversations held many years ago between Guicciardini's father and other
eminent Florentines shortly after the expulsion of Piero de' Medici and the
establishment of the new republic. The participants are Piero Guicciardini,
who in this work (as in his life) tends to remain neutral; two convinced
anti-Mediceans, Soderini and Capponi: and the man who is in general
Guicciardini's spokesman, Bernardo del Nero, a pro-Medicean who was
later to be decapitated for having knowledge of an anti-republican conspiracy which he did not reveal. Bernardo is approached by the others in his
country home and he extols to them the virtues of rural *ozio*, a classical
convention which is very soon turned to ironical use by Piero Guicciardini,
who says he is certain that there is as much prudence in this retirement as
there had been earlier in his political activity.[34] Bernardo is quickly charac-

possa ancora essere di qualche frutto ... E però non abbiamo a cercare di [nuovo]
uno governo immaginato e che sia piú facile a apparire in su' libri che in pratica,
come fu forse la republica di Platone; ma considerato la natura, la qualità, le condizioni, la inclinazione, e per strignere tutte queste cose in una parola, gli umori
della città e de' cittadini, cercare di uno governo ...'

33 *Dialogo*, p. 163: '... non ho forse parlato cristianamente, ma ho parlato secondo
la ragione ed uso degli stati, né parlerà piú cristianamente di me chi, rifiutata
questa crudeltà, consiglierà che si faccia ogni sforzo di pigliare Pisa, che non
vuole dire altro che essere causa di infiniti mali per occupare una cosa che
secondo la conscienzia non è vostra ... Il che ho voluto dire non per dare sen-
tenzia in queste difficoltà che sono grandissime, poi che chi vuole vivere totalmente secondo Dio, può mal fare di non si allontanare totalmente dal vivere del
mondo, e male si può vivere secondo el mondo sanza offendere Dio, ma per parlare secondo che ricerca la natura delle cose in verità, poi che la occasione ci ha
tirati in questo ragionamento, el quale si può comportare tra noi, ma non sarebbe
però da usarlo con altri, né dove fussino piú persone.'

34 *Dialogo*, p. 9: 'GUICCIARDINI. Deh, per lo amore di Dio, lasciati e' ragionamenti
dello ozio, nel quale siamo tutti certissimi che non manco vale la vostra prudenzia
che nelle faccende, seguitiamo el parlare di prima ...'

terized as an old man who has learned wisdom not from the books of
philosophers, but from experience, which is the true way to learn – though
he is allowed, once in a while, to quote Ficino.[35] As is fitting for such a
man, Bernardo insists on judging governments on a basis of practical efficacy rather than ideology. To know what kind of government is best or to
judge between one government and another, he says, we should not consider what type they belong to but what effects they produce: 'non dobbiamo considerare tanto di che spezie siano, quanto gli effetti loro.'[36] Thus
a good government is one that governs well and with regard to the utility
of its subjects, for government exists for the benefit of the governed and
not of the governors.[37]

The consequences of Bernardo's blunt insistence on the importance of
effects over form in government are significant and somewhat problematic.
Perhaps the most important is the obvious impetus such a view gives to historical study. If an event can only be known by its consequences, concrete
historical information is likely to be more useful than an abstract or theoretical discussion. And that, of course, is just what the first book of the
Dialogo is, an historical investigation of two types of government carried
out by means of dialogue.[38] There is just one problem, however. When the
conversations that the *Dialogo* reports were supposed to have taken place,
the popular regime was still in its early stages, so whereas the participants
can talk with great specificity about the evils of the Medici period, they
have greater difficulty when it comes to the republican period which followed. Guicciardini circumvents this problem by giving Bernardo a prophetic role, a stance which he can easily make credible since the actual compo-

35 *Dialogo*, p. 10: '... uno uomo di grande età e di singolare prudenzia, che non ha
    imparato queste cose in su'libri da' filosofi, ma con la esperienzia e con le azioni,
    che è el modo vero dello imparare.'
36 *Dialogo*, pp. 14-15: 'Perché io credo che a cognoscere quale spezie di governo sia
    piú buona o manco buona, non si consideri in sustanzia altro che gli effetti ...' And
    further: 'Dico che a volere fare giudicio tra governo e governo, non debbiamo con-
    siderare tanto di che spezie siano, quanto gli effetti loro, e dire quello essere migli-
    ore governo o manco cattivo, che fa migliori e manco cattivi effetti. Verbigrazia, se
    uno che ha lo stato violento governassi meglio e con piú utilità de' sudditi, che non
    facessi un altro che lo avessi naturale e voluntario, non diremo noi che quella città
    stessi meglio e fussi meglio governata?' But he goes on to explain that without go-
    ing into details, he would prefer a government that rules by consent to one that
    rules by violence since it is likely that the violent regime will be forced into bad acts.
37 See the preceding note, and further, *Dialogo*, p. 41: 'E' governi non furono tro-
    vati per fare onore o utile a chi ha a governare, ma per beneficio di chi ha a essere
    governato ...'
38 Historical discussions in this form were fairly common in the Renaissance, as for
    instance those of Dati, Cerretani, Pitti, and Vettori.

sition of the *Dialogo* occurred decades later, when he was in full possession of the facts. Bernardo himself justifies his pretended foresight by arguing that in history all things recur, though in different guises, and thus by examining the past one can calculate the future.[39]

Because of the fiction, common in Renaissance dialogues, that what is written down really was said on a particular occasion, Bernardo is required to make this argument for historical recurrence with special emphasis. Nevertheless we can assume that Guicciardini had no difficulty with the idea at this time, though later, as we shall see, he will change his mind. Like others, then, who look to history for political instruction, Guicciardini must accept the idea that *in its essence* history recurs: 'e ogni dì ritorna in esserre.' And so his insistence on political concreteness has led him, at least at this time, to disregard historical particularity, or rather to see it simply as a confusion to be penetrated, 'but covered and coloured in various ways so that he who does not have a very good eye doesn't recognize it and takes it to be new ...'[40]

Guicciardini's constitutional concerns undoubtedly gave added impetus to his interest in history, but threatened to subordinate historical writing to politics. The implications of this situation, which Guicciardini shares with others of his generation, have been very well described by Gilbert:

> *The problem of embodying a pragmatic view of history in accepted literary forms created the danger of a bifurcation of historical expression. On one hand, histories of a literary genre could be written according to humanist prescripts; on the other hand, the material of political history might be presented in political treatises. The result would have been that the contents of the literary histories would have no political relevance and the information about the past contained in political treatises would not be history. It is one of the crucial facts in the development of modern historiography that such a division into a rhetorically and politically oriented use of the past did not take place.*[41]

39 *Dialogo*, p. 17: 'Perché el mondo è condizionato in modo che tutto quello che è al presente è stato sotto diversi nomi in diversi tempi e diversi luoghi altre volte. E così tutto quello che è stato per el passato, parte è al presente, parte sarà in altri tempi ed ogni dì ritorna in essere, ma sotto varie coperte e vari colori, in modo che chi non ha l'occhio molto buono, lo piglia per nuovo e non lo ricognosce; ma chi ha la vista acuta e che sa applicare e distinguere caso da caso, e considerare quali siano le diversità sustanziali e quali quelle che importano manco, facilmente lo ricognosce, e co' calculi e misura delle cose passate sa calculare e misurare assai del futuro.'

40 (My trans.) *Dialogo*, p. 17: see footnote 39.

41 Gilbert, *Machiavelli and Guicciardini*, p. 236.

The *Dialogo* raises problems, too, for political theory, though they are less important to our main concern. Briefly, Guicciardini's insistence that government must be studied through its effects rather than its forms would appear to make constitutional discussions, such as the second book of the *Dialogo* less relevant. Potentially, Guicciardini might have been led to a Burkean idea of the organic growth of institutions; and there are elements of that approach in Bernardo's insistence that they talk not of the best possible form of government but of a good form of government that would be acceptable and practicable in the context of Florentine traditions. Nonetheless, in the end Guicciardini does present a constitutional proposal, and one can only assume that he thought he had resolved the inherent difficulty by giving that proposal as much concreteness as possible, since his discussion is meant simply as a proposal for Florence and not as a universal plan for good government.[42]

Finally, our 'back-to-front' examination of this work brings us to the 'Proemio.' In the three versions of this preface, Guicciardini elaborated a defence of his motives in composing the *Dialogo*. Here the principal interest lies in the evident tension Guicciardini felt between his obligations to the Medici and those to the *patria*. He attempts to reduce the seriousness of this problem in a number of ways, claiming, on the one hand, that he is simply reporting conversations that really took place which his father told him of many times, and, on the other hand, that he has written this work for his own pleasure, without any intention of publication. In either case he does not want it thought that he is ungrateful to the Medici for the honours they have given him, nor should it be inferred that he is against them in any way.[43] His 'true' political allegiance in all this is difficult to fix. In the beginning he speaks as though he is simply carrying out an abstract exercise which he no more expects to see put into effect than did Plato the *Republic*, a position which clearly is in contradiction to the pragmatism of the dialogue itself. A little later, however, he holds up the example of the government of Piero Soderini as one which approached his idea of good government and he states that his writing may still have some practical use, since, although the Medici are very strong because of the power of the pope and therefore Florence appears to have lost her liberty, nonetheless, human affairs are full of accidents and popular government may

42 For a contrary view cf. De Caprariis pp. 75 and 81.
43 *Dialogo*, p. 5: 'Alle quali obligazione non pare che si convenga nutrire pensieri contrari allo stato della casa loro; perché dallo scrivere mio, massime fatto per mio piacere e recreazione né con intenzione di publicarlo, non si può né debbe inferirne che io abbia animo alieno dalla grandezza loro, né che la loro autorità mi dispiaccia.'

yet return.[44] In the first two versions his position is perhaps a little clearer. Here, in a very interesting justification, he adds to his other thoughts the observation that his service to the Medici does not indicate that he is naturally inclined to favour tyranny ('governi stretti') because his service has always been to the pontificate and not to the regime in Florence.[45] Finally, in all three versions he concludes that his obligations to Florence must exceed those to the Medici and declares that above all he wants a government of honest liberty, well composed and well ordered.[46]

The *Dialogo* is an assured work, mature in style and in thought. And yet we have found it to be problematic in a number of ways, posing real tensions or dilemmas in terms of biography, historiography, and political ideas. For the resolution, or permanence, of these problems we must of course turn to other works, especially to the *Ricordi*, in which Guicciardini sifted through these same concerns over two decades. The *Dialogo* remains, however, significant evidence of three important aspects of Guicciardini's mind at this time: his developing concern with political history, now concentrated on the constitutional question and apparently quite removed from its earlier ambience of family and civic pride; his desire to lay bare the fundamentals of government without reference to anything but utility and practical efficacy; and finally, his sense of being caught by crossed allegiances to his patrons and his *patria*. All these concerns will reappear in the *Ricordi*.

44 *Dialogo*, pp. 3-4: 'Se bene per la autorità che hanno e' Medici in Firenze, e per la potenzia grandissima del pontefice paia perduta la libertà di quella, nondimeno per gli accidenti che tuttodì portono seco le cose umane, può a ogn'ora nascere, che così come in uno tratto dallo stato populare la venne allo stato di uno, possi ancora con la medesima facilità ritornare dallo stato di uno alla sua prima libertà.'

45 For these two earlier versions of the 'Proemio' see Francesco Guicciardini, *Opere*, ed. Emanuella Lugnani Scarano, I (Turin: UTET 1970), p. 483: 'E che le faccende in che ho servito e' Medici, che dependono dal pontificato, non dallo stato di Firenze, non fanno indizio che naturalmente e' governi stretti mi piaccino, né la qualità del vivere mio che è stato sempre modestissimo e incorruttibile, debbe apresso a chi lo considera torre fede che in me non possi essere animo quale si conviene a uno cittadino moderato e amatore della patria ...'

46 *Dialogo*, p. 6: 'Perché quando si proponessi uno modo di vivere con la libertà onesta, bene composta e bene ordinata, non potrei essere notato se dicessi piacermi sopra tutti gli altri; essendo notissimo quello che scrivono e' filosofi delle obligazione che s'hanno con la patria, e di quelle che s'hanno con gli altri; e che essendo nel vivere civile distinti e' gradi de' benefici e degli offici degli uomini, non si può chiamare ingratitudine el tenere più conto del debito ed obligazione che sono maggiore che delle minore.'

2 / The *Ricordi:*
The Development of
Structure and Language

Fragmentary, contradictory, exploratory, the *Ricordi* lack the coherence and accessibility we find in the public narratives of Guicciardini's successive histories. This brief work, so difficult to grasp by any single handle, has alternately been regarded as the master key to Guicciardini's mind or as a minor chapter among his writings.[1] Both viewpoints have some truth because in a sense the *Ricordi* is not so much a single work brought to perfection in a series of stages, as notes towards a work continually in progress. One might say that Guicciardini was labouring on two projects simultaneously: the first a distinguished collection of maxims having its roots in the Florentine tradition of family chronicles; the other, whatever it was originally intended to be, becomes the *Storia d'Italia.* It was not just

---

1 The moral judgements of De Sanctis and Symonds were, of course, based primarily on the *Ricordi*, which De Sanctis called 'the corruption of Italy, codified and exalted to a rule of life' (Francesco De Sanctis, *Storia della letteratura italiana*, II [Naples 1873] p. 118). Among recent interpretations, De Caprariis reacts against the tendency dating from Canestrini's publication of the *Opere Inedite* (Florence 1857-1867) to exaggerate the place of the *Ricordi*. He goes to the other extreme of downgrading their intellectual achievement as well as their value to the student of Guicciardini. Emanuella Lugnani Scarano reacts in turn against De Caprariis ('Le redazioni dei *Ricordi* e la storia del pensiero guicciardiniano dal 1512 al 1530,' *Giornale Storico della Letteratura Italiana*, CXLVII, 1970). Earlier, Fueter had minimized the value of the work, which he saw as brief notes thrown down quite carelessly, while emphasizing the overwhelming pre-eminence of the *Storia* (*L'Histoire de la storiographie moderne* [Paris: Alean 1914]). Fubini criticizes Fueter by demonstrating on a stylistic level the extreme care which went into the successive stages of the work's revision (Mario Fubini, 'Le quattro redazioni dei *Ricordi* del Guicciardini,' in *Studi sulla letteratura del Rinascimento* [Florence: Sansoni 1948]). For further discussion of the interpretation of the *Ricordi*, especially by earlier authors, in almost endless detail see V. Luciani, *Francesco Guicciardini and his European Reputation* (New York: Carl Otto 1936).

opportunism (or cannibalism, as Ridolfi calls it) that led Guicciardini a decade later to set so many of these fragments into the concrete realities of
the *Storia*. Despite the lapse in time between the two works, they bear the
marks of an intimate relationship, an almost perfect complementarity from
the beginning. These complexities must be borne in mind, since to ignore
them means to misjudge the character and tone of the work. The *Ricordi*
is neither an artless confession of cynicism and self-interest confided to a
private notebook nor a shorthand version of the *Storia d'Italia*; rather it is,
among other things, an indispensible record of the crystallization of Guicciardini's insights into politics and history and, more particularly, a powerful analysis of the uses and limits of political prudence.

The standing temptation for the reader of the *Ricordi* is to go too
quickly to the heart of the matter, be it autobiographical or political. Guicciardini is always a reticent author, one who must be approached indirectly
through his practice rather than directly by way of pronouncement; and,
though at first the explicit and concentrated formulations of the *Ricordi*
seem an invaluable exception to this rule, the rule holds. Trusting, as Law-
rence says, not the teller but the tale, let us begin our reading of the
Ricordi where his harshest critics began, with the self-revelation of the
author. We begin there not to rescue Guicciardini from their condemnation, for that is by now a remote though interesting issue, but to begin to
investigate the coherence of the work. In a fragmentary collection such as
this it is the voice of the author which holds together the disparate elements. But the *Ricordi* is not table talk and the voice we hear is not naive
but self-created. By insisting on the artfulness of this voice and of the
author's persona we not only distinguish our reading from that of Guicciardini's nineteenth-century critics but, more important, we distinguish
the author himself from his predecessors among the 'marchands écrivains'
of Florence.[2]

The *Ricordi* grows out of a popular genre in which old men, like Gino di
Neri Capponi, feeling themselves about to die, gathered up their thoughts,

2 'Ricordi' were by nature miscellaneous and could include a wide variety of elements, but the overall range of concern remains recognizable, as does the nature
   of their authority. It would, of course, be possible also to compare Guicciardini's
   Ricordi with more literary models of fragmentary meditation such as those of
   Marcus Aurelius, Erasmus, or Pascal. My feeling is that this would distort Guicciardini's intentions, however, and that his work should be seen as an organic out-
   growth of a native tradition. On this type of literature, see Christian Bec, *Les marchands écrivains* (Paris: Mouton 1967); and Claudio Varese *Storia e politica nella
   prosa del Quattrocento* (Turin: Einaudi 1961). See also Renzo Sereno, 'The
   "Ricordi" of Gino di Neri Capponi,' *American Political Science Review*, 52
   (1958), pp. 1118-22.

much as they gathered up their worldly possessions, for the enrichment of their sons. A man writing in such circumstances writes naively; he has neither time nor need to create a personality that will lend drama or authority to what he has to say. Patriarchy and the death-bed take care of that. Guicciardini, on the other hand, begins young; indeed many of his early *ricordi* have a stilted style that is the consequence of a man in his late twenties straining for the appearance of the wisdom of years. Moreover, he has the time and application to elevate the exercise into an art, albeit a minor one. The careful revisions he gave the five redactions of this work is evidence enough of that.[3] More specifically, we can discover, as we trace his thoughts from revision to revision, the creation of a speaking voice capable of sustaining our interest and commanding our respect. This voice remains impersonal and uncharacterized in most of the fragments, yet it is also capable of a degree of self-consciousness and self-dramatization far beyond the simple need to tell a few homely truths.

The fact is, of course, that Guicciardini's truths are far from homely; many of them are downright ugly. He cannot draw on the naive resources of a grandfather's authority because no conventional grandfather, even in so political and so cynical a place as Florence, would think of uttering the thoughts that Guicciardini polishes so carefully. The authority of the *Ricordi* is altogether different; it derives from Guicciardini's growing poli-

3 These five versions are generally identified as Q1 and Q2, A,B, and C. Redactions Q1 and Q2 are based on two notebooks of 1512 containing twelve and twenty-nine maxims respectively. The new autograph manuscript is that of 1528, called now the B version, which contained 181 'ricordi.' Guicciardini wrote at the head of this manuscript, however, that most of these had been written before 1525 in other notebooks and he was recopying them at this time. He then added ten more maxims in April of 1528. Finally, there is a manuscript of 1530, which is now identified as the C version, or final redaction, which contains 221 'ricordi.' Thus Q1 and Q2, B, and C can be definitely dated as being written in 1512, 1528 and 1530 respectively. However, a fifth version, called the A version, has been painstakingly reconstructed by Raffaele Spongano from later printed texts, and it is claimed that this represents the lost notebook from which Guicciardini copied the B text in 1525. I will discuss further the complicated problem of the A text below (and see also the introductions to Spongano's critical edition and to Domandi's translation). For the sake of ease and clarity, I will generally refer to Q, B, and C as the early, middle and late texts. Since the C version is the final redaction I will omit the letter prefix in my citations from this series. Because of the difficulties over dating and its supposititious character the A text will always be specifically identified. The reader will note that I have followed the usual practice of citing the available English translation in the text itself and of including the original in the footnote. There will be times, however, when inevitably the English does not carry the full sense or nuance of the original and in those cases I refer the reader to the Italian wording.

tical experience, his precision as a dissector of the human condition, and his utterly lucid style. Were it not for the commanding voice of the teacher and the analyst, the reader would not experience the thematic disunity of the *Ricordi* as a cumulative experience. It is important to remember in the following pages that, while for the purposes of analysis it is often convenient for us to take up fragments in isolation, the effect of reading the entire series is quite different. In fact, there is no need for the author to re-establish his authority or his personality at every opportunity, just as it is not necessary for him to reiterate his conclusions, because the reader carries with him a built-up experience of the writer's presence.

Let us begin with a *ricordo* whose ostensible subject is the necessity of learning the courtly arts:

> 179 *When I was young, I used to scoff at knowing how to play, dance, and sing, and at other such frivolities. I even made light of good penmanship, knowing how to ride, to dress well, and all those things that seem more decorative than substantial in a man. But later, I wished I had not done so. For although it is not wise to spend too much time cultivating the young toward the perfection of these arts, I have nevertheless seen from experience that these ornaments and accomplishments lend dignity and reputation even to men of good rank. It may even be said that whoever lacks them lacks something important. Moreover, skill in this sort of entertainment opens the way to the favor of princes, and sometimes becomes the beginning or the reason for great profit and high honors. For the world and princes are no longer made as they should be, but as they are.*[4]

Clearly Guicciardini will never replace Castiglione as a propagandist for the courtly graces! On the contrary, at every step of the way a gruff, austere voice is telling us to despise the entire argument the author seems to be making. Ostensibly, Guicciardini, now rich with adult experience, regrets

---

4 *Maxims*, p. 86. 'Io mi feci beffe da giovane del sapere sonare, ballare, cantare e simile leggiadrie: dello scrivere ancora bene, del sapere cavalcare, del sapere vestire accommodato, e di tutte quelle cose che pare che diano agli uomini piú presto ornamento che sustanza. Ma arei poi desiderato el contrario, perché se bene è inconveniente perdervi troppo tempo e però forse nutrirvi e giovani, perché non vi si deviino, nondimeno ho visto esperienza che questi ornamenti e el sapere fare bene ogni cosa danno degnità e riputazione agli uomini *etiam* bene qualificati, e in modo che si può dire che, a chi ne manca, manchi qualche cosa. Sanza che, lo abondare di tutti gli intrattenimenti apre la via a' favori de' principi, e in chi ne abonda è talvolta principio o cagione di grande profitto e essaltazione, non essendo piú el mondo e e prìncipi fatti come doverrebbono, ma, come sono.' *Ricordi*, p. 191.

that as a youth he did not learn the manners and arts that could have
served him later. Yet the folly of a youth spent in rejecting such frivolities
consistently appears as a kind of superior wisdom. There is still no doubt
that such graces are *leggiadrie*, more ornament than substance, and that for
all their utility in this corrupted world, they are ultimately a waste of time.
Only in the last line does the voice modify its consistently bourgeois anti-
courtly tone, as its puritanical edge softens in nostalgia for a period when
presumably princes and the world were just right.

The author's capacity for self-dramatization is naturally most obvious
when he takes himself for a subject. And given the circumstances of composition we must expect to hear changes in the author's voice. Let us contrast two *ricordi*, one from the early series (1512) and one from the late
(1530).

> Q 17 *I want to see three things before I die: a well ordered republic in
> our city, Italy liberated from all the barbarians, and the world delivered
> from the tyranny of these wicked priests.*[5]

There is no obvious subject here. Unlike most of the *ricordi*, this is not an
analysis of a problem. The content is all in the rhetoric. Direct, uncomplicated, would-be heroic and republican, it reminds one of Michelangelo's
Brutus. And with what perfect geometry it progresses in concentric circles
outward from its young author (who should be pictured perhaps in some
resolute pose) to his city, his 'nation,' his world.

By 1528 (the middle series) Guicciardini has modified his self-presentation at least to the point of introducing a more characteristic note of resig-
nation into the rhetoric of his youthful idealism. 'I want to see three things
before I die,' it now reads, 'but I doubt whether I shall see any of them, no
matter how long I live.'[6] Expectation is tempered; the voice is sadder and,
by implication, wiser. But Guicciardini's self-portrayal does not end here;
it is best reflected in another *ricordo* from the middle series, better known
but with a similar theme:

> B 124 *Naturally I have always wanted to see the ruin of the Papal State.
> But as fortune would have it, I have been forced to support and work*

5 *Maxims*, p. 144: 'Tre cose desidero vedere innanzi alla morte: uno vivere di republica bene ordinato nella città nostra, Italia liberata da tutti e barbari e liberato
   el mondo dalla tirannide di questi scelerati preti.' *Ricordi*, p. 239.
6 *Maxims*, p. 101. 'Tre cose desidero vedere innanzi alla mia morte, ma dubito
   ancora che io vivessi molto, non ne vedere alcuna.' *Ricordi*, B14, p. 239. Note also
   that the addition of the possessive pronoun (*mia* morte) may add a hint of emphasis and of personal concern to the expectation of death.

for the power of two popes. Were it not for that, I would love Martin
Luther more than myself, in the hope that his sect might demolish, or
at least clip the wings, of this wicked tyranny of the priests.

The final version reads:

28 *I know of no one who loathes the ambition, the avarice, and the*
sensuality of the clergy more than I – both because each of these vices
is hateful in itself and because each and all are hardly suited to those
who profess to live a life dependent upon God. Furthermore, they are
such contradictory vices that they cannot coexist in a subject unless he
be very unusual indeed. In spite of all this, the positions I have held un-
der several popes have forced me, for my own good, to further their in-
terests. Were it not for that, I should have loved Martin Luther as much
as myself – not so that I might be free of the laws based on Christian
religion as it is generally interpreted and understood; but to see this
bunch of rascals get their just deserts, that is, to be either without vices
or without authority. [7]

We have come a long way from the simple stalwart rectitude of the
early text to these perplexing tensions. In both the *ricordi* just cited, the
author presents himself in terms of unresolvable contradiction. No effort is
made to mitigate his difficulties or soften the abrasive conflict between his
ideals (indeed his faith) and his self-interest. But the late version (28) displays a greater tension. Both the wickedness of the clergy and Guicciardini's own essential orthodoxy are dramatized in the late *ricordo* – as they
were not in the middle one – in order to harden the terms of conflict. In
place of the flat declamatory tone of B 124, the author's voice in the later
version is in every sense richer. Its rhetoric is fuller ('the ambition, the ava-

7 *Maxims*, p. 126: 'Io ho sempre desiderato naturalmente la ruina dello stato eccle-
   siastico, e la fortuna ha voluto che sono stati dua pontefici tali, che sono stato
   sforzato desiderare e affaticarmi per la grandezza loro. Se non fussi questo rispetto, amerei più Martino Luther che me medesimo, perché spererei che la sua
   setta potessi ruinare o almanco tarpare le ale a questa scelerata tirannide de' preti.'
   Maxims, p. 48: 'Io non so a chi dispiaccia più che a me la ambizione, la avarizia e
   la mollizie de' preti: sì perché ognuno di questi vizi in sè è odioso, sì perché ciascuno e tutti insieme si convengono poco a chi fa professione di vita dependente
   da Dio, e ancora perché sono vizi sì contrari che non possono stare insieme se non
   in uno subietto molto strano. Nondimeno el grado che ho avuto con più pontefici
   m'ha necessitato a amare per el particulare mio la grandezza loro; e se non fussi
   questo rispetto, arei amato Martino Luther quanto me medesimo: non per liber-
   armi dalle legge indotte dalla religione cristiana nel modo che è interpretata e in-
   tesa communemente, ma per vedere ridurre questa caterva di scelerati a' termini
   debiti, cioè a restare o sanza vizi o sanza autorità,' *Ricordi*, p. 33.

rice, and the sensuality') and the condemnation of the priests both more
sweeping and better differentiated ('both because ... and because'). Once
more we have Guicciardini the despiser of cakes and ale. At the same time
the nexus that binds him to the service of ambitions and vices he loathes is
more accurately and honestly specified; no longer is he forced ('necessitato') to work for the popes by Fortune, but his service is dictated by his
own self-interest ('per el particolare mio'). Thus the author does not
escape his own self-censure; but as the condemnation is better distributed,
so is our interest and sympathy. In B 124 (as also in Q 17) the subject was
purely the author, or at least his anti-clerical posture. The later text broad-
ens its concern beyond the isolated figure of the author to the whole web
of self-interest that binds and motivates both Guicciardini and his patrons.
And, at the same time, the author's voice assumes a greater richness, tension, and perplexity.

We observe, then, that Guicciardini could shake off his early declamatory manner and abandon 'self-portraits' that show him as an isolated, pos-
turing figure, without at the same time losing his capacity for self-charac-
terization. Indeed, his characterization becomes subtler and more fluid as
it progresses from flat self-assertion to a dramatization of his own special
way of seeing the world. Increasingly, Guicciardini seems able to present
himself through a manipulation of voice and point of view rather than a
dependence on autobiographical content, though of course there are other
reasons for the abundance of autobiography in the *Ricordi*. The importance of this development lies not only in the more complex image that
we therefore receive of the author, but in the fact that through these techniques he is able to hold our respect and attention by compelling us so
often to identify his perspective with our own.

This point can be made clearer by looking at a *ricordo* in which the
autobiographical element has all but disappeared, and the self-assertive is
replaced by the self-dramatizing:

B 65 *It is generally believed, and it is often seen from experience, that
a dishonestly acquired fortune does not pass beyond the third generation. Saint Augustine says that God permits the man who had acquired
the wealth to enjoy it in return for whatever good he has done in his
lifetime. But then it may not pass on very far, for God has so ordained
against ill-gotten property. I once told my father that another reason
occurred to me. Generally the man who acquires the fortune, having
been reared in poverty, loves it and knows the art of keeping it intact.
But his children and grand-children, having been reared in wealth,
quickly dissipate it. For they have no idea what it means to earn a
fortune, nor do they know how to keep it.*

33 *The proverb tells us that a dishonestly acquired fortune is never en-*
joyed by an heir of the third generation. If this were so because such
wealth is contaminated, it would seem that the man who acquired it
ought to enjoy it least of all. The reason he is allowed to enjoy it was
once told me by my father. According to Saint Augustine, no one is so
wicked that he does not do some good. God, who leaves no good unre-
warded and no evil unpunished, gives such a man enjoyment in this
world as remuneration for his good deeds, only to punish him fully in
the next for his evil deeds. But since ill-gotten gains had to be purged,
they could not pass to a third heir. I answered that I did not know
whether the proverb itself was true, since one could cite many experi-
ences to the contrary. But if it were true, there might be another reason
for it. The natural vicissitude of human affairs brings poverty where
there once were riches. And this is more true for heirs than it is for the
founder of the fortune. For the more time passes, the more easily do
changes come about. Furthermore, the founder, the man who acquired
the fortune, is more attached to it. Just as he knew how to acquire it,
so he also knows the art of keeping it intact. And being used to living
frugally, he does not squander it. But heirs do not have the same attach-
ment to a fortune they have come by effortlessly. They have been
reared in wealth but have not learned the art of earning it. Who can
wonder, then that they let it slip through their fingers, either through
waste or carelessness?[8]

8 *Maxims*, p. 112: 'Si crede e anche spesso si vede per esperienza che le ricchezze
male acquistate non passano la terza generazione. Santo Augustino dice che Dio
permette che chi l'ha male acquistate le goda in remunerazione di qualche bene
che ha fatto in vita, ma poi non passano troppo innanzi, perché è giudicio così
ordinato da Dio alla roba male acquistata. Io dissi già a mio padre che a me occor-
reva una altra ragione: perché communemente chi guadagna la roba è allevato da
povero, la ama e sa le arte del conservarla, ma e figliuoli poi e nipoti, che sono
allevati da ricchi nè sanno che cosa sia guadagnare roba, non avendo arte o modo
di conservarla, facilmente la dissipano.' *Maxims*, p. 50: 'È in proverbio che delle
ricchezze male acquistate non gode el terzo erede; e se questo nasce per essere
cosa infetta, pare che molto manco ne dovessi godere quello che l'ha male acquistate. Dissemi già mio padre che Santo Augustino diceva, la ragione essere perché
non si truova nessuno sì scelerato che non faccia qualche bene, e che Dio, che
non lascia alcuno bene irremunerato né alcuno male impunito, dargli in satisfa-
zione de' suoi beni questo contento nel mondo, per punirlo poi pienamente del
male nell' altro; e nondimeno, perché le ricchezze male acquistate s'hanno a pur-
gare, non si perpetuare nel terzo erede. Io gli risposi che non sapevo se el detto en
sè era vero, potendosene allegare in contrario molte esperienze; ma, quando fussi
vero, potersi considerare altra ragione, perché la variazione naturale delle cose del
mondo fa che dove è la ricchezza venga la povertà, e più negli eredi che nel principale, perché quanto el tempo è più lungo tanto è più facile la mutazione. Di poi el

Let us begin, this time, with the later text. There can be no question here of a neutral voice evenly presenting both sides to a question. Instead, the 'I' here presents himself as a reliable and realistic guide to a subject about which others are likely to be moralistic and evasive. The key element in this self-presentation is, of course, the contrast he creates between himself and his revered but old-fashioned father, the quoter of St. Augustine and frequently in this work associated with expressions of bourgeois virtue worthy of a Ben Franklin. But the son has altogether another outlook. He begins by casting doubt on the proverb itself, looked at from the point of view of experience it seems dubious, and thus establishes his own greater discretion. Then, by resolutely emphasizing natural factors and common-sense psychology, he is able to persuade us that there is no need of high-flown theological argument to explain an intrinsically human problem ('che *maraviglia* è ...').

If all this seems quite ordinary and not really worth remarking on, it is useful to look back to the earlier version (B 65). Here is the evidence of the effort it cost Guicciardini to arrive at the simplicity of his final text. Already in the first version he seems to have the completed idea in mind, but without knowing quite how to accomplish it. The distinctiveness of his own voice is much less clear, in part at least because St. Augustine is allowed to do the talking in the first half, and the saint is not really a suit-able antagonist. Half of the effectiveness of the *ricordo*, after all, derives from its father-and-son theme. A man's relations to his father can be typed (and therefore do not need extensive characterization) in a way that his relations to a Father of the Church cannot be. That the 'I' here character-izes itself specifically as a son directly conditions the kind of truth we ex-pect to hear.[9] The B text is also more awkward in movement. Not feeling that he can do without his father, but not quite knowing what to do with him, Guicciardini inserts him as an auditor without any real function ('I once told my father ...'). Finally, the earlier text lacks several elements im-portant to the effectiveness of the final version: the expression of doubt

---

principale, cioè quello che l'ha acquistate, v'ha piú amore e, avendo saputo gua-dagnarle, sa anche le arte del conservarle, e, usato vivere da povero, non le dissipa; ma gli eredi, non avendo tanto amore a quello che sanza loro fatica si hanno tro-vato in casa, allevati da ricchi, e non avendo imparato le arte del guadagnare, che maraviglia è che, o per troppo spendere o per poco governo, se le lascino uscire di mano?' *Ricordi*, pp. 39-40.

9 How different this is, for example, from Guicciardini in one of his 'I've said it before and I'll say it again moods.' See No. 29, for example: 'Ho detto molte volte, e è verissimo ...' *Ricordi*, p. 34.

about the proverb itself, the important and powerful explanation in terms of natural variation, and the effective touch in the use of the word 'maraviglia.'

The controlling presence of the author, which is a major unifying element in the *Ricordi*, is felt also in meditations in which no 'I' is ever pronounced. Our next series of texts will indicate, among other aspects equally important, the way in which the manipulation of point of view can also reveal the author's hand. At the same time, we shall begin to look at some characteristics of structure in the *Ricordi*.

> 98 *Although a prudent tyrant will look with favor on timid wise men,*
> *he will also not be displeased by brave ones, if he knows them to be of*
> *quiet temperament, for he can always hope to satisfy them. It is the*
> *brave and restless men that he dislikes above all, because he cannot as-*
> *sume he will be able to satisfy them. And therefore he is forced to think*
> *about extinguishing them.*[10]

Here Guicciardini, looking at the problem from the perspective of the prudent 'tyrant,' makes a straightforward observation about which type of subject a ruler can hope to control and which he cannot. The matter-of-fact tone with which he contemplates a violent solution to the difficulty posed by a subject who is both 'brave' and 'restless,' and the implicit justification of such violent means in terms of political prudence rather than morality, are characteristic of Florentine political thinking in the Cinquecento. The substance of the *ricordo*, however, lies in the three-part classification of subjects: the 'timid wise,' the 'brave' but 'quiet,' and the 'brave and restless.' But the *ricordo* which follows it quickly complicates the problem:

> 99 *Unless the prudent tyrant consider me an enemy, I would rather he*
> *thought me restless and brave than timid. For he will try to satisfy me,*
> *whereas with the other sort, he will do as he pleases.*[11]

10 *Maxims*, p. 66. 'Uno tiranno prudente, benché abbia caro e savi timidi, non gli dispiacciono anche gli animosi, quando gli conosce di cervello quieto, perché gli dà el cuore di contentargli: sono gli animosi e inquieti quelli che sopra tutto gli dispiacciono, perché non può presupporre di potergli contentare; e però è sforzato a pensare di spegnerli.' *Ricordi*, p. 110.

11 *Maxims*, p. 66. 'A presso a uno tiranno prudente, quando non m'ha per inimico, vorrei piú presto essere in concetto di animoso inquieto che di timido, perché cerca di contentarti, e con quell'altro fa piú a sicurtà.' *Ricordi*, p. 110.

Here the observation seems in contradiction to the previous one. Indeed, the editor of the *Ricordi* suggests that 'restless' here may be a mistake.[12] An editor's anxiety to solve all problems on a purely textual level is only natural; but in the present context it only obscures what is most interesting about this series of *ricordi*: its contradictory structure. The obvious objection to considering 'restless' here as a slip of the mind or pen is that it makes *ricordo* 99 redundant, an uninteresting and simplified repetition of the proposition in 98. Why would Guicciardini bother to do this? Secondly, we must note the shift in point of view from the perspective of the prudent tyrant in 98 to that of the subject, presumably equally prudent, in 99. This shift will have important consequences. Third, an important qualification has been introduced ('Unless the prudent tyrant consider me an enemy'), which places definite limits on the application of the *ricordo*. Finally, the terms of the comparison have changed and its basis narrowed. The three types of subjects in 98 have now been reduced to a choice between two courses of action, timidity and temerity. Given a choice between two extremes, Guicciardini (still remembering that the subject is not on terms of open enmity with the tyrant) elects the bolder, more active, albeit more dangerous course. In doing so he upholds the dignity of the subject, which is entirely consistent with Guicciardini's habitual stress on honour and reputation.

But *ricordo* 99 does not yet represent the 'definitive' choice; it cannot because it poses only the simple either/or. The solution, prefigured in the tripartite categories of 98, finally emerges in 100:

> 100 *If you live under a tyrant, it is better to be his friend only to a certain extent rather than be completely intimate with him. In this way, if you are a respected citizen, you will profit from his power – sometimes even more than do those close to him. And if he should fall, you may still hope to save yourself.*[13]

The point of view is now emphatically that of the prudent subject. The tyrant has become someone to be manipulated and it is now *his* longevity

12 Spongano comments in a footnote: 'inquieto' è aggiunto sopra la linea, e certo mette in contraddizione questo ricordo col precedente.' And, in a note to the B text, he goes on to call it 'una contraddizione patente con tutti questi ricordi e fu pertanto un'aggiunta inopportuna, se non effetto di una vera e propria distrazione per "quieto."' Spongano, *Ricordi*, p. 110. Domandi agrees: *Maxims*, p. 66.
13 *Maxims*, p. 66. 'Sotto uno tiranno è meglio essere amico insino a uno certo termine che participare degli ultimi intrinsechi suoi, perché così, se sei uomo stimato, godi anche tu della sua grandezza, e qualche volta più che quell'altro con chi fa più a sicurtà: e nella ruina sua puoi sperare di salvarti.' *Ricordi*, pp. 110-11.

that is not to be taken for granted – a complete switch of roles from 98. At the same time, with the 'respected citizen' we have in effect returned to the median type of the first text, the 'brave and quiet' subject, rejecting the extremes of timidity and temerity posed in the second of the series. Of course, we return only in a limited sense; on the way we have explored other possibilities and contradictory perspectives. The initial contradictory language dismissed by Spongano was not at all a textual error, but a calculated element in the essentially dialectical movement of the three *ricordi*.

Characteristically, having led us this far, Guicciardini upsets the equilibrium for a final time by introducing a new problem. So far we have presumed to be dealing with a tyrant who is rational, self-interested, calculating, and therefore predictable, in Guicciardini's vocabulary a 'prudent' tyrant. But what if the tyrant proves not to be so conveniently rational? 'There is no rule or prescription,' he warns us, 'for saving yourself from a bestial and cruel tyrant, except the one that applies for the plague. Run as far and as fast as you can' (101).[14] This is the limiting case on all the previous observations; beyond this point no rules apply.

Once again, the nature of Guicciardini's intention can be clarified through a comparison with the less mature version of this reflection:

B 82 *If you are a man of rank who lives under a bloody and bestial tyrant, there is little good advice anyone can give you except to go into exile. But if the tyrant behaves decently, either out of prudence or necessity, or because of the circumstances of his position, you should strive to be highly respected and to be thought courageous but of a quiet nature, not anxious to change things unless forced. In that case, the tyrant will treat you gently and try not to give you any cause to think of making innovations. But he would not do that if he thought you were restless. In that case, knowing you would not keep still no matter what he did, he would be forced to look for an occasion to extinguish you.*

B 83 *In the above case, it is better not to be among the tyrant's confidants. For not only will he treat you gently, but in many matters he will take fewer liberties with you than he would with his friends. Thus you can enjoy his power, and if he should be overthrown, you can become powerful yourself. This* ricordo *is of no use to anyone who does not enjoy an important position in his country.*[15]

14 *Maxims*, p. 66. 'A salvarsi da uno tiranno bestiale e crudele non è regola o medicina che vaglia, eccetto quella che si dà alla peste: fuggire da lui el piú discosto e el piú presto che si può.' *Ricordi*, p. 111.
15 *Maxims*, p. 116: 'A chi ha condizione nella patria e sia sotto uno tiranno sanguinoso e bestiale, si possono dare poche regole che siano buone, eccetto el torsi lo

Here the text begins with what in the later version was the limiting case; and this leads smoothly into the major statement, for which the exceptional case chiefly figures as an introduction. Thus the case of the cruel or imprudent tyrant serves only to reinforce the compact, self-contained rule that is to come by previously excluding all areas of irregularity. In B the imprudent tyrant is only an exception; in C the effect is precisely the opposite: the limiting case still defines the areas of light and shade, but by its positioning it indicates a feebler light and casts a longer shadow. The major statement itself in B is flat. It embodies neither the contradiction of C 99 nor its shifting point of view. The possibility that one might be forced to choose between safe but timid mediocrity and risky but rewarding independence is not raised. The point of view of the subject is maintained throughout and the tyrant, prudent or otherwise, figures only externally in the calculation. Thus we lack the sense, so emphatic in the mature text, of the author (distinct from both the subject and the tyrant) turning a problem freely in his hand and examining its dimensions from a variety of perspectives.

In the preceding example, we saw Guicciardini deliberately structure his reflections on an initial contradiction, thus creating a kind of back-and-forth movement between the successive restatements of his theme. This contradictory structure is not unique to this short series, nor is it only a feature of the 1530(C) redaction.[16] But far more frequent are the related *ricordi* in which paradoxical or contradictory statements are contained within the compact shape of a single text. This is certainly consistent with Guicciardini's effort, particularly notable in the last redaction, to achieve the maximum clarity and economy.

essilio. Ma quando el tiranno, o per prudenza o per necessità e per le condizione del suo stato, si governa con rispetto, uno uomo bene qualificato debbe cercare di essere tenuto d'assai e animoso, ma di natura quieto, né cupido di alterare se non è sforzato, perché in tal caso el tiranno ti carezza e cerca di non ti dare causa di pensare a fare novità; il che non farebbe se ti conoscessi inquieto, perché allora, pensando che a ogni modo tu non sia per stare fermo, è necessitato a pensare sempre la occasione di spegnerti.' *Maxims*, p. 116: 'Nel caso di sopra è meglio non essere de' piú confidenti del tiranno, perché non solo ti carezza, ma in molte cose fa manco a sicurtà teco che con li suoi. Così tu godi la sua grandezza, e nella rovina sua diventi grande: ma non è buono questo ricordo per chi non ha condizione grande nella sua patria.' *Ricordi*, pp. 110-11.

16 An early example of Guicciardini's interest in contradictory statement is Q 9 and Q 10 in which he first asserts that 'few wise men are brave,' and then that 'only wise men are brave.' In this case, however, the later development of the thought is towards greater unity.

Paradox often provides a necessary and witty focus for Guicciardini's observations. True paradox, in the strictly logical sense, is rare in the *Ricordi*, but many of Guicciardini's analyses take their start from propositions that seem self-contradictory or contradictory to common sense. There is for instance the paradox that the more you attempt to make a conspiracy fail-safe the more likely it is to fail (20), or that in war if you are too tight-fisted you will only spend more in the end (148). Likewise if you try to win too quickly you will lengthen the struggle (149). A man's good fortune is often his worst enemy (164). We know that we are going to die, but we act as thought we were going to live forever (160). A prince or a master should know his servants or subjects best, but in fact he knows them least (165). In most of these examples the contradictory or paradoxical language is conventional; or as we shall see in a later example, it may be separable from the analytic core of the text. But Guicciardini is also capable of using the technique more organically and acutely.

89 *Unless my source is unimpeachable, I am loath to believe any news that seems probable. Since men are predisposed to believe such news, it is easy to find those who will invent it; whereas the improbable or the unexpected will not be so easily made up. Therefore, when I hear expected news from an unreliable source, I am more skeptical than when I hear unexpected news.*[17]

In this case there can be no separation of the technique from the content; the credibility of the news depends precisely on its being incredible.

Whether we want to term these *ricordi* paradoxical or simply problematic, Guicciardini seems in them to adopt the posture of a man tying and untying knots in a piece of string. Fairly typical is a *ricordo* from the reconstructed (A) redaction:

A 7 *Things which are universally desired rarely happen; the reason is that generally it is the few who set things in motion, and the objectives of the few are contrary to the objectives and appetites of the many.*[18]

---

17 *Maxims*, p. 63. 'Credo adagio, insino non ho autore certo, le nuove verisimile, perché, essendo già nel concetto degli uomini, si truova facilmente chi le finge: non si fingono così spesso quelle che non sono verisimile o non sono aspettate; e però, quando ne sento qualcuna sanza autore certo, vi sto più sospeso che a quell'altre.' *Ricordi*, p. 100.
18 (My trans.) 'Le cose che sono universalmente desiderate rare volte riescono: la ragione è che e pochi sono quelli che communemente danno el moto alle cose, e e fini de' pochi sono contrari a' fini e appetiti di molti.' *Ricordi*, p. 109.

The notion that what is most desired is least likely to happen is a problem that, once stated, requires explanation. The explanation, like the problem, is given with directness and economy. In the 1528 (B) text, the economy remains, but the directness has been affected by the introduction of a new element – a speaker:

> B 30 The marquis of Pescara once said to me *that things universally desired rarely happen.* If this is true, *the reason is that generally it is the few who set things in motion. And the objectives of the few are* almost always *contrary to the objectives and appetites of the many.*[19]

Here, though the form of the problem remains unchanged, it is no longer put forward as a universal truth but as the statement of a particular man on an unspecified occasion. This is also reflected in the addition of the qualifier 'If this is true' before the explanation. By moderating the absolute antithesis between the many and the few, Guicciardini not only exhibits his characteristic cautiousness about making absolute statements, but reduces the force of the initial contradiction. If the wishes of the few and the many are not intrinsically and universally opposed but only 'almost always,' the possibility exists, however remotely, of an end desired by both.

The 1530 (C) version carries these changes still further.

> 97 When Clement was made pope, *the marquis of Pescara said to me that this was perhaps the only time he had ever seen something happen which was universally desired. The* reason for this could be *that generally it is the few, not the many, who determine the affairs of the world. And since the aims of the few are almost always different from those of the many, they give birth to effects different from those desired by the many.*[20]

19 *Maxims*, p. 104. 'Mi disse già el marchese di Pescara che le cose che sono universalmente desiderate rare volte riescono: *se è vero*, la ragione è che e pochi sono quelli che communemente danno el moto alle cose, e e fini de' pochi sono *quasi sempre* contrari a' fini e appetiti di molti.' *Ricordi*, p. 109. Emphases here and elsewhere are mine.

20 *Maxims*, pp. 65-6. 'Dissemi el marchese di Pescara, *quando fu fatto papa Clemente*, che forse non mai più vedde riuscire cosa che fussi desiderata universalmente. La ragione di questo *detto può essere* che e pochi e non e molti danno communemente el moto alle cose del mondo, e e fini di questi sono quasi sempre diversi da' fini de' molti, e però partoriscono diversi effetti da quello che molti desiderano.' *Ricordi*, p. 109.

Here the anecdotal overcomes the paradoxical and the contradictory becomes simply improbable; now we have not only a speaker but an occasion. The universally desired event, the election of Pope Clement, originally almost a contradiction in terms, has in fact occurred, and is the starting point for the reflection. With the shift from a problematic to an anecdotal structure, the author takes up a more neutral position. The universality of the statement has been further reduced by calling it a 'saying,' for which Guicciardini then gives us a likely explanation without fully standing behind either the maxim or its explanation. Finally, compared to the strict parallelism in A of problem and solution, of the knot tied and untied, the switch to anecdote in C allows a slightly uncertain connection between the various elements. Between the occasion and the comment a little room for play has crept in. Irony, the play of expectation against fulfilment, of appearance against reality, is frequently the child of story-telling. Is there not a hint of irony here in the choice of this particular occasion for the marchese's maxim? Do things universally desired succeed after all? Clement's pontificate, as it turned out, saw the sack of Rome and the defection of the English church.

While giving us an example of irony in the *Ricordi*, 97 also points to an explanation of the comparative rarity of irony as opposed to paradox in this work.[21] Aphoristic fragments distill experience into a few lines, encouraging the author to pointed observation and sharp statement while leaving him free of the burdens of theme and narration. This too is their limitation. Without the external necessities of plot and character, the fragments tend toward the exploration of the paradoxical rather than the truly ironic. Moreover, lacking anyone to be ironical about except himself, Guicciardini creates a persona here quite different from that in his other works. The fragmentary statements of the *Ricordi* are a limitation on, as well as a vehicle for, Guicciardini's embittered thoughts in the years of the sack of Rome and siege of Florence. Later, in the pages of the *Storia d'Italia*, he can turn his anger and cynicism outward and exercise his ironic wit on the characters of his great story; in the *Ricordi* the author is the principal character and Guicciardini's irony is directed largely at himself.

21 For other examples of irony in the *Ricordi*, see 18 on Tacitus; 209 on how the complete randomness of Turkish justice gives one at least a fifty-fifty chance, which is better than in a Christian court; 124 on the wide-spread distribution of certain devotions and how this proves that God's grace is for everyone; 161 on how surprised he is to see an old man or a good harvest. Trivial irony of the latter type, an ironic pose rather than a real statement about anything, is Guicciardini's equivalent in maturer years to the earlier poses of idealism and civic ambition.

Guicciardini revised his brief work most thoroughly, leaving not a single reflection unchanged from the earliest texts. Many *ricordi* were dropped and a large number were added in the final text. The extent of these changes testifies presumably not only to his thoroughness but to the substantial alteration of his outlook from 1512 to 1530. Thus, those *ricordi* which appear in each of the five series must be given an especially important place in Guicciardini's intellectual biography. They offer us a unique chance to survey the changes in his style and ideas over almost two decades.

Let us begin with a *ricordo* that we have already looked at as an example of Guicciardini's early republicanism:

> Q 2 *Citizens who seek reputation in their city are praiseworthy and useful, provided they seek it not by faction or usurpation but by striving to be considered good and prudent and by doing some good works for the public. Would to God that republics were full of such ambition!*[22]

Here plainly speaks the young man of 1512, the patrician republican of the *Storie fiorentine*. Every word is redolent of his civic aspirations, of his thirst for esteem and success within the walls of Florentine politics. Here is the rare Guicciardini of uncomplicated integrity who cried out for a well-ordered republic, a free Italy, and an end to the tyranny of priests. He is idealistic and ambitious at the same time because he has not yet discovered that ideals and ambition can conflict. Here, in sum, is the very opposite of that other Guicciardini of complicated integrity who details so honestly the conflict between his own ambition and ideals.

The *ricordo* is reworked in the reconstructed A series (1525) and totally transformed:

> A 78 *Ambition for honor and glory is praiseworthy and useful to the world, because it gives men cause to conceive of and do generous and excellent things. Not so is the desire for grandeur because he who takes that for his idol wants to have and to keep it by any means, and it is the cause of infinite evils. Thus we see that rulers and others who have this for their object, are restrained by nothing, and will trample over the possessions and lives of others, if it will help maintain their grandeur.*[23]

---

22 *Maxims*, p. 142. 'Quelli cittadini che appetiscono riputazione nella città, pure che non la cerchino per via di sette o di usurpazione, ma collo ingegnarsi di essere tenuti buoni e prudenti e fare qualche buona opera pel publico, sono laudabili e utili alla città: e dio volessi che le republiche fussino piene di questa ambizione.' *Ricordi*, p. 37.

23 (My trans.) 'La ambizione dell'onore e della gloria è laudabile e utile al mondo, perché dà causa agli uomini di pensare e fare cose generose e eccelse. Non è così

The civic references, the factions, the parochial horizons of the early redaction have gone, as have God and the republic. Of the two key words in the first version, ambition and reputation, Guicciardini now concentrates on the first. Whereas in the original text, ambition is simply defended, in the more mature reflection two types of ambition are distinguished, both as to ends and means, and their good and bad effects catalogued, with considerable emphasis on the bad.

The lines of Guicciardini's development seem clear enough; yet in the B text (1528) we witness a surprising return to the earlier outlook.

> B 1 *Citizens who seek honor and glory in their city are praiseworthy and useful, provided they seek it not by faction or usurpation but by striving to be considered wise and good, and by serving their country. Would to God our republic were full of such ambition! But citizens whose only goal is power are dangerous. For men who make power their idol cannot be restrained by any considerations of honor or justice, and they will step on anything and everything to attain their goal.*[24]

Though the new text retains the vital distinction between good and bad ambition developed in A, it is full of the civic and republican language of Q (1512). The first two-thirds, that part describing worthy ambition, is for all practical purposes identical to the earliest text; the last third, on the other hand, expresses the same thought as the latter part of A, but without repeating any major phrases. In all, the feel of B, the 1528 text, is far closer to Q, the 1512 text, than to the supposed intermediate version A. Given the generally accepted dating of the texts, the only reasonable hypothesis seems to be that Guicciardini retained an interest in both of his previous versions while leaning strongly towards the earlier and attempted to combine them in B (1528). This hypothesis, however, while remaining possible, seems less reasonable when we look finally to the last redaction, C (1530).

quella della grandezza, perché chi la piglia per idolo vuole averla e conservarla per fas et nefas, e è causa di infiniti mali. Però veggiamo che e signori e simili, che hanno questa per obietto, non hanno freno alcuno, e fanno uno piano della roba e vita degli altri, pure che così gli conforti el rispetto della sua grandezza.' *Ricordi*, p. 37.

24 *Maxims*, p. 99. 'Quelli cittadini che appetiscono onore e gloria nella città sono laudabili e utili, pure che non la cerchino per via di sette e di usurpazione, ma con lo ingengnarsi di essere tenuti buoni e prudenti e fare buone opere per la patria; e dio volessi che la republica nostra fussi piena di questa ambizione. Ma perniziosi sono quelli che appetiscono per fine suo la grandezza, perché chi la piglia per idolo, non ha freno alcuno né di giustizia, né di onestà, e farebbe uno piano di ogni cosa per condurvisi.' *Ricordi*, p. 37.

It is perhaps surprising that an author would revive almost word for
word a text now sixteen years old while bypassing the forms and much of
the thought of another so much more recent – and, one might add, so
much more mature. It is especially surprising since the reconstructed A
text is supposed to represent the lost manuscript from which Guicciardini
copied when he wrote the B version. It is altogether astonishing, however,
that when we examine the 'final' version, C (1530), we find ourselves once
again on the path laid down in A.

> 32 *Ambition is not a reprehensible quality, nor are ambitious men to*
> *be censured, if they seek glory through honorable and honest means.*
> *In fact, it is they who produce great and excellent works. Those who*
> *lack this passion are cold spirits, inclined more toward laziness than*
> *activity. But ambition is pernicious and detestable when it has as its*
> *sole end power, as is generally the case with princes. And when they*
> *make it their goal, they will level conscience, honor, humanity, and*
> *everything else to attain it.* [25]

We can now look at the development of the *ricordo* as a whole. The
final version clearly takes up where the second, A, left off, but in language
that is both stronger and more subtle. The theme is now announced at its
most general level ('Ambition is not ...') and is then immediately made
concrete in the person of the *ambizioso*, the ambitious man. This replaces
the limited, civic context of the early and middle versions ('citizens who ...')
and the abstractness of A. In a number of places the language has become
more precise and conditional: 'Citizens whose only goal' in B and 'rulers
and others' in A becomes 'generally the case with princes ... when they
make it their goal ...' The positive side of ambition is amplified on the level
of character ('those who lack this passion are cold spirits'), which is consistent with the personification of the *ambizioso*. At the same time, the
whole reading is far more emphatic. Not only does the theme announce
itself from the very beginning by pronouncing the key word 'ambition,'
unlike the early and middle versions where it is left almost to the end, but
it is strengthened along the way by the phrase beginning with the emphatic

25 *Maxims*, 'La ambizione non è dannabile, né da vituperare quello ambizioso che ha
   appetito d'avere gloria co' mezzi onesti e onorevoli: anzi sono questi tali che ope-
   rano cose grande e eccelse, e chi manca di questo desiderio è spirito freddo e incli-
   nato piú allo ozio che alle faccende. Quella è ambizione perniziosa e detestabile
   che ha per unico fine la grandezza, come hanno communemente e prìncipi, e
   quali, quando se la propongano per idolo, per conseguire ciò che gli conduce a
   quella, fanno uno piano della conscienza, dell'onore, della umanità e di ogni altra
   cosa.' *Ricordi*, p. 37.

conjunction *anzi* ('In fact') and the rhetorical repetition at the end ('conscience, honor, humanity ...') Most of all, the reflection takes on a sense of completion and weight that grows out of its balance and parallelism. In each half a general pronouncement is immediately made concrete through a personification ('Ambition is not reprehensible' 'ambitious men'; 'But ambition is pernicious' 'princes'). And in the same way the key contrast between *gloria* and *grandezza*, which is the heart of the *ricordo*, is tightened. None of the early versions, including A which otherwise shares the same basic structure, possesses this feel of even-handedness and a progression that is both unhurried and unimpeded. In Q (1512) the major statement is interrupted by a gaggle of qualifications, and the possibility of bad ambition never enters, though bad means are recognized. The B (1528) text is overstuffed with the virtues of ambition (this is the section inherited from Q) and almost comes to a standstill at the end of the first thought. On the other hand, A, the reconstructed version, is overbalanced on the negative side, where it is even somewhat repetitious, and suffers from an abstract and unrelieved diction.

Some of the lines of development of the *ricordi* have, I hope, been clarified in this analysis; there remains, however, the problem of the strange zig-zag course Guicciardini's revisions of the basic text seem to have followed. It cannot be denied that the generally accepted chronology of the texts and their stylistic and conceptual logic seem totally contradictory. And there are several others in which the accepted sequence poses the same difficulty. Given the existence of these anomalies, it seems more reasonable to see the problem as being located in the hypothetical A text than in the well authenticated B manuscript. To do otherwise would mean calling into question the apparent sequence of Guicciardini's intellectual development. Specifically, it would mean considering the B redaction a kind of regression, and one scholar has said just that. But the fact remains that although the reconstruction of the A text was a remarkable scholarly achievement, there is no way to prove conclusively that the A redaction as we now have it is entirely identical to the lost 1525 manuscript. Rather than distort the growth of Guicciardini's ideas, I would argue, it makes better sense to leave the editorial question moot.[26]

I began this survey of the style and structure of the *Ricordi* by considering the author's 'literary' persona. This led me to emphasize the distinctiveness of Guicciardini's work compared to conventional writers of *ricordi*. It is perhaps appropriate to conclude this part of our critique of the *Ricordi* by looking at a facet of the work in which its essential continuity

26 For fuller discussion of this problem see the Appendix.

with such predecessors as the *Ricordi* of Morelli or the *Libro Segreto* of
Goro Dati is clearly to be seen. What ties these works together and allows
us to discuss them as a unit is nothing specifically literary. In fact, as I indicated at the start of this chapter, it is in its specifically literary character
that the *Ricordi* pulls away from its predecessors. Rather, the continuity
of such works is the continuity of the class that generated them, its language, mental habits, and material concerns.

The true record of Francesco Guicciardini, Florentine bourgeois and
Doctor of Laws, is the *Ricordanze*, the private and wholly traditional records Guicciardini, like so many other Florentine businessmen, kept of his
personal affairs. Nevertheless, the *Ricordi* are hardly, or more accurately
they are not only, that work of a 'carattere squisitamente teorico' to which
one scholar refers.[27] The man who carefully records his income and outgo
in the *Ricordanze* does not make way entirely for the speculative mind of
the *Ricordi*, nor does the lawyer-businessman disappear behind the historian. It sometimes comes as a shock for us, intent as we are on retracing
the early steps of the later great historian, to find, for example, that when
Guicciardini warns about the falsification of documents, he does so strictly
in the context of legal and business practice, without a glance at the historical implications.[28]

Even in a casual reading it is not hard to find a good deal of mercantile
language in Guicciardini. In particular he seems fond of using the market
place as a metaphor for political life, or even human relations in general:
'When men see that your condition forces you to do their will, they have
little respect and take advantage of you ['fanno buono mercato']...'[29]
More significant than the simple transfer of mercantile language to other
areas in life is the carry-over of the habit of rational analysis and calculated self-interest in Guicciardini as in other members of his class. So often
the *Ricordi* seem to be instruments of measurement which weigh the advantages and disadvantages of any given action. The balanced structure
which characterizes these maxims, particularly in the final series, corresponds admirably to this mental habit:

> A 18 *Men remember offences longer than favors. Indeed, thinking*
> *themselves more deserving than they are, even if they remember the*
> *favor at all, they recall it as being smaller than it was. The opposite is*

27 Lugnani Scarano, 'Le redazioni dei *Ricordi*,' p. 231.
28 See *ricordo* 119.
29 *Maxims*, p. 91. 'Come gli uomini si accorgono che tu se' in grado che la necessità
   ti conduca a quello vogliono, fanno poca stima di te e ne fanno buono mercato ...'
   Ricordo 196, p. 208.

*true of offences, which always hurt more than they reasonably should.
Therefore, other things being equal, be careful about doing favors for
one person if that necessitates offending someone else to the same extent, because, for the reason just stated, you will, on the whole, lose
more than you gain.*[30]

A 19 *You can better rely on someone who needs you or who has, in a
given case, common interests, than on someone who has received a
favor from you, because one sees from experience that men are not generally grateful. Therefore in making your calculations and in planning
how to deal with men put more reliance on one whose interests are involved than on one who is only moved by gratitude, because when it
comes down to it people forget favors.*[31]

This is Guicciardini 'well-chilled,' the man De Sanctis had in mind when
he called the *Ricordi* the codification of Italian corruption, the stereo-
typed cynic and calculator who still appears in books like Luigi Barzini's
and in the Italian press. The principal feature of reflections like these is
their rational exploration of a calculus of self-interest. Every item is added
up; balances of profit and loss are strictly kept; what will I gain and what
might I lose are the only questions raised. The spirit of mercantile investment seems to be carried over indiscriminately into the calculation of
human relations, and no distinction is made between business and politics,
between commodities and men: 'nel fare e *calculi* tuoi e nel *disegnare* di
disponere degli uomini ...' There is no indication here of the theatre of
operations; the reflection applies equally to politics and trade in a society
in which the two were so closely linked.

In the later versions of these *ricordi* some of the more blatantly mercantile language has been suppressed for reasons of decorum, as Guicciardini

30 (My trans.) 'Più tengono a memoria gli uomini le ingurie che e benefici; anzi,
quando pure si ricordano del beneficio, lo fanno nella immagine sua minore che
in fatto non fu, reputandosi meritare piú che non meritano: el contrario si fa della
ingiuria, che duole a ognuno piú che ragionevolmente non doverria dolere. Però,
dove gli altri termini sono pari, guardatevi da fare quelli piaceri a uno, che di
necessità fanno a uno altro dispiacere equale, perchè per la ragione detta di sopra
si perde in grosso piú che non si guadagna.' *Ricordi*, p. 30.
31 (My trans.) 'Piú fondamento potete fare in uno che abbia bisogno di voi o che
abbia in quello caso lo interesse commune, che in uno che abbia ricevuto da voi
beneficio, perché si vede per esperienza che gli uomini communemente non sono
grati; però, nel fare e calculi tuoi e nel disegnare di disponere degli uomini, fa maggiore fondamento in chi ne consegue utilità che in chi si ha da muovere solo per
remunerarti, perché in effetto e benefici si dimenticano.' *Ricordi*, p. 29.

suppressed other popular and specifically local elements in his language.[32] Nonetheless, the same spirit remains. Guicciardini's language remains the reflector of the class of burgher politicians who rationalized both economics and politics. Yet, as we shall see in the next chapter, Guicciardini does not offer observations like these entirely without apology.

---

32 See Fubini, 'Le quattro redazioni dei *Ricordi*,' p. 153: 'tendono naturalmente ad esprimersi in una forma eletta ... schiva di ogni locuzione che abbia del popolare ...' Fubini likewise shows that Guicciardini eliminates the Latin phrases common in the A version and avoids localism. The exception that proves the rule is 104: 'di natura liberi e reali e, come si dice in Firenze, schietti.'

3 / The *Ricordi:*
The Rules of Prudence and the
Limits of Prediction

We began our reading of the *Ricordi* by examining the persona which Guicciardini establishes in the work, thus giving unity and control to an otherwise fragmentary book. From this starting point we were led into broader considerations of structure, technique, and style. But we have not yet faced directly any questions about the meaning and purpose of the maxims. Guicciardini, always a reticent author, never states his purpose in general terms, but he does offer some partial explanations of his intentions.

> B 43 *I have written the preceding* ricordi *so that you may know how to live and how to weigh things, and not to stop you from benefitting others. Because, aside from being a generous thing a benefit will be repaid – sometimes even to such an extent that makes up for many others. It is quite possible that the Power above us likes noble actions and therefore will not consent to their always being fruitless.*[1]

Let us pass over the cynicism of the final sentence, and concentrate on the beginning. Clearly Guicciardini is aware of the cramped and airless moral atmosphere of some of his reflections, the ones specifically referred to here (A 18 and A 19) are those with which we concluded the last chapter. He appears to be saying, however, that it is not his purpose to exhort us to either moral or immoral action but to show us the hard realities of life. Idealism is not to be discouraged – it can even bring rewards! – but the first purpose of Guicciardini's curriculum is to know how to live and how

---

1 *Maxims*, p. 107. 'Ho posto e ricordi prossimi perché sappiate vivere e conoscere quello che le cose pesano, non per farvi ritirare dal beneficare; perché, oltre che è cosa generosa e che procede da bello animo, si vede pure che talvolta è remunerato qualche beneficio, e anche di sorte che ne paga molti: e è credibile che a quella potestà che è sopra gli uomini piaccino le azione nobile e però non consenta che sempre siano sanza frutto.' *Ricordi*, p. 15.

to weigh things ('sappiate vivere e conoscere quello che le cose pesano'). Presumably this kind of knowledge is to be gained through the type of rational calculation and prudent weighing up of the advantages and disadvantages that we noticed in A 18 and A 19.

We still do not know a great deal about the purpose for which the *Ricordi* were written, but it has something to do with useful knowledge that will allow us to act realistically through understanding how things stand in the world. We find further and more revealing discussions in the series of *ricordi* associated with *ricordo* 6 of the final version. We begin with Q 12: 'Rules are found written in books; exceptional cases are written in your discretion.'[2] This statement has that straightforwardness characteristic of the early series. There are rules and there are exceptions; the rules can be written down, but the exceptions are a matter of discretion. We do not know, however, what the rules are for, or how many or how important the exceptions will prove to be.

The middle version (1528) is less straightforward but fuller:

B 35 *These* ricordi *are rules that can be written in books. But particular cases have different circumstances and must be treated differently. Such cases can hardly be written anywhere but in the book of discretion.*[3]

Two vital elements have been introduced. The first is a self-consciousness about his own procedures which is the consequence of Guicciardini's identifying the *ricordi* themselves as rules. The second change is the shift from an emphasis on the exception to the particular. Thus we are made aware of the fact that the difficulty of judging the exceptional case lies precisely in its particularity, and we are really only one step away from the recognition of the particularity of all cases and the irregularity of all particulars.

In this *ricordo* the relative maturity of the A (reconstructed) and B (1528) redactions is harder to judge:

A 11 *These* ricordi *are rules which have exceptions in particular cases in which different reasons pertain; but which these particular cases are only discretion can really teach us.*[4]

2 *Maxims*, p. 144. 'Le regole si truovano scritte in su' libri: e casi eccettuati sono scritti in sulla discrezione.' *Ricordi*, p. 11.
3 *Maxims*, p. 105. 'Questi ricordi sono regole, che si possono scrivere in su' libri; ma e casi particulari, che per avere diversa ragione s'hanno a governare altrimenti, si possono male scrivere altrove che nel libro della discrezione.' *Ricordi*, p. 11.
4 (My trans.) 'Questi ricordi sono regole, che in qualche caso particulare, che ha diversa ragione, hanno eccezione; ma quali siano questi casi particulari, si possono male insegnare altrimenti che con la discrezione.' *Ricordi*, p. 11.

Here Guicciardini finally abandons the vague and static metaphor – implicit
in the early text and explicit in the middle one – of the two books: the
book of the *Ricordi* and the 'book' of discretion. What is lost in rhetoric is
more than made up in clarity. The relationship between the particular and
the exceptional is made more explicit and discretion becomes an active
quality.

These lessons are recapitulated in B 121 (A 99 is identical); more than
just a restatement, though, it seems a definite advance on the texts we have
just examined. It is impossible to say, of course, how much time has
elapsed between B 35 and B 121, but the fact that Guicciardini repeats and
amplifies his restrictions on the scope of the *Ricordi* after recording eighty-
six more maxims indicates a continuing preoccupation with this thought:

> B 121 *Remember what I said before: these* ricordi *should not be fol-
> lowed indiscriminately. In some particular case that presents different
> circumstances, they are of no use. Such cases cannot be covered by any
> rule, nor is there any book that teaches them. Rather, such illumination
> must be given you first of all by nature and then by experience.*[5]

Here the unemphatic phrasing of A 11 and the vague metaphor of B 35
have both been overcome. Guicciardini is clearer and more precise, particularly on the sources of discretion, and his emphasis seems steadily shifting
towards the irregular.[6]

We now have a better idea of the purpose and application of the *Ricordi*. Clearly these maxims are intended to be a guide to the same points
that discretion teaches, albeit a less reliable one that needs to be supple-
mented by good sense. In a word, the aim of the *Ricordi* is to teach *prudenza*, though their success will depend on experience and natural gift.
What we still lack, however, is information about the relationship of the
particular to the general and the exception to the rule. Are the exceptions
largely insignificant, for instance, or are they so frequent as to make any
application of rules extremely risky? With this question we come finally to
the last version:

---

5 *Maxims*, p. 125. 'Ricordatevi di quello che altra volta ho detto: che questi ricordi
  non s'hanno a osservare indistintamente, ma in qualche caso particulare, che ha
  ragione diversa, non sono buoni: e quali siano questi casi non si può comprendere
  con regola alcuna, né si truova libro che lo insegni, ma è necessario che questo
  lume ti dia prima la natura e poi la esperienza.' *Ricordi*, p. 11.
6 On experience as the teacher of discretion, see also *ricordo* 10 of the final redaction: *Ricordi*, p. 14.

6 *It is a great error to speak of the things of this world absolutely and
indiscriminately and to deal with them as it were, by the book. In
nearly all things one must make distinctions and exceptions because of
differences in their circumstances. These circumstances are not covered
by one and the same rule. Nor can these distinctions and exceptions be
found written in books. They must be taught by discretion.* [7]

Now we enter fully into Guicciardini's equivocal world. Though the
scope of the *Ricordi* was already limited by the knowledge that exceptional cases exist and cannot be handled by the book, it now appears that
the exceptional immeasurably predominates over the regular. More than
just the utility of the *Ricordi* is undercut as Guicciardini comes close to
denying any basis for an ordered understanding of society. Though by now
we may have accepted Guicciardini's earlier argument that no rule of human behaviour is elastic enough to match the variety of realities, it must
still come as a shock to discover here that, in a sense, reality is by its very
nature – in its variety, in its particularity, in its distinctions and pervasive
exceptions – not the kind of thing to which rules apply. The whole sphere
of human life seems to have been swept into a subjunctive mood. [8]

Clearly we have followed Guicciardini into a paradoxical thicket. The
author of the *Ricordi*, our guide to the world of prudent politics, is in the
perplexing situation of writing brief generalizations about human conduct
while all the time knowing – or perhaps we should say while constantly re-
discovering – that all generalizations are inadequate when tested against
specific circumstances. The most important generalization of all, it appears,
and the most prudent, is the one that says all generalizations are false.
Guicciardini has not given up being prescriptive, as some have claimed. [9] It
is his prescription itself that is paradoxical. No wonder then that so many
of the maxims take the form of prudential warnings – 'beware of this,'
'watch out for that,' and 'don't count on the other.'

We seem to be approaching the kind of paradox represented by the Cre-
tan who claimed that all Cretans are liars. But Guicciardini's desire for

7 *Maxims*, p. 42. 'È grande errore parlare delle cose del mondo indistintamente e
   assolutamente e, per dire così, per regola; perché quasi tutte hanno distinzione e
   eccezione per la varietà delle circunstanze, le quali non si possono fermare con
   una medisima misura: e queste distinzione e eccezione non si truovano scritte in
   su' libri, ma bisogna le insegni la discrezione.' *Ricordi*, p. 11.
8 Fubini writes about this maxim: 'in questo più maturo pensiero, la stessa esis-
   tenza di regole ed eccezioni accolta nelle precedenti redazioni, è in certo senso
   messa in dubbio ...' ('Le quattro redazioni dei *Ricordi*,' p. 160). In general I find
   Fubini's commentary the best available on the *Ricordi*.
9 Both De Caprariis and Lugnani Scarano make this a central point of their analyses.

knowledge is always directed towards action and he would clearly be dissatisfied with mere conundrum. He is not interested in paradox for its own sake or simply for the purpose of wit. His 'anti-rule' – if I might call it that – that rules do not work, is a genuine if perplexing discovery made in the course of a sustained effort to apply knowledge to the needs of action. In view of his later achievements as a historian, it is a discovery of the highest significance. And in terms of the *Ricordi* themselves, it is an uncertainty principle that colours and limits every fragment of the work.

To appreciate the true nature of the discovery made, or at least signalled, in *ricordo* 6, we must for the first time investigate an extended theme in the *Ricordi*. Though this 'anti-ricordo' is the sharpest statement that Guicciardini makes about the nature of the maxims themselves, this topic is itself only a sub-section of what must be counted the major theme of the work taken as a whole: the problem of the relationship of knowledge to action, or more exactly, to successful action.

This problem is approached negatively in a number of *ricordi* in which the possibility that knowledge might be a bar to action is examined. Pope Clement – Guicciardini's own Prince Hamlet – is the star of these maxims. In *ricordi* 59 and 60 Guicciardini juxtaposes a discussion of Clement's timidity with the assertion that a superior intellect is given men 'only to make them unhappy and tormented. For it does nothing but produce in them greater turmoil and anxiety than there is in more limited men.'[10] It is interesting to note here that Guicciardini has dropped the humanistic consolation in the earlier version which asserted that *lo ingegno nobile* (noble intellect) also allows man to transcend the human condition and approach the celestial.[11] In another place Guicciardini admits that many so-called wise men will be afraid to act because they recognize all the dangers that a fool ignores, but concludes that the truly wise do not overvalue the perils of their situation (96). Equally negative is the possibility that fools may succeed where the wise fail because of the power of fortune. This can happen because the wise man trusts much to reason and little to fortune, while the 'madman' does just the opposite – and fortune often brings amazing results (136). Yet in the end neither the wise nor the foolish can resist fate, but the wise man allows himself to be led by what he cannot resist (138). Thus success is limited from the start by forces that we can neither fully understand nor control.

10 *Maxims*, pp. 56-7. 'Per loro infelicità e tormento, perché non serve loro a altro che a tenergli con molte piú fatiche e ansietà che non hanno quegli che sono piú positiva.' *Ricordi*, pp. 68-9.
11 *Ricordi*, B 115, p. 69: 'ma l'uno participa piú di animale bruto che di uomo, l'altro transcende el grado umano e si accosta alle nature celeste.'

On the positive side, Guicciardini praises learning (47), damns ignorance (168), asserts the necessity of action and spurns a life of chance:

187 *Remember this: whoever lives a life of chance will in the end find himself a victim of chance. The right way is to think, to examine, and to consider every detail carefully, even the most minute. Even if you do, it takes great pains to make things come out right. Imagine how things must go for those who drift.*[12]

This horror of the arbitrary, the uncontrolled, or irrational is characteristic of Guicciardini. We have already seen that his advice on how to deal with an irrational tyrant is to treat him like the plague and run for your life. And in another pair of maxims (167 and 168) he states his preference – common I think among elitist intellectuals – for an evil rather than a stupid man. Evil, unlike stupidity, is calculable and thus you can hope to guard against it. But to return to the text at hand, Guicciardini gives us here, though without naming it, a statement of the essence of *prudenza*, the doctrine that is for him the principal mediator between the restraints on successful action and the necessity to act. Prudence, at least for Guicciardini, is a cognitive virtue, as the repetition 'to think, to examine, and to consider ... carefully' emphasizes. The prudent man, the protagonist of the *Ricordi*, must penetrate reality even into its smallest details in order to understand his situation and devise the means for success. Even so his task is very difficult, the effort tremendous, and the results by no means guaranteed. But the only alternative, Guicciardini believes, is abandonment to whim and chance.

A vast number of obstacles stand in the way of a man wanting to apply understanding to action. One's knowledge is frequently very limited, particularly of 'public' affairs; governments and princes have many secrets. Do not marvel, he writes, that one knows so little of times past or places far away, because if you think about it, one has little real knowledge of things done every day in his own city. Often there is such a thick cloud between the palace and the market place that no one can penetrate it. As a result the people know as little about what the rulers are doing, or their reasons for doing it, as they know about India. And so, says Guicciardini, the world is quickly filled with erroneous opinions.[13]

12 *Maxims*, p. 88. 'Sappiate che chi governa a caso si ritruova alla fine a caso. La diritta è pensare, essaminare, considerare bene ogni cosa etiam minima; e vivendo ancora così, si conducono con fatica bene le cose: pensate come vanno a chi si lascia portare dal corso della acqua.' *Ricordi*, p. 199.
13 *Ricordi*, 141, p. 153: 'Non vi maravigliate che non si sappino le cose delle età passate, non quelle che si fanno nelle provincie o luoghi lontani: perché, se considerate bene,

Again and again Guicciardini stresses the need for detailed understanding and for long and arduous examination. 'Small beginnings hardly worthy of notice,' he warns, 'are often the cause of great misfortune or of great success. Thus, *it is very wise to note and to weight everything, no matter how tiny.*'[14] And this maxim is immediately followed by another which holds out the hope, based on his own experience, that repeated application will bring increased understanding. Whereas he once believed that what he did not grasp immediately would never be clear to him, Guicciardini says that he now believes just the opposite: the more and the better you consider things, the better they are understood and carried out.[15] In short, Guicciardini asserts here the prudent man's need for intellectual discipline and stresses the unity of understanding and action. At the same time, he recognizes that a weaker mind may become confused when confronted with this necessary mass of detail (155). On the other hand, there are many men who cannot put their knowledge to use. How different is theory from practice! There are so many who forget or cannot use their knowledge. Using a metaphor from the counting-house which vividly expresses his persistent anti-theoretical bias, Guicciardini asserts that such knowledge is like treasure stored in a chest which can never be opened.[16]

Guicciardini's rigorous insistence on knowledge of particulars and his vivid sense of the difficulties of acquiring such knowledge make him very sceptical about the possibility of any sort of prediction. To act successfully, he says, you must keep many contingencies constantly in mind. Most wise men, he has observed, select two or three probable courses on which to found their deliberations, but this is not enough. Other contingencies may easily arise to confound your plans (182). Moreover, the timing of events is often a most difficult factor to judge, as public affairs in particu-

non s'ha vera notizia delle presenti, non di quelle che giornalmente si fanno in una medesima città; e spesso tra 'l palazzo e la piazza è una nebbia sì folta o uno muro sì grosso che, non vi penetrando l'occhio degli uomini, tanto sa el popolo di quello che fa chi governa o della ragione perché lo fa, quanto delle cose che fanno in India. E però si empie facilmente el mondo di opinione erronee e vane.'

14 *Maxims*, p. 82. 'Piccoli principi e a pena considerabili sono spesso cagione di grande ruine o di felicità: però è *grandissima prudenza avvertire e pesare bene ogni cosa benché minima.*' *Ricordi*, 82, p. 93.

15 *Ricordi*, 83, p. 94: 'Fui io già di opinione che quello che non mi si rapresentava in uno tratto, non mi occorressi anche poi, pensandovi; ho visto in fatto in me e in altri el contrario: che quanto più e meglio si pensa alle cose, tanto meglio si intendono e si fanno.'

16 *Ricordi*, 35, p. 42: 'Quanto è diversa la pratica dalla teorica! quanti sono che intendono le cose bene, che o non si ricordono o non sanno metterle in atto! E a chi fa così, questa intelligenza è inutile, perché è come avere uno tesoro in una arca con obligo di non potere mai trarlo fuora.'

lar tend to move or decline more slowly than you expect, and this may
cause your discomfiture. And, after all this, once you have made your decision, you may be tempted to withdraw, seeing now only the drawbacks of
your resolution, where before taking sides you saw the difficulties pro and
con equally (156).

Counteracting these difficulties is the necessity of acting. The imperfection of any given situation cannot restrain you from action because all
situations in which men find themselves are by their very nature flawed:

> 213 *In all human decisions and actions there is always a reason for do-
> ing the opposite of what we do, for nothing is so perfect that it does
> not contain a defect. Nothing is so evil that it does not contain some
> good, just as nothing is so good that it does not contain some evil. This
> causes many men to remain inactive, because every tiny flaw disturbs
> them. They are the overconscientious, awed by every minute detail.
> That is no way to be. Rather, having weighed the disadvantages of each
> side, we should decide for the one that weighs less, remembering that
> no choice is clear and perfect in every respect.*[17]

Clearly Prince Hamlet (and Pope Clement) will find no comfort here; nor
is this merely a conventional lament over the imperfections of this world.
A lament it is not because lamentation brings no results and requires no
action. And 'imperfection' lies too much on the surface to describe what
troubles Guicciardini. Given his preoccupation with the problematic, the
paradoxical, and the irregular, there is little doubt that Guicciardini speaks
here of persistent contradiction and tension that he finds in the very centre of all political life. No action, however prudent and considered, can
hope to overcome this tension, and yet the prudent man must not allow
himself to be overcome by his own recognition of the contradictions in all
actions and all situations. Even understanding itself is thus seen to be contradictory, being both an essential prerequisite to action and too often the
prudent man's self-created barrier to success.

Set side by side, *ricordi* 6 and 213 – the one shattering all rules, the
other demanding action in the face of all contradiction – describe a world

17 *Maxims*, p. 96. 'In tutte le resoluzione e essecuzione che l'uomo fa, s'ha *ostaculo
di ragione in contrario*, perché nessuna cosa è sì ordinata che non abbia in com-
pagnia qualche disordine: nessuna cosa sì trista che non abbia del buono, nessuna
sì buona che non abbia del tristo; donde nasce che molti stanno sospesi, perché
ogni piccola difficultà dispiacce loro: e questi sono quelli che di natura si chia-
mano rispettivi, perché a ogni cosa hanno rispetto. Non bisogna fare così, ma,
pesati gli inconvenienti di ciascuna parte, risolversi a quelli che pesano manco;
ricordandosi non potere pigliare partito che sia netto e perfetto da ogni parte.'
Ricordi, p. 225.

in which one is forced to reason without certainty and act without assurance. By now the easy certainties of the earliest *ricordi* seem as remote as the age of Lorenzo.

A question which is closely related to the theme of knowledge and action, and one which traditionally has engaged historians, is the problem of prediction. Given the fragmentary, non-linear structure of the *Ricordi*, Guicciardini is not forced to present an entirely consistent point of view. There is instead a range of emphasis from outright denial of any useful foreknowledge to a limited admission of the future as an object of rational speculation. One point is clear, however: non-rational means of prediction are totally disallowed and its practitioners mocked.

> 57 *How much luckier astrologers are than other men! By telling one truth among a hundred lies, they acquire the confidence of men, and their falsehoods are believed. Other men, by telling one lie among many true statements, lose the confidence of others, and no one believes them even when they speak the truth. This comes about because of the curiosity of men. Desirous of knowing the future, and having no other way to do it, they go running after anyone who promises to reveal it to them.* [18]

And in the earlier (B) version, such credulity is compared to the faith of a sick man in a doctor who promises him health. The same point of view is put less ironically and more emphatically in *ricordo* 207. It is madness, says Guicciardini, to speak of astrological prediction. Either, he states with typical judiciousness and care, it is not a true science, or all the things it is necessary to know cannot be known, or human capacity itself is insufficient. Changing his emphasis slightly from *ricordo* 57, he concludes that to think one can know the future by these means ('per quella via') is a dream. [19]

18 *Maxims*, p. 56. 'Quanto sono più felici gli astrologi che gli altri uomini! Quelli, dicendo tra cento bugie una verità acquistano fede in modo che è creduto loro el falso; questi, dicendo tra molte verità una bugia, la perdono in modo che non è più creduto loro el vero. Procede dalla curiosità degli uomini che, desiderosi sapere el futuro *né avendo altro modo*, sono inclinati a correre drieto a chi promette loro saperlo dire.' *Ricordi*, p. 66.

19 *Ricordi*, p. 219. 'Della astrologia, cioè di quella che giudica le cose future, è pazzia parlare: o la scienza non è vera o tutte le cose necessarie a quella non si possono sapere o la capacità degli uomini non vi arriva. Ma la conclusione è che pensare di sapere el futuro per quella via è uno sogno.' Domandi, we might note, translates the first sentence as follows: 'It is mad to believe in astrology – that is to say, in the sciences that judges (sic) future events.' (*Maxims*, p. 94). But Guicciardini in fact seems to be introducing here a distinction between two or more kinds of astrology. In other words he appears to be condemning only that kind of astrology which pretends to read the future.

But a final irony remains, since Guicciardini is known to have consulted astrologers. How different, as he himself remarks, is theory from practice!

Elsewhere, Guicciardini quotes with approval the dictum that 'de futuris contingentibus non est determinata veritas' (58). But presumably this still leaves open the possibility of partial or contingent knowledge, and in general this seems to be where the weight of his opinion falls. I have already referred to the maxim in which Guicciardini emphasizes the need, in view of the contingency of all future things, to hold more than just a few alternative courses of action in mind. Similarly, though a general trend may at times be foreseen quite accurately, the particulars are far more difficult to predict. The difficulties are so great in fact that the wise and foolish seem to enjoy an equal lack of success.[20] And given Guicciardini's insistence on particular knowledge, this reservation about the detailed knowledge of the future has far more importance than might at first appear. Hence *ricordo* 114, perhaps the most significant of his statements on this theme:

> *Some men write discourses on the future, basing themselves on current events. And if they are informed men, their writings will seem very plausible to the reader. Nevertheless, they are completely misleading. For since one conclusion depends upon the other,* if one is wrong, all that are deduced from it will be mistaken. *But every tiny, particular circumstance that changes is apt to alter a conclusion.* The affairs of this world, therefore, cannot be judged from afar but must be judged and resolved day by day.[21]

We could not ask for a clearer demonstration than this that Guicciardini's insistence on a rigorously detailed understanding of politics is rooted in his perception of the particularity and contingency of the historical process itself. Our understanding, if it is to be a useful guide to action, must be as detailed, flexible, and contingent as the realities it explores. The utility of rational investigation is thus simultaneously confirmed and severely limited.

20 *Ricordi*, 23, p. 28: 'Le cose future sono tanto fallace e sottoposte a tanti accidenti, che el più delle volte coloro ancora che sono bene savi se ne ingannano: e chi notassi e giudici loro, *massime ne' particulari* delle cose – perché ne' generali più spesso s'appongono – farebbe in questo poca differenza da loro agli altri che sono tenuti manco savi.'

21 *Maxims*, p. 70. 'Sono alcuni che sopra le cose che occorrono fanno in scriptis discorsi del futuro, e quali, quando sono fatti da chi sa, paiono a chi gli legge molto belli; nondimeno sono fallacissimi, perché, dependendo di mano in mano l'una conclusione dall' altra, *una che ne manchi, riescono vane tutte quelle che se ne deducono*; e ogni minimo particulare che varii è atto a fare variare una conclusione. *Però non si possono giudicare le cose del mondo sì da discosto, ma bisogna giudicarle e resoverle giornata per giornata.'* *Ricordi*, p. 125.

From one day to the next the individual actions that make up historical and political processes can be comprehended, though with difficulty; but over the long run the complexities multiply impossibly as contingency hinges on contingency and exhaust human understanding. Guicciardini stands here like a physicist theoretically predicting the paths of billiard balls to which he has assigned an infinite elasticity – after only the briefest of time, the caroms escape prediction and assume the appearance of randomness. No wonder then that he would shift his attention from the future to the past, where the patterns of completed action, though still terribly complex, are yet finite.

In a more positive mood, Guicciardini is willing to admit a continuity or even a repetitiveness between past and future, and acknowledges that some future events are so probable as to be predictable, if only in outline. Everything that existed in the past and exists in the present, he writes, will be in the future: 'But the names and appearances of things change, so that he who has not a discerning eye will not recognize them. Nor will he know what line to take or what judgement to form.'[22] Though we recognize here a considerably different direction from some of the more sceptical reflections, nonetheless the emphasis remains as always on the difficulties of judgement. Nor is it clear whether Guicciardini wishes to assert a simple continuity of historical process or is subscribing to the traditional notion of cycle or repetition. The idea of cycles seems clearer in an earlier version where he states that 'the same things recur' ('le cose medesime ritornano'); by comparison the maturer reflection seems to climb down from the outright assertion of the earlier text that 'past events shed light on the future' ('le cose passate fanno lume alle future'). Nonetheless, this *ricordo* seems to contradict several of Guicciardini's cautions on historical judgements; however this may be, we should read it in conjunction with the strong warning against acting on historical analogy, a warning to be repeated at the expense of Piero de' Medici in the *Storia d'Italia*. Judging on the basis of example, he admonishes, is very false, because if the two situations are not entirely analogous in every particular the effects may be totally different. And to discern such tiny differences, he concludes, takes an extremely good eye.[23] Thus, whatever the theoretical possibilities, in practice it is

22 *Maxims*, pp. 60-1. 'Ma si mutano e nomi e le superficie delle cose in modo, che chi non ha buono occhio non le riconosce, né sa pigliare regola o fare giudicio per mezzo di quello osservazione.' *Ricordi*, 76, p. 87. We encountered this maxim earlier in the *Dialogo*.
23 *Ricordi*, 117, p. 128: 'È fallacissimo el giudicare per gli essempli, perchè, se non sono simili in tutto e per tutto, non servono, conciosia che ogni minima varietà nel caso può essere causa di grandissima variazione nello effetto: e el discernere queste varietà, quando sono piccole, vuole buono e perspicace occhio.'

clear that for Guicciardini the past offers little concrete guidance to political action.

To understand the originality of Guicciardini's arguments against the use of historical analogy and the conviction with which he made them, we must remind ourselves of the context in which he wrote. Renaissance humanists leaned very heavily on arguments from example, as did Machiavelli for whom the study of the past was a sure guide to political success. Roman history especially was the inspiration of the humanist and Machiavelli alike, but Guicciardini adds to his general admonitions against historical analogy the specific warning that Rome is a most unsuitable exemplar. For any comparison to be valid, he writes, you would have to have a city with similar conditions and a similar government. Otherwise the comparison is much like asking a jackass to race like a horse.[24] Only when we see Guicciardini's argument against this background can we understand what deeply ingrained intellectual habits he was fighting against. His arguments about the force of analogy are not simple ideas arrived at abstractly. They are an attack on a fundamental feature of contemporary intellectual practice. His conviction that all political action is contingent and that in practice the future is unpredictable was leading him to formulate historical ideas totally at odds with Renaissance tradition.

Parallel to the problem of knowledge and action is the question of morality and power. Though it does not possess the same importance for Guicciardini's personal development as a historian, it nonetheless occupies a major place among the fragmentary themes of the *Ricordi* and was destined, of course, to become a central topic in all political literature from the Renaissance on.

For Guicciardini the effects of moral righteousness on political success are at best indirect. At times, however, the conviction that right is on your side can be a surprisingly powerful asset. The very first *ricordo* of the final series sees the then contemporary siege of Florence in this light. Faith, says Guicciardini, can move mountains because faith breeds obstinacy and in a world subject to a thousand accidents ('sottoposte a mille casi e accidenti') obstinacy often pays off. The explanation is acidly secular, as in the equation of faith and obstinacy and in the definition of faith itself. 'To have faith,' announces Guicciardini, 'means simply to believe firmly – to deem almost a certainty – things that are not reasonable; or if they are reason-

---

24 *Ricordi*, 110, p. 121: 'Quanto si ingannano coloro che a ogni parola allegano e Romani! Bisognerebbe avere una città condizionata come era loro, e poi governarsi secondo quello essemplo: el quale a chi ha le qualità disproporzionate è tanto disproporzionato, quanto sarebbe volere che uno asino facessi el corso di uno cavallo.'

able, to believe them more firmly than reason warrants.'[25] It is a long way from the 'evidence of things unseen' to this belief in things unreasonable! Defined in this way, the problem of the efficacy of faith becomes the obverse of the question of knowledge (or reason) and success. In other words, the question becomes when is *lack* of reason a condition of political success, and the possibility is raised that ignorance and irrationality may sometimes be a better guide than prudent calculation.

Guicciardini's insistent secularity is even more evident in a maxim that we have already examined, in which St. Augustine, Guicciardini himself, and his father are the protagonists of a discussion on ill-gotten gains (33). His father is also associated with the unusually moralistic (for Guicciardini) *ricordo* 44:

> Do all you can to seem good, for that can be infinitely useful. But since false opinions do not last, it will be difficult to seem good for very long, if you are really not. My father once told me this.[26]

Nevertheless, the emphasis is primarily on utility rather than goodness, and we tend, on the evidence of things unseen, to attribute the utility to the son and the moralism to the father. Even so, in another maxim (91) Guicciardini professes himself unable somehow to grasp the idea that God's justice would allow the sons of Lodovico Sforza to enjoy their inheritance. Significantly, however, Lodovico's sins are as much historical as moral – he usurped Milan wickedly and in doing so was the ruin of the whole world.[27] This is one of the few times, incidentally, when the *Ricordi* seems to provide marginal notes on the *Storia*. But deliberately juxtaposed to this thought is a denial of the very sentiment he had just expressed: Never say that God helped someone because he was good or that someone else failed because he was bad, because very often we see that the opposite happens. But Guicciardini concludes, very traditionally, one should not therefore say that God's justice is lacking, only that his counsel is too profound.[28]

25 *Maxims*, p. 39. 'Fede non è altro che credere con openione ferma e quasi certezza le cose che non sono ragionevole, o se sono ragionevole, crederle con più resoluzione che non persuadono le ragione.' *Ricordi*, 1, p. 3.

26 *Maxims*, p. 53. 'Fate ogni cosa per parere buoni, ché serve a infinite cose: ma, perché le opinione false non durano, difficilmente vi riuscirà el parere lungamente buoni, se in verità non sarete. Così mi ricordò già mio padre.' *Ricordi*, p. 53.

27 *Ricordi*, 91, p. 102: 'Difficilmente mi è potuto entrare mai nel capo che la giustizia di Dio comporti che e figliuoli di Lodovico Sforza abbino a godere lo stato di Milano, el quale lui acquistò sceleratamente, e per acquistarlo fu causa della ruina del mondo.'

28 *Ricordi*, 92, p. 103: 'Non dire: "Dio ha aiutato el tale perché era buono, el tale è capitato male perché era cattivo"; perché spesso si vede el contrario. Né per questo dobbiamo dire che manchi la giustizia di Dio, essendo e consigli suoi sì profondi che meritamente sono detti *abyssus multa*.'

These considerations are effectively summed up in *ricordo* 47: it is an
error to believe that justice or injustice affect success, because every day
one sees the opposite. Not right, but prudence, arms (*forze*), and good fortune bring victory. Indirectly having a just cause can help by giving confidence, but it is false to think it does so directly.[29] What is the reason for
this disjunction between justice and success? The question is never put
directly but the answer may lie in the amoral character of political units
themselves:

> 48 *Political power cannot be wielded according to the dictates of good
> conscience. If you consider its origin, you will always find in it violence
> – except in the case of republics within their territories, but not beyond.
> Not even the emperor is exempt from this rule; nor are the priests,
> whose violence is double, since they assault us with both temporal and
> spiritual arms.*[30]

The category of republics abiding within their own territory being almost
an empty set in sixteenth-century Italy, the violent nature of political
authority is practically a universal. And in the earlier version he especially
singles out the Romans as the greatest usurpers of all.

Although it is clear that Guicciardini was as aware as Machiavelli of the
disjunction between morality and power, he did not make the theme his
own nor exploit its tremendous potential shock value. On the contrary, he
seems to have been troubled by the relationship, or lack of it, which is not
surprising in view of his personal scrupulousness and conservative outlook.
Moreover, he seems to have been especially interested in the ways in which
some relationship, albeit indirect, did exist between success and a just
cause. The fact that the final version of the *Ricordi* was being written at
the time of republican Florence's heroic, desperate, and surprisingly successful last stand against both pope and emperor undoubtedly focused a

29 *Ricordi*, p. 159: 'Erra chi crede che la vittoria delle imprese consista nello essere
   giuste o ingiuste, perché tutto dì si vede el contrario: che non la ragione, ma la
   prudenza, le forze e la buona fortuna danno vinte le imprese. È ben vero che in
   chi ha ragione nasce una certa confidenza, fondata in sulla opinione che Dio dia
   vittoria alle imprese giuste, la quale fa gli uomini arditi e ostinati: dalle quali due
   condizione nascono talvolta le vittorie. Così l'avere la causa giusta può per indi-
   retto giovare, ma è falso che lo faccia direttamente.'
30 *Maxims*, p. 54. 'Non si può tenere stati secondo conscienza, perché – chi considera
   la origine loro – tutti sono violenti, da quelli delle republiche nella patria propria
   in fuora, e non altrove: e da questa regola non eccettuo lo imperadore e manco e
   preti, la violenza de' quali è doppia, perché ci sforzano con le arme temporale e
   con le spirituale.' *Ricordi*, p. 57. We have, of course, already encountered this
   thought in the *Dialogo*.

brighter light on the problem. But his concern was more than topical. It was an expression of Guicciardini's lasting concern with the contrast of appearance and reality – for instance, the fact that it is really obstinacy rather than faith that moves mountains – and his fascination with the irregular and unprecedented. And the occasional triumphs of fools and madmen represent, as I have already said, a limiting case on Guicciardini's central preoccupation with *prudenza*. If fools rush in and sometimes succeed where wise men fail, that also is something for the prudent man to note:

136 *It sometimes happens that fools do greater things than wise men ...
The wise men of Florence would have given in to the present storm; the
fools, having decided against all the dictates of reason to oppose it, have
until now done things which it would have been impossible to believe
our city could ever accomplish.*[31]

Guicciardini was one who had a hand in the purge that followed the fall of the republic, but earlier, in the detached, though difficult conditions of exile, he could allow himself the luxury of grudging respect for his adversaries. Though himself firmly committed to prudence and reason, he was continually fascinated by the imprudent and unreasonable, by the exceptions to his own rules. Perhaps in such bleak times they provided a hint of relief from the burden of history.

If Guicciardini did not choose to work the vein of amorality so fully as Machiavelli, there is a closely linked theme that he too exploited to shock conventional minds, and with which he has been associated in the Italian imagination ever since. What the celebration of ruthlessness and amorality is for Machiavelli, the cultivation and the analysis of self-interest is to Guicciardini, and the nineteenth century at least seems to have found the latter more shocking.

That human beings act first and foremost out of self-interest is central to Guicciardini's concept of human nature and hence to his concept of history. The world is composed therefore of millions of competing egos and the prudent man can trust no one. Law exists, in classic conservative fashion, to coerce people to be good, not because men are inherently evil (as they are for Machiavelli) but because human nature is fragile and temptations are frequent. On the other hand, anyone who genuinely prefers doing bad to doing good is more a monster than a man (134-5). Self-interest

31 *Maxims*, p. 75. 'Accade che qualche volta e pazzi fanno maggiore cose che e savi ... E savi di Firenze arebbono ceduto alla tempesta presente; e pazzi, avendo contro a ogni ragione voluto opporsi, hanno fatto insino a ora quello che non si sarebbe creduto che la città nostra potessi in modo alcuno fare.' *Ricordi*, p. 148.

can obviously be a powerful stimulus to evil-doing.[32] But it is clear from broader contexts that Guicciardini does not consider the pursuits of self-interest in itself to be an evil.

Law is one protection against the self-interestedness of individuals; prudence is another. Of course, prudence itself is only another way of saying that the prudent man acts knowledgeably in his own interest. Looked at from this point of view, most of the *ricordi* are prescriptions for self-interest: how to protect yourself from tyrants, princes, fortune, or the ingratitude of men; how to get the maximum utility from friends and family; how to win favour, reputation and so forth:

> 157 *To get a reputation for being suspicious and distrustful is certainly not desirable. Nevertheless, men are so false, so insidious, so deceitful and cunning in their wiles, so avid in their own interest, and so oblivious to other's interests that you cannot go wrong if you believe little and trust less.*[33]

This is Guicciardini's prudential philosophy at its grimmest, most pessimistic, least generous. Certainly the fact that men are not *inherently* evil seems to have little effect on a practical level.

Although the concept of self-interest is most often left as an undifferentiated characteristic, a universal of human behaviour, it can also be broken down further or its operations analysed with respect to specific types of men or situations. *Ricordi* 61-3, for instance, investigate the balance or conflict between fear of loss and hope of gain and then examine the avariciousness of old men as a specific case. On the other hand, self-interest is not entirely universal. An imprudent man when carried away by the desire for revenge may even work against his own interest (150). Nor do men always recognize what is in their own best interest. Thus you should act on what experience shows a prince is most likely to do rather than what is most reasonable (128). Yet in the end it seems to be self-interest that underlies most actions, even when they seem (perhaps especially then?) most disinterested. Do not believe those who preach liberty, he warns, because perhaps without exception they have only their own

32 *Ricordi*, A 14, p. 145: 'Sono sì varie le corruttele del mondo e fragilità loro, che facilmente e spesso per lo interesse proprio inclinano al male.' This is an earlier version of 134.

33 *Maxims*, p. 81. 'Non è bene vendicarsi nome di essere sospettoso, di essere sfiducciato; nondimeno l'uomo è tanto fallace, tanto insidioso, procede con tante arte sì indirette, sì profonde, è tanto cupido dello interesse suo, tanto poco respettivo a quello di altri che non si può errare a credere poco, a fidarsi poco.' *Ricordi*, p. 170.

interests in mind.[34] Similarly, Alexander and Caesar, both famous for their clemency, only used it toward their enemies when it increased their reputation without risking their security (76).

Evidently, self-interest is cousin to prudence. But what about honour and generosity? Is the prudent man capable of no more than selfish action? We have already seen that Guicciardini professes to having no desire to discourage generous actions, while feeling obliged to point out how things really stand in the world. And generosity, aside from being its own reward, might even bring something more tangible in return! As for honour, this is a more serious topic with Guicciardini and his praise for it is less stinted. Honour is not only an end in itself, worth maintaining at great cost (e.g. by vendetta), but it is also an essential stimulus to success; the man who values honour highly will succeed in everything since he disregards dangers, money, and fatigue. From his own experience, Guicciardini affirms, he can say that actions which lack this powerful stimulus are worthless ('vane e morte').[35] Thus, while recognizing self-interest as the common denominator of all human action, even among great men like Caesar or Alexander, Guicciardini is definitely not reconciled to a soulless world lacking both in glory and moral principle. The marriage of honour and interest is performed in a chapel dedicated to the great Renaissance cult of reputation. Self-interest is a legitimate standard only if it is understood in a wide and generous sense. Reputation, whose importance and utility is proclaimed in a number of *ricordi*, is as valuable as hard cash:

218 *In this world of ours, the men who do well are those who always* have their own interests in mind and measure all their actions accordingly. *But it is a great error not to know* where true interest lies; *that is, to think it always resides in some pecuniary advantage rather than in honor, in* knowing how to keep a reputation, *and in a good name.*[36]

---

34 *Ricordi*, 66, p. 76: 'Non crediate a costoro che predicano sì efficacemente la libertà, perché quasi tutti, anzi non è forse nessuno che non abbia l'obietto agli interessi particulari ...'

35 *Ricordi*, 118, p. 129: 'A chi stima l'onore assai succede ogni cosa, perché non cura fatiche, non pericoli, non danari. Io l'ho provato in me medesimo, però lo posso dire e scrivere: sono morte e vane le azione degli uomini che non hanno questo stimulo ardente.'

36 *Maxims*, p. 97. 'Quegli uomini conducono bene le cose loro in questo mondo, che hanno sempre innanzi agli occhi *lo interesse propio, e tutte le azione sue misurano con questo fine.* Ma la fallacia è in quegli che non conoscono bene *quale sia lo interesse suo,* cioè che reputano che sempre consista in qualche commodo pecuniario più che *nell'onore, nel sapere mantenersi la riputazione* e el buono nome.' *Ricordi*, p. 230.

One could hardly ask for a better example of Weberian rationality, trade-mark of the bourgeois spirit, than this careful measuring of our actions as means towards ends that have themselves been selected by rational self-interest. Whether this spirit can be married quite so easily to a traditional concept of honour is another question.

The real treasure house of *egoismo* is of course the *Storia d'Italia*, so much so that Montaigne complained that he could find in it not a single in-stance of generous action. But if Montaigne was annoyed that Guicciardini applied the standard of self-interest so consistently to others, the nine-teenth century was outraged that he did not flinch to apply it to himself. Not pausing to reflect on, much less celebrate, his remarkable honesty, his critics hurried to accept as literal his most acid self-criticism. Paradoxically, they seem to have assumed the unimpeachable authority of their witness while damning him for dishonesty and selfishness. 'His phlegmatic and per-sistent egotism, his sacrifice of truth and honor to self-interest, his acquies-cence in the worst conditions of the world, if only he could use them for his own advantage, combined with the glaring discord between his opinions and his practice, form a character which would be contemptible in our eyes were it not so sinister,' writes Symonds in his marvellous entry in the eleventh edition of the *Encyclopaedia Britannica*, more denunciation than biography. O corruptor of a corrupt age! Machiavelli's *Prince*, on the other hand, redeems itself with a 'divine spark of patriotism yet lingering in the cinders of its frigid science, an idealistic enthusiasm surviving in its moral aberrations ...' Almost anything, apparently, can be forgiven an idealist.

It is a pleasure to contemplate the indignation Symonds must have felt when he read the following unpatriotic 'sentiment':

> 189 *All cities, all states, all reigns are mortal. Everything, either by nature or by accident, ends at some time. And so a citizen who is living in the final stage of his country's existence should not feel as sorry for his country as he should for himself. What happened to his country was inevitable; but to be born at a time when such a disaster had to happen was his misfortune.*[37]

No doubt Guicciardini aimed to shock the collective values of his day with this invocation of individualism, this philosophy of *sauve qui peut*, but he

---

37 *Maxims*, p. 89. 'Tutte le città, tutti gli stati, tutti e regni sono mortali; ogni cosa o per natura o per accidente termina e finisce qualche volta. Però uno cittadino che si truova al fine della sua patria, non può tanto dolersi della disgrazia di quella e chiamarla mal fortunata, quanto della sua propria: perché alla patria è accaduto quello che a ogni modo aveva a accadere, ma disgrazia è stata di colui abattersi a nascere a quella età che aveva a essere tale infortunio.' *Ricordi*, p. 201.

found his truest mark in the soft, rhetorical hearts of Risorgimento patriots like Symonds. And yet what is most remarkable about this maxim is how desperate its individualism is. Given the clear-sighted recognition of the decline of Florence, or perhaps of all Italy, the conclusion seems inevitably to look to the survival of the individual. Yet Guicciardini considers no individualist alternative. No consolation of philosophy or pastoral escape is offered, nor is there any garden to cultivate. The situation of the individual born at the death of his city seems tragic to Guicciardini precisely because he is still wholly attached to political values. If consolation is directed at the individual, it is because the city has failed him by offering no scope for his talents and no opportunity to serve the community with glory.

Once again we find Guicciardini's individualism, and the concept of self-interest that goes with it, softened by a yearning for honour and service. But that the reconciliation between honour and self-interest was not always easy we know from Guicciardini himself in his famous self-accusatory *ricordo* – presumably one that would rile Symonds more than any other for its forthright recognition of self-interest. Here he describes the conflict between his anti-clerical principles and his Medicean ties in terms of barely suppressed fury, yet without any excuses. It is gratuitous of Symonds to remark on 'the glaring discord' between opinions and practice; no one could have put it more strongly than Guicciardini himself. His hatred of the clergy stems from his moralism, which goes back, perhaps, to the influence of his Savonarolan father. More than the viciousness of the clergy, he cannot bear the fact that they enjoy both spiritual authority and material glut. Regularity and order in the Church, as in politics, is his prime desideratum. And for the same reason he despises Luther's rebelliousness. But his career tied him to the service of the clerics: 'a amare per el particulare mio la grandezza loro.' Were it not for this, I would have loved Martin Luther, he says, ironically echoing 'el particulare mio,' as much as myself. The polarities here do not represent real choices for Guicciardini (his employment in Rome seemed at the time to be over and he was an orthodox Catholic with no interest in Lutheranism) but he presents himself with a choice between extremes in order to emphasize the irony of his situation. Rather than disguise or diminish the extent to which he has been led by self-interest, he deliberately exaggerates it.

That Guicciardini was gripped by an internal conflict between honour and interest remains clear; the exact balance he struck between the two cannot be worth much worry half a millennium later. What is significant, from the point of view of his intellectual biography, is the habit he developed of looking for the interested motive, his sense that such is human nature and that, where self-interest does not lead to ill effects, it is not in itself to be condemned. Later we will observe his extraordinary clarity in analysing and describing self-interest as a force in politics; but here in the *Ricordi* what may be most remarkable is his uncomfortable rigour in measuring his own stature by the common standard.

Prudence, self-interest, and success, these are the focal points of the *Ricordi*. But Guicciardini's exploration of these themes twists and turns on itself without finding any settled answers. In the end he cannot do much more than issue a series of cautions. Thus in turning from the form to the themes of the *Ricordi* we have found once again a preoccupation with the problematic and irregular. It would be misleading, however, to consider this orientation as something which Guicciardini arrived at freely and brought to his work as an aphorist. On the contrary, it is inseparable from the *Ricordi* itself and grew out of a contradiction in the very purpose for which the work was written. Guicciardini set out to teach prudence, yet somewhere along the way he discovered that prudence is unteachable. He attempted to formulate rules, but sometime between 1512 and 1530 he perceived that the world is almost totally irregular. And yet these discoveries only reinforced the conviction that without knowledge – the careful consideration of a prudent man - our acts are blind and ultimately futile. In practice the pressure of this conflict led to an emphasis on the particular event and the individual man, on pragmatic understanding rather than theoretical speculation. Thus the author was challenged to attempt a description of the political world that is, as much as that world itself, built up from concrete, particular, and contingent units. The contradiction between his scepticism and his desire for understanding impelled him towards the creation of the most comprehensive possible description of contingent political realities – and to do this he turned again to historical narrative, first in the *Cose fiorentine* and then in the *Storia d'Italia*.

4 / The Critique of Machiavelli and the *Cose Fiorentine*

In the early years of his active career we found Guicciardini occupied by a range of political, historical, and personal writings that show him closely tied to Florentine traditions. Now in the late 1520s, when he was involuntarily freed from the daily pressures of diplomacy and administration, a new series of works indicates directions which are more distinctly his own. The *Ricordi*, whose long evolution bridges the two periods, reveals certain lines of development and establishes what will become new points of departure. Two other works, companions to the later *Ricordi*, show Guicciardini applying himself to more concrete tasks: a critique of Machiavelli's *Discourses* and a second Florentine history. Though separated in genre these three works are united in the thrust of their inquiry, and taken together they amplify our understanding of Guicciardini's mind.

In the *Ricordi* Guicciardini's analysis of political action led him on to an analysis of political knowledge. This analysis in turn has important implications for historical knowledge, though in the *Ricordi* these remain for the most part in the background. But what is implicit in the maxims becomes explicit in the *Considerazioni sopra i Discorsi di Machiavelli*. This short and incomplete commentary, less complex and less challenging than the *Ricordi*, is therefore an invaluable confirmation of earlier explorations. Here Guicciardini argues some specific points of great interest, such as the debate over the historical role of the Church in fragmenting Italy, or his observations on the psychology of tyrants and the corruptions of power. But beyond any specific topic of concern, one thing must stand out in any reading of the *Considerazioni*: when confronted with the most powerful political theory of the day, Guicciardini did not so much respond to Machiavelli's political conclusions as to his historical means. Over and over he subjects Machiavelli's arguments to a sceptical critique focusing on the inadequacy of his historical evidence and the simplicity of his historical analysis. Thus the debate between the two Florentines assumes a wider character and becomes a debate over the uses of history. It may be that their generation, so fruitful in both historical and political thought, was the first in which such a debate could have occurred. And yet, for all the importance of the debate, we are also attracted by the personal confrontation. We have the real pleasure of seeing Guicciardini face to face with Machiavelli, making concrete much of what unites and divides them. Although there is nothing in this work to match Machiavelli's passionate exclamation, 'I love Messer Francesco Guicciardini, and I love my country more than my own soul,' what we hear of Guicciardini's voice (and imagine of Machiavelli's) is just as characteristic, and it gives this brief work the sense of an occasion.

The *Considerazioni*, like all of Guicciardini's writing, was the fruit of a hiatus in his involvement with political affairs. It seems likely that the work was composed in Rome in the year 1530. Guicciardini had been declared a rebel by the Florentine Republic and his goods were confiscated. In Roman exile he was safe from the republicans but also from service against the Republic. Here he found the leisure to compose a commentary on the *Discorsi* of Machiavelli, who had died three years earlier. But like so much of Guicciardini's work the *Considerazioni* was never finished.

Shortly after abandoning work on the *Considerazioni* Guicciardini resumed his protracted labours on the *Ricordi* and recast it in its final form. Not surprisingly, then, the *Considerazioni* has much in common with the other work. Guicciardini's interest in particulars is evident here too, but without the same abstract insistence on it as a principle. And though similar in its careful use of prudential language, the *Considerazioni* lacks the paradoxical structure of the *Ricordi*. The two writings are separated by circumstance and by genre. The *Ricordi* were the product of a long preparation, reaching back into the author's early manhood, and were crystallized into their final form in the quixotic last days of the Florentine republic. The chagrin of exile, evident in the *Considerazioni*, had turned to a half-admiring puzzlement in the first of the new series of the *Ricordi*. There we find a mood of detachment which comes from Guicciardini's perverse pride in Florentine obstinacy and his sure knowledge that, faith and obstinacy notwithstanding, the fate of the Republic was sealed. Only a few months earlier his mood was different. In exile and under sentence, he was concerned in the *Considerazioni* to justify his opposition to the regime which still held the loyalty of his brother, an opposition which he felt had been thrust upon him by the hostile republican government. And in this work, the product of a single moment, there was no residue of earlier circumstances and earlier drafts to resist or mollify the frustrations of the present.

Coupled to the change in political background is the choice of a different genre. The *Considerazioni* is strictly a commentary and the critic refuses to argue beyond his text. The provocation to thought already existed in Machiavelli's work, so there is no need for Guicciardini to begin with self-inspection. Thus his mind need not search within itself for ambivalence or paradox, the author need not regard himself with irony. Freed from the necessity to be both protagonist and antagonist Guicciardini now presents himself in more straightforward terms and against a strong and clear opponent. Against the vision, passion, and simplification of Machiavelli, Guicciardini puts order, analysis, and above all discrimination. Against the profound imagination of his friend and antagonist he sets his own equally profound intelligence.

In the twelfth chapter of the first book of the *Discorsi*, Machiavelli makes a famous indictment of the Church, which he blames for the corruption and disunity of Italy. He begins by asserting that religious order is essential to political order. One can have no better symptom of the decay of a country, Machiavelli says, than to see religion disparaged. Had the original purity of Christianity been preserved free of corruption, the Christian republics would today be happier and more united than they are. And the best evidence of the decline of religion and the corrupting influence of the Roman Curia is that the peoples closest to Rome are the least religious. Politically, too, the presence of the Curia in Italy has been damaging. Too weak herself to unite the peninsula, the Church has always managed to frustrate the attempts of others to do the same, often by calling in the foreigner. Thus Italy, disunited and weak, became easy prey to any invader.

Typically, Guicciardini accepts both of Machiavelli's major conclusions but, by posing the problem against a different historical background, discovers in them an altogether different significance. He accepts, and redoubles, Machiavelli's invective against Rome. You cannot, he says, exaggerate the evil of papal Rome; it is an infamy, an exemplar of all that is worthy of vituperation and opprobrium in the world.[1] Further, Guicciardini fully accepts Machiavelli's contention that the Church has frustrated the unity of Italy. But, asks Guicciardini, is disunity the curse or blessing of Italy? Unity might have been glorious for the name of Italy and for the city that dominated, but for the rest it would have been a disaster. If a divided Italy has endured calamities that might have been avoided in a unified country, on the other hand Italy has had in past centuries ('in tutti questi tempi') so many flourishing cities, impossible under a unified republic, that unity would have been more unfortunate than fortunate.

1 *Considerazioni sui 'Discorsi' del Machiavelli*, ed. Roberto Palmarocchi, in Francesco Guicciardini, *Scritti Politici e Ricordi*, VIII: *Opere* (Bari: Laterza 1933), p. 22ff.

Typically, while Machiavelli is preoccupied by beginnings and ends, Guicciardini's concern is the historical middle. Hurt by the present crisis, but not transfixed by it as Machiavelli is, he has understood the essential precondition of Italy's Renaissance greatness, while not denying that it is also the key to her fall. We admire Machiavelli's urgent dedication, but we must equally admire Guicciardini's historical understanding, his ability to comprehend the immediate calamity within a broader pattern.

Guicciardini remembers a longer history than Machiavelli does. He points out that even before the days of the Church it was never easy to unify Italy because of the strong appetite of its people for liberty. Only by virtue of great skill and violence did the Romans unify Italy, and yet they could not prevent frequent invasion by foreigners. Against the stark single-mindedness of Machiavelli's condemnation Guicciardini's conclusion is measured and balanced:

> *Hence if the Roman Church has opposed unity I would not easily agree that it was the misfortune of this province, since it has preserved her in that way of living nearest her most ancient habit and inclination.*[2]

This division over the role of the Church in Italian history has great topical interest; less topical but far more telling for their historical methods is their disagreement over Rome. For Machiavelli, as for his humanist predecessors, Roman history was exemplary; more than any other history, the history of Rome was the source and justification of historical teaching. Guicciardini, on the other hand, further removed from the culture of humanism and by now deeply sceptical of historical arguments from analogy, saw in the peculiar conditions of Rome's greatness not the validation but the invalidation of any argument from Roman example. Chapter IV of the first book of the *Discorsi* and Guicciardini's commentary demonstrate concretely the divergence of their views. Machiavelli's argument here is that 'the disunion of the senate and people rendered the Republic of Rome powerful and free.' Rejecting what will be Guicciardini's main argument in advance, Machiavelli admits that fortune and a fine army created Roman greatness, but insists that Roman military discipline reflected Roman political virtue and created her good fortune. He argues that it was the clash of opposing interests that made Romans free, and concludes with a general warning that one should be careful of disparaging Roman government since

2 *Selected Writings*, p. 82. 'Però se la Chiesa romana si è opposta alle monarchie, io non concorro facilmente essere stata infelicità di questa provincia, poi che l'ha conservata in quello modo di vivere che è piú secondo la antiquissima consuetudine ed inclinazione sua.' *Considerazione*, p. 23.

such great success could only have arisen from very good causes. This final note is more than an historical argument, it is a signal of the almost-sacred status of Roman institutions and history. In effect Machiavelli puts the institutions of Rome beyond criticism so that they may be a measuring post for others.

Machiavelli's emphasis is on conflict and his concern is with the liberty of the people and the power of the state; Guicciardini's overwhelming desire is for order, and he cannot see strife as anything but a threat. Praising disunity, he says, is like praising a sickness for the remedy which it necessitates. No republic is perfect from its origins, so it is always necessary to apply remedies. But in the case of Rome, it is implied, the fundamental clash between the popular and aristocratic factions was a permanent fault in the constitution. Rome was held together, despite serious flaws, by her military virtues, and thus is not a model to hold up to others:

> I do not think they were such that those seeking to establish a republic should take them as a model. Their military discipline was excellent and their great qualities sustained all the other defects of the government, which matter less in a city which depends on force of arms than in those which are ruled by the struggles, ever-changing circumstances, and arts of peace.[3]

Of course, Machiavelli could never accept such an argument, and had rejected it in anticipation. Without a comprehensive example of ancient virtue – Guicciardini's grudging allotment of special virtues would never do – his whole appeal for a political reformation arrived at through the study of history would collapse. Nevertheless Machiavelli's remaking of Roman history as an archetype is not slavish, but critical and self-conscious. This is made clear in the prologue to the second book of the Discorsi, one of the most exciting pieces of writing in the work, where he argues powerfully against the common assumption that former times are always superior to our own. Machiavelli's psychological analysis of the need that is served by this distortion is subtle and perceptive. Less subtly but no less interestingly, he argues in world-historical terms for a kind of law of the conservation of virtue and vice. In all times, he says, the total quantity of each seems equal, only the distribution from place to place changes. Thus

3 Selected Writings, p. 69. 'Non credo fussino tali, che chi avessi a ordinare una republica, gli dovessi pigliare per esempio. Fu eccellentissima la disciplina militare, e la virtù sua sostenne tutti gli altri difetti del governo, e' quali importano manco in una città che si regge in sulle arme, che in quelle che si governano con la industria, con le girandole e con le arte della pace.' Considerazione, p. 11.

the virtue that was once gathered together in Rome was later dispersed and transferred to Arabs, Turks, and others.

But all this, ironically, is only a prelude to a lament for the loss of ancient virtue. Machiavelli's conviction of the corruption of his age is so strong, his sense of the gulf between Rome and Italy so profound, that he cannot admit that he too may be exaggerating the perfection of the ancients. The text is touched with the poignant sense that he has been failed by his times. Whoever has been born in Italy or Greece, he writes, and was not born an ultramontane in Italy or a Turk in Greece, has reason to blame his age and laud the past. Truly, he says later, if it were not that the virtue that reigned then and the vice that reigns now were as clear as the sun, he would speak more cautiously for fear of committing the error that he had condemned in others. Touching finally a personal note, and displaying at the same time his purest affinities with humanism, he declares his intention of using his writings to excite the minds of the young to imitate the virtues of the ancients and flee the vices of the present, which is the duty of the good man ('Perché gli è offizio di uomo buono, quel bene che per la malignità de' tempi e della fortuna tu non hai potuto operare, insegnarle ad altri'). Among the many he has instructed, he hopes, perhaps there will be one more favoured by heaven to put into practice what the author himself has been unable to do.[4]

Guicciardini's response, lacking that tinge of personal regret, is neither so moving nor so personal, but it demonstrates a subtler discrimination and historical sense. He accepts enthusiastically ('la conclusione è verissima ...') the idea that men exaggerate the virtue of ancient times. On the other hand, he refuses to go along with Machiavelli's rigid and unhistorical assumption that all ages show an equal amount of virtue and vice. To prove his point, Guicciardini cites the idea of a renaissance of the arts, an interesting note in a writer so devoid of aesthetic reference and an indication of the pervasiveness of the metaphor of rebirth. Who does not know, he writes, what excellence there was in painting and sculpture in the time of the Greeks and the Romans, and how after many centuries of obscurity these arts were revived one hundred and fifty or two hundred years ago? Military discipline, on the other hand, has disappeared, leaving few traces. And the same variation from time to time can be seen in religion and in letters.

Both Florentines affirm that human affairs are always in motion, but for Machiavelli they move on a fixed track, rising and descending like an eleva-

4   N. Machiavelli, *Il Principe e Discorsi*, ed. S. Bertelli (Milano: Feltrinelli 1971), p. 274.

vator or a point on a spinning wheel.[5] His fundamental assumption, essential to his didacticism, is sameness, not in the sense of stability but of repetition. By contrast, as we already know from the *Ricordi*, Guicciardini's bias is toward the uniqueness of each historical act and of each historical judgement. We can imagine how simplified Machiavelli's statement that the world has always been the same[6] would have seemed to Guicciardini, though in the *Ricordi* he had uttered, somewhat contradictorily, similar sentiments. But now he responds with complication, discrimination, variation:

> *As a result of the changes in arts and religion and the movements of human affairs it is not surprising that men's customs too should vary, which often take their direction from an institution, from chance, or from necessity.*[7]

This is not a matter of an endless repetitive rising and falling, but of variation in all aspects of human life. Institutions, occasions, needs, arts, letters, war – 'the customs of men' – all seem in motion, all are seen as variables. The product of this freer view of change, this escape from the rigidity of Machiavelli's 'law,' is Guicciardini's understanding that from one age to another there can be real historical gain or loss. Thus he concludes his commentary with the reflection that, while it is true that antiquity is not always to be preferred to the present, it is not true that all ages are the same ('ma non è gia vero el negare che una età sia qualche volta piú corotta o piú virtuosa che l'altre').

Curiously, then, Machiavelli, while arguing against the slavish assumption of the superiority of the ancients and maintaining that in all ages there is an equal quantity of vice and virtue, sees his own nation as utterly corrupt, and struggles against the vision of an almost unbridgeable gap between Italy and Rome. Guicciardini, on the other hand, admits that some ages are truly greater than others, but fails to comment on the supposed baseness of his times or draw the lesson that total reformation is required. The conviction that the times were out of joint was no less strong in Guicciardini, but he was less inclined to see the world in simple dichotomies.

5 'Perché essendo le cose umane sempre in moto o le salgano o le scendano.' Machiavelli, *Discorsi*, p. 272.
6 '... giudico il mondo sempre essere stato ad uno medesimo modo, ed in quello essere stato tanto di buono quanto di cattivo.' Machiavelli, *Discorsi*, p. 272.
7 *Selected Writings*, p. 108. 'Dalle quali variazione delle arte, della religione, de' movimenti delle cose umane, non è maraviglia siano anche variati e' costumi degli uomini, e' quali spesso pigliano el moto suo dalla instituzione, dalle occasione, dalla necessità.' *Considerazione*, p. 50.

If there is a single persistent criticism of Machiavelli in the *Considerazioni*, it is the charge of oversimplification. Again and again Guicciardini accuses his antagonist of failing to consider all the possibilities and, particularly, of creating false dichotomies. Machiavelli's mind is swift and his speech muscular. Driven by the need to establish new truths, he slices quickly through old ones. The need for action dominates his thinking, as the inevitability of action and the need for prudential calculation dominate Guicciardini's. Not as for Guicciardini a preparation for politics, writing became for Machiavelli a sublimation of action called upon to provide the excitement, daring, and decisiveness of politics itself. It is no wonder that Guicciardini finds reasons to attack his friend for simplification and bookish theorizing.

It is frequently Machiavelli's habit, as I have already remarked, to launch his reflections with a dichotomy, often a false one. 'There are two kinds of men,' he seems often to be saying, 'thin men and fat. Now if your enemy is a fat man ...' On one occasion at least in the *Considerazioni* Guicciardini's reaction to this habit approaches open annoyance. Regarding the question of whether it is better to attack or wait to be attacked, he writes:

> *And if one wants to discuss it thoroughly, it requires many considerations which have been omitted by the author. For it is not enough to make that one distinction: either I have armed subjects, or they are without arms, but it is necessary to think beyond that.*[8]

Either, he continues, my subjects are loyal or they are inclined to rebel; either my towns are weak or they are strong; either I can sustain a long conflict, even with the war on my own territories, or I cannot. Moreover, writes Guicciardini, warming to his subject, you must consider the condition of the enemy – what troops he has, what lands, what revenues, what resources he has to pursue war on home ground and abroad. Swept up in his army of distinctions, Guicciardini seems triumphant and unstoppable. There is a difference, he continues, between saying I will carry the war into his territory and saying I will meet him outside of my own country and also outside of his. There is a difference between saying I will start the war on his lands before he can start it on mine, and, having the war already in my home territory, beginning hostilities also on his. And so, like a supermarket competing with a corner store, Guicciardini adds variety after variety to the simple choices offered by his friend.

8 *Selected Writings*, p. 110. 'Ed a volerlo bene deliberare ha bisogno di molte considerazione che sono state pretermesse dallo autore. Perché non basta sola quella distinzione: o io ho e' sudditi armati o e' sono disarmati; ma è necessario pensare piú oltre ...' *Considerazioni*, p. 51.

Guicciardini's attack on Machiavelli's habit of simplification is a criticism of his logic; but in Guicciardini's eyes this habit of posing simple black and white alternatives is more than a question of method; it is also a matter of political choice. Chapter 26 of the first book of the *Discorsi* and Guicciardini's reply to it pose very clearly the confrontation of these two very different 'realists' over the issue of what may as well be called 'machiavellianism' in politics. Machiavelli's argument here is that a new prince in a city or province conquered by him should organize everything anew. He articulates the difference between private and public moralities in advocating a policy of total destruction and total regeneration. Cities must be destroyed and new ones created; the rich must be made poor, and the poor rich; nothing should be left unchanged so that everything – honours, wealth, rank – may be recognized as coming from the new prince. Admittedly such means are cruel and inimical to all Christian or even human values. One should prefer to flee such a course and be a private man rather than a prince at the cost of the ruin of so many. Nevertheless, whoever is not willing to follow the right course, to establish a legitimate monarchy or civic republic, must follow the opposite, evil one, if he wishes to maintain his power. But because princes do not know how to be either all bad or all good they usually follow the middle way, which is the most dangerous.

Guicciardini reacts to this in two characteristic ways: he accepts the harsh repugnant core of Machiavelli's dictum, but attempts to limit its application.[9] First, he makes several distinctions about types of cities and citizens and indicates his belief that not all need be dealt with in such cruel fashion. Some cities, unused to liberty and less attached to their laws and their liberties, can tolerate a despot. And as for private citizens, the prince has ways of contenting them as long as their displeasure is based on personal interest, not principle. The real difficulty comes when the people as a whole are against the new government. Those who are really devoted to liberty cannot be put off with blandishments because they cannot bear to see others rule over them. In this case, says Guicciardini, harsh measures are required. Thus, having attempted to limit and to discriminate, Guicciardini shows no obvious qualms about accepting 'machiavellianism' where it is 'necessary.' Even so he argues against cruelty for those few who can be gained by kindness, because violence creates its own weaknesses. Thus the prince must have the courage to use extraordinary measures ('questi estraordinari') and yet he must be 'prudente' too, and not miss any chance to establish himself through favours and kindness. Separating himself from the extremism of Machiavelli, he warns his reader not to take

9 *Considerazioni*, pp. 32-3.

what this author writes as an absolute rule, because he was always too partial to violent and extraordinary measures ('al quale sempre piacquono
sopra modo e' remedi estraordinari e violenti').

Let us freely admit impediment to the marriage of these two minds.
Yet behind the divergence of style, method, and mission, there remains a
fundamental bond. Machiavelli has no interest in the establishment of despotism and his whole discourse follows from the assumption that you have
chosen against 'quella prima via del bene' that leads to a legitimate monarchy or civil republic. The real thrust of his argument is a warning against
failing to make a choice and muddling along in compromises. And Guicciardini, whose politics differ from Machiavelli's only in degree, makes no
objection to the structure of the discourse. The argument of both Florentines requires, then, a suspension of our (and their) disbelief in the intended
political goal. We must forget our preference for the humane or Christian
life, our belief in the superiority of republican governments, and enter into
the world of argument. There is no attempt to convince us of the virtues
of despotism; rather there is in each man a fascination with politics as a
science or game. Both can argue the enemy's case, not in order to convince,
but to explore. They have become temporarily more interested in the process than the conclusion.

As one might expect, however, Guicciardini shows even greater talent at
this exercise in detachment than Machiavelli, whose political passions more
frequently rage across his pages, winning him our sympathies but losing
that sense of alternatives on which perspective is built. Too frequently
Machiavelli wants to change the rules of the game, and Guicciardini is the
first to point this out. Chapter 10 of the first book of the *Discorsi* is a passionate and highly rhetorical set-piece lauding the virtues of founders of
legitimate republics and monarchies and damning the founders of tyranny.
Nowhere is Machiavelli's debt to humanism clearer and the transmutation
that humanist rhetoric undergoes in his hands more evident. The traditional scheme of virtue praised and vice condemned is as naked here as in
any homily. But while the condemnation of Caesar and praise for Brutus
and Scipio are familiar humanist themes, Machiavelli's interest in the charismatic founder of the new order is his own:

> *And surely, if he be a man, he will be shocked at the thought of re-*
> *enacting those evil times, and be fired with an intense desire to follow*
> *the example of the good. And truly, if a prince be anxious for glory and*
> *the good opinion of the world, he should rather wish to possess a corrupt*
> *city, not to ruin it wholly like Caesar, but to re-organize it like Romulus.*[10]

10 Luigi Ricci, trans. Niccolò Machiavelli, *The Prince and Discourses* (New York:
   Modern Library 1950). 'È sanza dubbio se e' sara nato d'uomo, si sbigottirà da

This is Machiavelli's version of the highest good, and it is the heart of his political myth. Truly, he says, the heavens could not give you a greater occasion for glory than this, nor could a man want more.

The vision of reformation is noble, but vulnerable. Carried away by generous enthusiasm for his hero, the charismatic founder of a new state, Machiavelli suggests that having once founded the new order he might want to step aside. It is his conviction that the new order is best established by a single individual but best preserved by a republic; thus, the self-denying founder who, like Solon, does his work and disappears is a convenient answer to an obvious dilemma. Guicciardini, predictably, is not so easily satisfied. He is far more aware than Machiavelli of the intimacy of charisma and tyranny, far more fearful of unchecked power. Already in the previous chapter he had written that not only may the potential tyrant deliberately hide his intentions under the colour of honesty, but a good man may be corrupted by power. Foreshadowing Acton, he argues that 'the sweetness of power and unlimited authority may change his earlier good intentions to bad ones.'[11]

In the present text, Guicciardini returns to the same theme with greater intensity and harsher criticism of Machiavelli's idealism. After the by now expected distinctions between various cases and types ('But because cases are so different, and the author does not distinguish properly between examples ...') he focuses on the idea that the prince or tyrant already in power will voluntarily lay down his authority. Without Machiavelli's rhetoric or his humanism, Guicciardini accepts the fundamental proposition that founders of tyranny are to be blamed as the founders of republics are to be lauded. But the distinction is not always so obvious; just as in the previous chapter he saw the tyrant behind the hero, now he points to oppression in the guise of liberty. Many things, he says, are often called freedom which are not. As so often in this work, he has in mind the Florentine republic, now approaching its last days. Justifying the choice of those who, like himself, chose ultimately for the tyranny of the Medici against the 'liberty' of the Republic, he writes:

> These were forced either to desire the change of a government, which, under colour of liberty was tyrannous and destructive of the liberty of

ogni imitazione de' tempi cattivi, ed accenderassi d'uno immenso desiderio di seguire i buoni. E veramente cercando un principe la gloria del mondo, dovereb-be'l desiderare di possedere una città corotta, non per guastarla in tutto come Cesare, ma per riordinarla come Romolo.' *Discorsi*, p. 159.
11 *Selected Writings*, p. 76. 'La dolcezza della potenzia e la licenzia del principato gli faccia mutare in mala la intenzione che da principio fussi stata buona.' *Considera-zioni*, p. 18.

*the nation, or to allow themselves in silence, and unjustly, to be de-
prived of their country and their possessions.*[12]

Ideally one should put the love of country before one's own safety, but
because 'questo amore o questa fortezza' is more often desired than found
among men, those who act from such reasons deserve to be excused, especially where, as in the case of the republic of 1527-30, the government is a
bad one.

It must be said that Guicciardini's argument is somewhat oblique to the
bulk of Machiavelli's text. And just as there is a large element of wishful-
ness in Machiavelli's proposition, there is a considerable amount of self-
justification in Guicciardini's. On the other hand, Guicciardini fully accepts
Machiavelli's principal contention – the condemnation of the founders of
tyranny and praise for the founders of legitimate regimes – and thus leaves
himself free to probe the weaknesses in Machiavelli's rhetoric. The chief
weakness, aside from the usual failure to distinguish between various cases
and types, seems to be Machiavelli's idealistic refusal to take seriously the
psychology of tyrants. Turning from the case of a newly established tyranny to a tyranny that is inherited, Guicciardini agrees that it would be
wonderful if a tyranny should be relinquished voluntarily, but doubts that
it has ever happened. And no wonder. Those brought up in tyranny do not
have the eyes to see the glory of liberating their country. Accustomed to
that way of life, the tyrant believes power to be the highest good and nothing will persuade him to give it up.[13] Moreover, a tyrant always makes enemies, and such a step would be filled with danger for himself and his sons.

Guicciardini here demonstrates himself capable of understanding a situation not from his own perspective but from the standpoint of the actor.
Furthermore he seems aware of this capacity in himself and contrasts it to
what he considers Machiavelli's utopianism. These thoughts of tyrants giving up their tyrannies and kings depriving their posterity of the succession
are much more likely in theory than in practice. Like the *regole* that he
attacks in the *Ricordi*, such idealistic notions are only to be found in
books: '[these ideas] are more easily given form in books and in men's
imaginations than carried into effect.'[14] Thus, concludes Guicciardini, can

12 *Selected Writings*, p. 78. 'E' quali la necessità ha condotti o a desiderare la mutazione di uno stato che sotto nome di libertà è tirannico e distruttore della patria,
   o tacitamente lasciarsi con somma ingiustizia torre la patria e le facultà.'
   'Considerazioni,' p. 20.
13 *Considerazioni*, p. 20: 'Assuefatto a quello modo di vivere, giudici che el sommo
   bene sia nella potenzia ...'
14 *Selected Writings*, p. 79. 'Si dipingono più facilmente in su' libri e nelle immagina-
   zione degli uomini, che non se ne eseguiscono in fatto.' *Considerazioni*, p. 21.

we really blame men for failing to do things which few or perhaps none has ever done?

Much of the *Considerazioni* can be seen as the concrete application to Machiavelli's text of lessons that Guicciardini had already taught himself in the earlier redaction of the *Ricordi*, though there are also new ideas of great intrinsic interest, such as the defence of the disunity of Italy. Yet if we look back across the major arguments of the commentary we must recognize great consistency in the work, a quality less characteristic of the *Ricordi*. This, more than anything else, suggests that the *Considerazioni* is a work of consolidation rather than discovery. Guicciardini's fundamental criticisms of Machiavelli's style of thought – the charges of utopianism, extremism, oversimplification, failure to distinguish between cases, and the mythological use of Roman history – are easily gathered together into a single and clear position on historical knowledge, the same position naturally enough that we have already examined in the *Ricordi*. It is easier, of course, to be consistent in a work of criticism than in an essay in primary analysis, but most of all Guicciardini was helped by having a strong and clear opponent in Machiavelli. The consistency of the *Considerazioni* can be taken as a sign of maturity in the author, but it is the sense of fully worked out positions on both sides that gives this confrontation the stamp of a significant occasion. Although Guicciardini had the last word, the argument could not be anything but equal. The two antagonists articulate not just private views but two permanent positions on the uses of history, and the significance of each is enhanced by its awareness of the other.

The poet, T.S. Eliot said, should write something every week so that when a great conception comes someday, he will not lack a vehicle. Perhaps a similar prescription applies to historians; certainly when we measure Guicciardini against other political intellectuals of his generation in Florence, one thing that stands out is his continued application to the craft of history. Others wrote single histories under the commission of the governing house or a ruling idea, and taken collectively the generation was remarkably prolific. Clearly men like Vettori and Nerli were members of a class and society peculiarly aware of the differences time had made. And yet alone among them Guicciardini demonstrates a life-long commitment to the historian's craft. Of course, his first choice was, almost until the end, for the active political life. But when disbarred from politics and thus possessing a sort of obligatory leisure, Guicciardini turned to reflecting upon and writing history. Thus, in late 1527 in the aftermath of the overthrow of the Medici regime, Guicciardini for the second time began to compose a Florentine history. He began the work in retirement at his villa near Florence. Later, in 1529 he left Florence to travel in safer places and ended up

in Rome. There he was able to resume the work but without benefit of
books and documents that he had left behind. In 1530 he was again in
Florence, though now with less leisure, and there he continued the work,
which finally was abandoned except for some minor corrections when he
left to become Governor of Bologna in 1531.[15] This second Florentine history, named the *Cose fiorentine* by Ridolfi, who recovered and published
it after four hundred years, marks the exact middle of Guicciardini's career
as an historian. Here we find an increasing perfection of the vehicle, un-
matched yet by a conception of equivalent force. In retrospect we can see
clearly the masterpiece to come; but in the fragmentary work itself we find
something more conventional than either the spontaneous writing of his
youth or the idiosyncratic genius of his age. Here more than anywhere else
Guicciardini attempts to fit a pattern and here, too, it becomes obvious
that he questions history and examines its materials in a way that will produce a new design.

More than the *Storie fiorentine*, the *Cose* can be taken as a kind of progress report. The unfinished state in which Guicciardini left his text, full of
queries, undigested documents, and loose ends to be followed up, does not
in fact permit us to do much more. But precisely because of its incomplete
form, the *Cose* reveals the works and mechanism which the historian elsewhere conceals behind a taut narrative and intricate prose. Only the last
books of the *Storia d'Italia*, also left unfinished, give us the same direct
view of his technique, which does not seem to have changed much in the
intervening decade. Moreover, we are fortunate that Ridolfi's belated *editio
princeps* not only gives us a thorough discussion of Guicciardini's use of
sources but preserves the evidence in the printed text. With regard to this
aspect of the *Cose*, then, we need do nothing more than follow in Ridolfi's
steps.

The *Cose fiorentine* is Guicciardini's second attempt to write a comprehensive narrative of Florentine history from the late Trecento, but he
seems to have embarked on this more ambitious history without even a
backward glance to the *Storie fiorentine*.[16] Thus, rejecting his earlier work
but operating very much in the tradition of the humanists, Guicciardini
went back to the large body of chronicles and histories that Florentines
had created, most notably, of course, the humanist histories of Bruni and
Poggio and the chronicles of Villani, Stefani, and Buoninsegni. But many
other sources are cited and used as well, including Flavio Biondo, Aeneas

15 For the dating of the work see Ridolfi's 'Introduction' to his edition of *Le Cose
   fiorentine* (Florence: Olschki 1945), pp. xxiv-xxvii.
16 For what follows see Ridolfi, 'Introduction,' *Cose*, pp. xxiv-xl.

Silvius Piccolomini, Gino and Neri Capponi, Luigi Guicciardini's *Ricord-anze*, and to a lesser degree such sources as Froissart, S. Antonino, Platina, Sabellico, and Dati. The evidence of his judiciousness is everywhere as he carefully weighs one source against another or notes their reliability. Thus he reminds himself in his margins that Stefani's position in the city put him in a good place to understand the external affairs of Florence, but that in internal matters he is biased by factionalism. And in citing some evidence that contradicted an assertion of Machiavelli's he notes the contradiction and admonishes himself to look into it carefully.[17]

These sources took Guicciardini through his first two books, which begin with a summary of the origins of the city and bring the main narrative from 1375 to the opening of the fifteenth century. And so far, for all his undoubted critical acuity, Guicciardini's methods have, of necessity, been a refinement of the conventional, though the conventional is not to be despised when we recall the high standards a historian like Bruni had set. But with the beginning of Book III Guicciardini came to a point at which he could make larger use of documents preserved in his extensive family archive. We should remember that this collection had already served him well in the composition of the *Storie fiorentine*. But this time the results of contact with the archive seem different. There ensued, according to Ridolfi, a 'profound crisis of method' which stood in the way of the progress of the work.[18] While continuing to draw the central thread of his narrative from previous histories, principally for this period Poggio and Buoninsegni, Guicciardini began to fill out his margins with documentary evidence taken from such sources as the *Commissioni* of Rinaldo degli Albizzi and the papers of Piero Guicciardini.[19] Even in its external appearance, notes Ridolfi, the text changes, as the narrative center diminishes and the margins flourish with data increasingly independent of the narrative thread. And finally, Guicciardini abandoned the text altogether, attracted perhaps (as Ridolfi speculates) by another history which he himself had lived and for which the sources would be so much more adequate.

17 *Cose*, p. 55 n. 3: 'Adverte che Marchionne è assai fedele auctore delle cose di quelli templ, dico di fuora, perché si travagliava et andò imbasciadore et hebbe magistrati; ma in quelle di drento è passionato, chè andava alla via degli Octo della Guerra et della moltitudine.' See also *Cose*, p. 59 n. 1: 'Questo passo è contro al Machiavello; però vedilo diligenter.'
18 'Introduction,' *Cose*, xxvi: 'una profonda crisi di metodo che, salutare per se nocque al progresso dell' opera.'
19 Also the *Ricordanze* of Michele Castellani and the *Esamina* of Niccolo Tinucci. See Ridolfi, 'Introduction,' *Cose*, xxxiv.

It seems clear that Ridolfi regards Guicciardini's exploration of archival sources as the key feature of the *Cose fiorentine*. Not only is Guicciardini's technique remarkable and precocious and therefore demands our attention, but it also seems to be the critical element of the work which helps to determine the shape of other elements. With regard to its precocity I have no quarrel; Guicciardini's remarkable carefulness as a researcher is well known and the *Cose* clearly represents the decisive moment in the development of this technique from the more elementary use of the family archive in the first history to the fuller use of the archives of Dieci in the composition of the *Storia d'Italia*. But whether we can accept the notion that this is the key feature of the history, a feature that determines something so basic as the final abandonment of the narrative and leads to the choice of a new and more contemporary theme, is an entirely different matter. In the most general terms, it seems dubious that any historian before the modern age of professionalism was motivated primarily or even largely by questions of research technique. And from what we now know about Guicciardini in particular it seems clear that this scrupulousness of his was far more than a way of using documents. On the contrary, it seems more reasonable to say that the critical acumen that Guicciardini demonstrates with regard to his sources in the *Cose* is the application to historical practice of a long process which we have traced in the *Ricordi* and the *Considerazioni*, in which Guicciardini re-examined the nature of historical knowledge and abandoned much of the traditional humanist framework of historical writing. Moreover, Guicciardini's scrupulous use of documents should not be taken in isolation as the only evidence of his critical sense. His rejection of dogmatism and didacticism, humanist or Machiavellian, his cool and analytic tone and careful language are equally features of his new, more critical sense of history.

We have noted that Guicciardini's collection of documents for the *Cose* proceeded further than the narrative portion of his text, but this is not the only element of the intended history that outruns the central story-line. Equally, there exist finished speeches of the type familiar from classical historiography which Guicciardini intended to compact with the documents themselves into a fuller narrative. Thus, the elementary story of events which the historian drew from his predecessors became increasingly distinct from the intended narrative, a sort of builder's chalk line marking the areas of future construction. But none of this indicates a lack of interest in narrative history; on the contrary, it indicates a more complex and ambitious sense of what narrative history might be. And in that expanded narrative, the imagined orations, hypothetical mirrors of the minds of historical actors, were intended to have as serious a place as the rougher materials quarried from documents.

A few years after abandoning the *Cose*, in a 'Commentary' that represents the germ of the *Storia d'Italia*, Guicciardini makes a rare programmatic statement about history that may help us to see the value of these
fragments. The true value of history, he writes, consists more in understanding motives (*consigli*) and the origins of things than in knowing the
effects. The reason is that what actually happened is well known to everyone (here Guicciardini speaks as a contemporary historian) whereas the
origins of events and motives are hidden. And perhaps most important of
all, he associates the enquiry into these hidden parts of history with highly
detailed narrative, saying that he will press himself to narrate with as much
particularity and minuteness as he can.[20] Perhaps it is risky to cast the light
of this statement back over the earlier history, but the *Cose* is an unfinished
work which in a sense did not live long enough to make its own statement.
The words of the later text seem to make explicit the sort of unity which
Guicciardini must have had in mind for the *Cose* when he lavished care on
the seemingly opposite tasks of uncovering documents and composing
speeches. Thus, caring less for the outward appearance of events – the
diminishing stream of story, already well known or easily derived from
earlier histories – he gave minute attention to the investigation of motives
and causes.

Guicciardini's careful use of the invented speech also draws our attention to other sides of the *Cose fiorentine*. It is clear that these orations
have an analytic function, especially when presented in pairs arguing the
pros and cons of a particular policy. Felix Gilbert has noted the political
concreteness which Guicciardini gives his compositions as compared to his
humanist predecessors.[21] But the speech also has a more purely rhetorical
function of embellishing the work and establishing its classical seriousness,
a purpose which Gilbert associates with the attempt to write 'true history'
as the humanist defined it.[22] It is impossible to know precisely how far
Guicciardini, never a literary man, had the explicit prescriptions of the

20 'Le quali cose mi sforzerò narrare piú particularmente et piú minutamente che io
   potrò, perché el fructo vero della hystoria consiste piú in intendere e' consigli et
   le origine delle cose che in sapere gli effecti, perché questi sono noti a tucti, quegli
   occulti et, che è peggio, divulgati spesso molto falsi et alienissimi dalla verità.'
   Ridolfi, *Genesi della 'Storia d'Italia' Guicciardiniana* (Florence: Olschki 1939),
   Appendice 1, p. 41. For further discussion of this 'Commentary' text, see below.
21 'Poggio elaborated the arguments by linking them with general philosophical reflections; Guicciardini strengthened them by adding factual details on the political situation under discussion. To this extent Guicciardini was much more concrete and realistic.' Gilbert, *Machiavelli and Guicciardini*, p. 246.
22 'We have suggested that Guicciardini embarked on writing a second Florentine
   History because he realized that his first one failed to meet the accepted standards
   for a "true history."' Gilbert, *Machiavelli and Guicciardini*, p. 247.

humanists in mind when he wrote. But it certainly is clear that the *Cose* approaches the classical convention far more closely than either the earlier *Storie fiorentine* or the later *Storia d'Italia*. Like the first Florentine history, the *Cose* is a civic history, but it includes the classical speeches and a summary of the origins of the city, also a humanist feature. More generally, the *Cose* displays a greater sense of proportion in the narrative, and in style it begins to resemble the studied gravity of the later work. Guicciardini has cast off the colloquialisms of the earlier history in this middle work but he has not yet fully elaborated the complexity and qualification of his late prose. Let us look, for example, at the opening of Book III:

> *The death of Gian Galeazzo, at a time when it was least expected by the Florentines and most desired, changed the state of affairs in Italy, because it left those who had thought to subjugate others in danger of losing the State and, on the contrary, made stronger those who had little hope of defending themselves.*[23]

A reader who comes to this passage from a knowledge of the *Storia d'Italia* will have no difficulty in recognizing the largeness and weightiness of such a sentence; typical, too, is the balancing of ironies, albeit obvious ones. We also note the essentially Italian frame of reference. But as we read further, this sense of recognition blurs and there emerges an author who is distinctly different from his older or younger self:

> The oldest men used to recount *that there were two other times when the death of an enemy was very opportune for the salvation of Florence. The first was when the Emperor Henry who had unsuccessfully beseiged the city returned with great machines and with his will stubbornly set on destroying her. The other time was when Castruccio 'Signore' of Pisa and Lucca, a man very skilled in military arts and very famous for many victories, recovered Pistoia and aided by the Ghibelline forces, which at the time were powerful in Italy because of the coming of the Bavarian and for other reasons,* was entirely intent on our destruction. God, who loves republics, wanted to demonstrate with these unexpected aids how much liberty pleased him. That grace *being well understood, many devout processions were made and signs of gratitude to God ...*[24]

23 (My trans.) 'La morte di Gian Galeazo, in quello tempo che da' Fiorentini era manco aspectata et piú desiderata, mutò le conditione delle cose di Italia, perché resorono in pericolo di perdere lo Stato quegli che credevano soctoporre gl'altri, et, pel contrario, superiori coloro che havevano pocha speranza di potere difendere sè medesimi.' *Cose*, p. 123.

24 (My trans.) '*Raccontavano e' piú vecchi* due altre volte la morte degli inimici essere stata molto opportuna alla salute di Firenze: prima, quando Herrico im-

I have used roman type to set off the most notable elements. First, there is the odd and artificial literary device which refers back to an archaic notion of history as a kind of oral collective memory. Then, as we proceed, the earlier Italian framework is entirely displaced by a narrower Florentine civic viewpoint, as expressed by the appeal to a Florentine audience. And finally there is the appeal to divine protection for republics, almost shocking for the reader familiar with the later Guicciardini. Nor does one know whether to be more surprised at the strength of Guicciardini's republicanism or his introduction of an historically active God. Of course this passage is not typical, at least in its tone. The struggle of the city against Visconti 'tyranny' at the end of the fourteenth century is the *locus classicus* of Florentine civic humanism. Thus Guicciardini may be responding here to sentiments transmitted in his sources and in the preceding historiography; but we should not forget too that Guicciardini began the *Cose* in a period when republicanism and *libertà* were once again the leading political issues in the endangered Republic. Guicciardini's civic loyalty may be expressed more forcefully and rhetorically in the passage we have read than elsewhere, but it is not a unique instance.[25] And it is this specifically Florentine element in the *Cose*, which the reader familiar with the *Storia d'Italia* is likely to experience as a limitation in the earlier work, that most sharply distinguishes Guicciardini's sense of history in 1530 from that of nearly a decade later. It has been said that Guicciardini was consciously adopting the classical form of the history of a city-state when he wrote the *Cose*, a form which he later abandoned for the wider horizons of the *History of Italy*. But it should be clear from the passage we have been examining that more than a matter of form is involved. In the *Cose fiorentine* Guicciardini still writes as a man of local loyalties with a civic audience - or is it that he

---

peradore, che invano era stato ... alle mura de la cictà, ritornava con grandi apparati et con animo molto obstinato alla destructione sua; l'altra, quando Castruccio, signore di Pisa et di Lucca, huomo peritissimo nella arte militare et riputatissimo per molte victorie, recuperata Pistoia et appoggiato dalle forze de' ghibellini, che allora per la venuta del Bavero et altri accidenti erano grandissime in Italia, *era tucto intento alla nostra debellatione: Dio amatore delle republiche havere voluto con questi rimedii non aspectati dimostrare quanto gli piaceva la libertà de' popoli.* La quale *gratia* essendo bene ricognosciuta, furono facte molte procissione devotamente et segni di ringratiare Dio ...' *Cose*, p. 123.

25 For example, commenting on the beginning of the same set of wars, he writes; 'Non fu nessuno che con animo generoso non confortassi che più presto si pigliassi la guerra con ogni pericolo che si maculassi la fede o la libertà.

Seguita la guerra gravissima che hebbe el popolo fiorentino con Giovan Galeazzo Visconti conte di Virtù, della quale nessuna hebbe mai più memorabile et in quale apparissi più la potentia e virtù sua, havendo a fare con uno inimico potentissimo a chi obbediva quasi tucta la Lombardia ...' *Cose*, p. 93.

writes that way once again? Less than a decade later he will deliberately
obliterate the traces of any such tie and appear to become a historian without citizenship.

Clearly the second Florentine history recalls the first in some respects,
but the differences are remarkable. In the simplest terms, the author of
this work is also the creator of the *Ricordi*, which he was putting into a
final form at much the same time. The most obvious connection between
the two works is the way in which various maxims get transferred to the
Cose, just as later they will find a setting in the *Storia d'Italia*. Not surprisingly, these reflections frequently find their way into the speeches which
Guicciardini has invented for his historical characters. And it is an interesting feature of both the *Cose* and the *Storia d'Italia* that it is not always the
wiser of the contending orators who is loaned the use of one of Guicciardini's maxims.[26] But even where Guicciardini does not draw directly on the
formulae of the *Ricordi* it is clear that their counterpointed and ironic
mode of presentation has become a part of his style. Thus, for example,
when the Duke of Milan precipitates war by refusing Venetian conditions
for peace, we are told that:

> *Even though it seemed to him dangerous, nonetheless he nobly decided
> to accept (the war) not wanting to accept through timidity or baseness
> conditions imposed by others, though shortly before he had hoped to
> impose them on all Italy.*[27]

And of the beginning of an earlier war he writes that Italy had been at
peace, nor could one see the seeds of a future war, had it not been for the
fact that new fires were lit by those whose office it is to extinguish them.[28]
The special interest of the statement, in addition to the obvious irony, is
that this is precisely the formula that Guicciardini will call upon over and
over again in the *Storia d'Italia* in condemnation of princes, popes, and republics. And I should not omit to add that, as it comes at the end of a

---

26 An example, perhaps, of what Keats called 'negative capability.' See, for instance,
the very fine pair of speeches in which an anonymous opponent of the highly respected statesman, Niccolò da Uzzano, in effect quotes Guicciardini on the difficulties of judging the future (*Cose*, p. 155). Niccolò has his own chance later,
however. See p. 206.

27 (My trans.) 'Benché a lui paressi grave et pericolosa, nondimanco deliberò genero-
samente acceptarla, né per timidità o ignavia piglare per sè medesimo le legge da
altri, le quali pocho innanzi haveva sperato dare a tucta Italia.' *Cose*, p. 192.

28 *Cose*, p. 38. 'Stava Italia allhora socto questi governi assai in pace, et e' Fiorentini già anni si erano riposati, né si vedeva seme di futura guerra, se non havessino
acceso nuovo fuoco coloro lo uficio de' quali era spegnerlo se fussi stato suscitato
da altri.' I might add that the formula is stated a little clumsily here.

summary of the state of affairs in Italy, this text is also a corrective to what has been said about Guicciardini's civic allegiance. Certainly Guicciardini, however strong his Florentine loyalty, is already very much aware of the extent to which Tuscan history depends on Italian affairs.

In the *Cose* Guicciardini is a less reticent author than he will later be. His voice intrudes more often into the narrative, making explicit judgements on men and events. It seems reasonable to link this to the proximity of his two non-historical works of the same period. At times, in fact, he seems to be carrying on the same arguments, as for example when he recounts how in its early history Florence, like other provincial cities, remained small because of the overwhelming domination of Rome.[29] More generally, this is a highly political history in which the political vocabulary and arguments of his generation are frequently reflected. Indeed, in the sense of possessing a specifically political language, the second Florentine history can be said to be more political than the first. To take an example, the ghost of Machiavelli seems near when Guicciardini asserts in connection with a factional dispute that there is no more imprudent policy than to overthrow opponents and yet not take away from them every possibility of revenge.[30] And a typically Machiavellian preoccupation with the distinction between means and ends, though adapted to Guicciardini's own language of prudence, appears in the following: 'The conditions in the city were difficult, and too late was the realization that it is not enough to engage in a war with justice and nobility if one does not also use prudence.' It is not, he adds, in the beginnings or the means of an affair but in its end that honour consists.[31] Like Vettori, Guicciardini saw all government as violent. But he is more subtle than Vettori (or Machiavelli on the unarmed prophet) when he says that the early Christian emperors wished to command the popes because princes have always wanted certain things that neither force alone nor persuasion alone could procure. And among the ways of compelling men, that which compels them without arms or the appearance of force is far from the weakest.[32]

29 *Cose*, p. 10.
30 *Cose*, p. 52: 'Non è piú imprudente consiglo che crollare gl'homini et non tòrre loro tucta la forza di potersi vendicare.'
31 (My trans.) 'Dure erano le conditione della ciptà et tardi el cognoscere che non basta piglare le guerre con giustitia et con generosità, se anche non si piglano con prudentia, et che non ne'principii et ne' mezi delle imprese, ma nel fine consiste l'honore.' *Cose*, p. 62.
32 *Cose*, p. 23. See also his discussion in the *Cose* of the election of Charlemagne as emperor (p. 24): 'Non voglo affermare che questa electione di Carlo fussi iuridica, ma consentirò facilmente a chi dirà el contrario, se mi mostrerrà che anche fussi iuridica quella degl'altri imperadori, et che e' tituli degli Stati et de' principati

The impression the *Cose* makes upon the reader is an amalgam of the rough and the smooth, the sophisticated language of politics and oratory combined with fragments from archives and the historian's shorthand. Before leaving the work we must at least sample the last of these, the notes and queries with which Guicciardini plotted his way towards his history. Here his concern for detail, his diligence, and his curiosity are most evident. Speaking of so well known a Florentine institution as the Parte Guelfa, he admonishes himself to look more closely at its character, its mode of government, and its rules for membership.[33] Similarly, he asks himself whether the Arte della Lana, the wool guild, was much larger then than now. And speaking of the revolutionary wool workers, the Ciompi, he is not content to bring them into his story without a historical introduction, but directs himself to investigate their progress since the days of the Duke of Athens.[34] And in another place he outlines what is in effect a plan for a short but detailed history of the Monte, the communal funded debt.[35] When a peace is signed he wants to know not only the month but the day and makes a note to himself to search for a copy of the treaty.[36] A league concluded by the Venetians draws the comment that it seems more ceremonial than real, but still he instructs himself to think about it further.[37] And quite often, of course, these marginal comments are directed at discrepancies between his-

naschino piú dalla dispositione delle legge che dalla forza delle arme o dalla occasione delle cose, dalle quali piglano anchora regola le congiunctione o le inimicitie de' principi.'

33 *Cose*, p. 50: 'Vedi che cosa era questa università de' guelfi et el modo del governo loro, et se ognuno ne poteva essere o bisognava approvatione.'

34 *Cose*, p. 72: 'Vegghisi bene el progresso de' ciompi dal duca d'Athene insino a questo tempo.'
   'Se la Arte della lana era molto maggiore che hora.'

35 *Cose*, p. 109: 'Et hinc, capta occasione, dichiarisi largamente che cosa sia el Monte, come hebbe origine et in che tempo, quanto si allargassi, delle dote de' maschi et femine, de' danari de' forestieri, et come in progresso di tempo per la soma grande ha perduto riputatione, et molte volte si è facta diminutione et qualche volta beneficio. Fu invenzione da principio salutifera, perché in molte necessità della cictà è stato causa et e si truovino danari piú promptamente, ma male usata, perché questa commodità di far danari ha facto gl'huomini piú prompti a piglare le guerre non necessarie o male misurate, donde, oltre a travaglosi accidenti che spesso ne sono seguiti, si è facta questa soma del Monte che tiene affogata la ciptà, in modo che, come fu già decto, o el Monte disfarà Firenze o Firenza disfarà el Monte.'

36 *Cose*, p. 107: 'Vedi in che mese et dí fussi facta la pace, et, se si può, la copia de' capitoli.'

37 *Cose*, p. 116: 'Questa lega de' Vinitiani mi pare piú presto cerimoniale et per dare riputatione che per altro; pero considerala bene.'

torians. Similarly the veracity of an historical narrative may be weighed against common sense or documentary evidence.[38]

What cannot be conveyed from this list is the way in which the text progressively crumbles into its most basic elements, as not only the narrative attenuates but references to narrative sources become thin and the page swarms with notes from government documents, letters, treaties, and dispatches. But impressive as all this apparatus is, we should not forget that it is all preliminary to something larger. Because Guicciardini never came close to completing the history, it is impossible to say what his intended goal was. We know that as he composed the *Cose* he made no use at all of his earlier *Florentine History*, and it seems safe to assume that he now had new ambitions which made the first work unacceptable. It is clear that he consciously elevated his style. Drawing on the conventions of humanist and classical historiography, he moved away from the Florentine chronicling tradition which was still important in the *Storie fiorentine*. Thus he gave his new work some of the seriousness and prestige that adheres to the classical tradition. But Guicciardini's seriousness was not just some trick of rhetoric. The apparatus of the *Cose*, the aphorisms of the *Ricordi*, and the criticisms of the *Considerazioni* all demonstrate that he was troubled by the simplicities of the inherited historiographical tradition and its Machiavellian extension. He was distrustful of its didacticism and sceptical of its generalizations. Increasingly in his mind particularity and truthfulness became synonymous. Where others would tend to take an event as a unit which can then be combined with other like units to form a didactic pattern, he had come to see the individual event itself as a complex of a large number of intentions, circumstances, and accidents. Thus, narrative itself becomes a significant achievement.

It is difficult to draw conclusions from this unfinished work. All that seems clear from the *Cose* is that Guicciardini's response to the challenge of his problematic view of history will take the form of arduous research and a narrative of great particularity. To see the finished shape of such a narrative, however, we must wait for the *Storia d'Italia*.

---

38 *Cose*, p. 160: '... dice Poggio che e' Fiorentini la negorono per non dare occasione di muovere l'ire al duca, il che non è verisimile, perché non vi era cause; però credo più presto, come dice in lettere Rinaldo, che la difficultà nascessi perché e' Fiorentini volessino includervi drento el signor Braccio ...'

PART TWO

The *Storia d'Italia*

Introduction

The enforced leisure and isolation from political power that mark Guicciardini's last years are the indispensible setting for his final work, the
Storia d'Italia. Although Guicciardini may once have entertained hopes of
guiding the young Cosimo de' Medici, even perhaps of marrying a daughter
to him, the old patrician found himself respected but without authority
after many years of service in which much had been sacrificed as well as
won. Power had stripped him of idealism, and service to absolute rulers
had dissolved the solidarities of class. He was rich, of course, but without
sons, and on his death his wealth would be divided among his brothers.
Two of the brothers, Iacopo and Girolamo, had maintained the business
interests traditional to their class. Luigi, the eldest had, on the other hand,
devoted himself professionally to politics, while a fifth brother, Bongianni,
retired to a cultured and gentlemanly leisure on inherited estates. The patriciate was changing. The sons of Piero Guicciardini had, in different de-
grees, veered away from the Albertian ideals still cautiously pursued by
their father. Piero had combined careful investment with careful politics.
For him, in significant contrast to two of his sons, politics was a duty of
his class which he undertook often reluctantly and from which he neither
expected nor received great profits. Francesco inherited his father's position in the city, but economically as well as politically he seems far removed from the family traditions that he had chronicled as a young man
and from the virtues which he had praised in his father.

How Guicciardini perceived these changes must remain largely a matter
of conjecture. Even a relatively concrete matter such as his personal view
of the Medici and his relationship to their regime is not easy to specify
with confidence. Guicciardini was above all a prudent and reticent man.
His correspondence, which we might expect to reveal his more personal
side, is largely official, offering few clues to his private life or character.

And because all of his extended writings belong to intervals of retirement, his collected correspondence, the *Carteggi*, is fullest for the years of political activity and bare in the periods of literary engagement. Thus if we try to pursue the question of Guicciardini's relationship to the Medici, the *Carteggi* offer a little evidence for the early 1530s but none for the last years of the decade in which the *Storia* was actually composed.

There can be no question about the fact that by 1530, after the fall of the last republic, Guicciardini saw his fortunes as entirely bound up with the political success of the Medici. But this only begs a further question. Was the Medici regime an absolute one to which Guicciardini felt tied as a servant to his masters? Or did he participate in the new government as a partner, albeit a minor one, and preserve some sense of independence? Clearly it is beyond our scope to attempt to analyse the character of Medici rule in Florence after 1530, but we can get a feeling from the *Carteggi* of Guicciardini's own sense of his rights and duties. In certain of these letters it seems apparent that, in his own mind at least, Guicciardini maintained some independence, and that he did not see the Medici as absolute authorities to whom he had to accommodate himself at all costs. Evidence of this attitude comes in the series of letters Guicciardini wrote in connection with his expectation of being reappointed to the Presidency of the Romagna, the lucrative office he had held before the troubles. He was anxious to leave behind what Ridolfi calls 'the bitterness of Florence' and to begin to recoup his fortunes, which had been wasted by the exactions of the Republic and the loss of his official salary. When rumours began that his rival Valori would be given his old job, Guicciardini was incensed, and the offer of the equally prestigious position of Governor of Bologna did not assuage him, especially as he expected that at Bologna he would have to maintain a more ostentatious and costly establishment. The reader who wades through this protracted correspondence re-experiences in part Guicciardini's fretful boredom as he waited for the vacillating pope to act on the appointment. Finally, having accepted the governorship of Bologna, Guicciardini, vexed at still further delays, allowed his rage to boil over into a highly undiplomatic letter to Rome:

> *I thought it would have sufficed him [Pope Clement] to have taken away from me the office of the Monte with as much dishonour as if I had murdered the entire commune, to have treated me over the Presidency of Romagna as you well know how, after forcing me against my will to have the grievances of the Romagnoli brought up in Rome, and so made a fool of me, without now doing this further thing to me, which in the space of four months would be too much for any base*

fellow. I am determined to complete my arrangements to take the governorship and quite decided that any end to this affair will be better than going on like this. And if His Holiness thinks otherwise, I will send the brief and the patents to Cybo at once, and will take what resolve for myself God inspires me with. I will not do this out of pride or anger nor because I am unaware of the gravity of such an action and the consequences it must have. But although I value His Holiness's good graces at their true worth, and my service in his house, yet in all my actions I have always valued and will always value my own honour more than any other consideration, and with this style of living I shall go on until my death, come what may.[1]

Concluding his diatribe, he asks his correspondent to see that Clement reads his letter: 'And I commend myself to you praying you to show this to His Holiness.'

Naturally this outburst does not represent the normal tone of Guicciardini's correspondence with Rome, but it does at least suggest the limits of his subservience. Although the exaggeration of his reaction might lead us to dismiss it as something momentary and uncontrolled, there is other evidence in the *Carteggi* along the same lines. His comments on the future form of the Medici government, as we will see, not only demonstrate a willingness to tell the Medici unpleasant truths, but also show that his political assumptions continue to be basically patrician. The restoration of Medici rule in Florence had given the city a government that was somewhat provisional in character. Clement held the real power but he was pope and he was in Rome, so neither his office nor his location permitted him to

---

1 Ridolfi, *Life*, p. 214. 'Credevo bastasi havermi tolto l'uficio del Monte così honorevolmente, come se io havessi assassinato el commune, havermi tractato nella Presidentia di Romagna della sorte sapete voi, doppo havermi astrecto contro a mia voluntà a fare venire a Roma le querele de' Romagnuoli et messomi per questo verso una mitera in testa, sanza che hora mi facessi questa altra, che in quattro mesi sarebbono pure troppe a ogni vile cencio. Io sono risoluto a seguitare lo expedirmi totalmente per andare al governo, deliberato che questa cosa habbia più presto qualunque fine che stare così. Et se Sua Sanctità la intenderà altrimenti, gli rimanderò subito el breve del governo et le patente a Cibo, et piglerò di me quello partito che Dio mi spirerà, il che non farò nè per superbia nè per collera nè per mancare di cognoscere quello che importi el governarsi così et quello che habbia a tirarsi drieto. *Ma ancora che io stimi quanto è conveniente la gratia di Sua Santità et la servitù con casa sua, 'tamen' in tucte le actione mie ho sempre stimato et sempre stimerò più l'honore mio che qualunque altro rispecto et con questo stile et modo di vivere andrò insino alla morte et seguiti che vogla.*' Letter of 19 May 1531, *Carteggi di Francesco Guicciardini*, ed. Pier Giorgio Ricci, XV, no. 35, p. 62.

give day to day attention to Florence. Furthermore, Clement was hoping
to avoid the dangers of the tumultuous past, which had twice seen his
family expelled from the city. He was determined to establish a more autocratic and less vulnerable regime, but he was anxious at the same time to
avoid the appearance of having imposed this on Florence. It was with the
hope, then, that others would do his work for him that the Pope solicited
a number of high-ranking Florentines for their thoughts on a new constitution, and certainly it was not in a spirit of free and liberal enquiry that
their advice was asked. Guicciardini, being absent from the city, gave his
advice formally in a number of briefs in which he takes a moderating
stand.[2] More informally in letters written after Clement had taken the decisive step of setting up Alessandro, his illegitimate son, as Duke, he gave
further advice and notified Rome of the reaction of the citizens. Typically,
Guicciardini does not believe that the form of the constitution as such is
the vital point. We may presume that he saw the constitution as an abstract
question that, like other abstractions, should be distrusted or discounted.
What will matter, he says, is the day-to-day running of the government and
the selection of the best men.[3] As for the specific innovations, he warns
that there is displeasure with the changes in the city, which were only
made because they had to be and not because they were desired. Men are
by nature fearful of innovation and in Florence, he says, there could hardly
be a greater change than putting an end to the Signoria and closing the
Palazzo, which for so long have been venerated. This fear of change may
be the result of ignorance, but the people of higher quality are worried
too because it seems that this may be the start of the establishment of a
new authority which will leave no room for the participation of the citizens ('un'altra autorità che non habbia bisogno di ministerio di cittadini').
And even the best friends of the regime are worried because these measures

2 See Felix Gilbert, 'Alcuni discorsi di uomini politici fiorentini e la politica di
   Clemente VII per la restaurazione medicea,' *ASI*, XCIII (1935: II), pp. 3-24.
   The *pareri* were published by Canestrini in *Opere inedite*, II, pp. 354-82 as
   Discourses VII-IX.
3 Letter of 17 April 1532 to Lanfredini, *Carteggi*, XV, no. 111, p. 142: 'Però non
   si può dire schiectamente che la cosa sia approvata et satisfaccia, ma, quanto al
   gusto mio, importa pocho, perchè tucto consiste nel procedere quotidiano che si
   farà poi; el quale, se sarà buono et prudente, la cosa acquisterà alla giornata con
   ognuno, et riputatione et gratia, ma quando si facessi altrimenti, e medesimi che
   hora la desideranno et laudano la detesteranno et gli dispiacerebbe. Però *hinc
   pendent leges et prophete*: giuchare continuamente questo giuocho a ragione. Et
   perchè la importanza principale di quello che s'ha a fare hora consiste in eleggere
   bene questi huomini et piglare per fondamento dello Stato le persone che importano più et tenere manco conto di chi importa meno ...'

have made them so odious that should there be another revolt they would find no safety. The changes, Guicciardini repeats once again, will be useful and provide stability only if things are well managed and if reasonable and appropriate steps are taken to ensure the loyalty of the friends of the regime. But this cannot be done while they are persuaded that the regime will not confide in them, because there can be no faith where it is not reciprocated, and where there is no faith there cannot be any love.[4]

These are Guicciardini's most serious and measured thoughts in which, unlike the very personal matter we first examined, there is no trace of temperament or momentary outburst. It could hardly be plainer that Guicciardini's view of government in this letter, intended for the advice of the pope, remains fundamentally patrician. In his mind there is still a political class in Florence on whom the survival of any government depends, and any government, no matter how absolute in pretension, must placate this class. These people (himself included) will only give their support to a regime which looks after their interests, and their interests include some participation in government. And he clearly does not rule out, should his advice not be followed, the possibility of yet another rebellion. As one vitally interested in the survival of the regime, he certainly does not want to see new upheavals, especially given the stigma which he says the new measures have attached to them all. But it seems clear that he believes the proper conduct of the government matters as much to men like himself, the minor partners, as to the Medici. And presumably it is because of this urgency that he feels obliged to displease Clement with these opinions.

4 Letter of 13 May 1532, *Carteggi*, XV, no. 116, pp. 149-50: 'Dico che a molti delli amici ha dato alterazione una innovatione sì grande, essendo natura degli huomini, massime di quelli che non intendono molto, aombrare delle cose nuove, nè potendo quasi a Firenze essere maggiore novità che levare la Signoria, che è durata presso a CCC anni et serrare il Palazzo che è stato tanto tempo, si può dire, adorato ... Altri, et questi sono di più qualità, hanno dubitato et dubitano che questo non sia stato un principio per pigliare poi di nuovo un'altra autorità che non habbia bisogno di ministerio di cittadini. Ci sono stati delli altri che, benchè amino questo Stato et desiderino parteciparvi et essere adoprati, nondimanco vorrebbono sempre havere un poco di riservo o di spiraglio, donde potessino sperare di potere uscire se le cose si mutassino ... Et a questi tali è parso che questo nuovo modo imbratti tanto et faccia tanto odioso ciascuno che ne partecipa che non resti loro luogo da potere sperare salute, se si facessi mutatione ... Et io tengo per certo che questo modo nuovo farà utile et stabilità se le cose saranno governate bene et che con le vie che sono ragionevoli et convenienti si cerchi di intratenere et conservare bene disposti li amici, e quali non si potranno mai incarnare nè essere di quel buono animo bisognerebbe mentre si persuadono che non si confidi di loro, perchè la fede non può essere dove non è reciproca, et dove non è fede non può essere amore.'

It is hard to say how far this picture of Guicciardini's relationship to the Medici changes in the last part of the decade, the period of our greatest concern. His biographer suggests a growing alienation following the death of his old master, Clement VII. And the same suggestion of distance can be read beneath the impersonal surface of the *Storia*. In the end perhaps the history remains our best evidence. An 'objective' work written in retirement by an aging man, this public history shows none of the compromise with present political realities that private political letters might be expected to contain. And there is no doubt that Guicciardini intended his history as the supreme witness of his thoughts. Here he shows his former patrons little love, excuses them nothing, and in the most brilliant of his character studies, pitilessly reveals all the inadequacies of the two Medici popes.

I suspect that Guicciardini may have envied the Medici. Perhaps he reflected that the Guicciardini were as old a family as the Medici, and his own talents superior to theirs. And yet his career committed him ever more firmly to their cause. The tide was running against patricians who did not wish to be courtiers. The last republic had shown that the alternative to absolutism was not oligarchy but Savonarolan populism. There would be no return to the ideal Lorenzo had symbolized of harmonious relations between an uncrowned ruler and the old merchant patriciate, an ideal Guicciardini had condemned as tyrannical in his early days but which won his approval in later, more difficult years. So for Guicciardini after 1530 there were no choices, for himself or for Florence. He was one of the leading men of the restored regime and appeared before the Emperor as the Medici advocate against the republican exiles. And yet in 1537 he could still make that futile attempt to impose conditions on Cosimo, an act which inevitably appears in the history books as quixotic gesture, though it might equally be seen as the last expression of the tradition of the mixed constitution, undertaken by one of the few of the old guard neither compromised by the recent republic nor wholly committed to absolutism.[5] In any case, quixotic or not, the inevitable aftermath of the succession of Cosimo was the further isolation of the aging counsellor, already an enemy to the exiled republicans. As never before, Guicciardini now had the time and incentive to write.

In the end, an acceptance of political polarization out of cynicism, pessimism, or self-interest was the only answer short of retirement or exile, and the *Storia d'Italia* was both a retirement and a kind of self-exile. Some,

5   In the older biography of Guicciardini by Otetea this is in fact how the episode of the election of Cosimo is seen.

like Nerli, found the accommodation to absolutism easy, since they saw it as the inevitable solution to the perennial Florentine problem of faction. But in Guicciardini there remains a tension, a resistance to the inevitable, which reflects not only his own biography but the collective fate of his class. Guicciardini's dark view of history, which many since Montaigne have found objectionable, is more than the personal prejudice of a man always shrewd and cynical and now grown old in difficult times. It is also an expression of the despair of a displaced class that has lost its independence and could only maintain its dignity and privilege by serving a prince who had once, not long since, been their equal. Searching for parallels, I think of Burckhardt or Weber, uneasy patricians caught out in a world of democrats and absolutists. Guicciardini's work, like theirs, is an alienated masterpiece; his history is a product of his resistance to history.

There is a clear pattern to Guicciardini's literary activity. In youth he had written because politics was not yet open to him. In mid career he had taken it up again when events had temporarily disqualified him from active life. Now, disqualified again and perhaps disaffected, he wrote with a vengeance. But it was not only the leisure to write that mattered on each of these occasions. There was always something he wanted to do with his writing – some effect to be produced, some decision to be prepared – for Guicciardini was not primarily a man of letters. With his pen he could indulge a lawyer's passion for argument, an intellectual's taste for analysis, a bureaucrat's love of fact. Now it was a matter of a great retrospect in which all these faculties could be combined. Of course, in a practical sense there was nothing that could be done about the tragic history of Italy in the last half century. Guicciardini had neither Machiavelli's mission as a prophet nor the humanist faith in the lessons of history. But in written history living history could be collected, given shape, analysed, and explained. Blame could be assigned with an independent rectitude not permitted to the Medici office-holder. And so without any hesitation he named his villains: the rulers of Italy, the Medici, Sforza, Borgia, Della Rovere and the rest, including the republican regimes of Florence and Venice. In writing, then, there could be a kind of redress and there might be a different kind of fame. The failure of his own counsels, which had led to the sack of Rome, could be shown to be a small part of the massive breakdown of Italian politics. Bit by bit it would be seen that the traditions of the Italian states had been abused and their vitality destroyed until the inevitable conclusion was reached in the spectacle of Rome in plunder and Italy held in sullen subjection.

In dealing with a man of Guicciardini's reticence we have had to approach his intellectual biography through hints and conjecture, and for

these last years this limitation is even truer. Our best resource, naturally
enough, is the *Storia d'Italia*, and there we do find a few major clues. The
first of these is the genesis of the work, as Ridolfi has uncovered it.[6] Guicciardini opens his history with his own decision to write: 'I have determined to write about those events which have occurred in Italy within our
memory, ever since French troops, summoned by our own princes, began
to stir up very great dissensions here.' But when Guicciardini first began in
1535 to write of the history of his own times these were not his intentions.
Instead, in the preliminary work that is now known as his 'Commentary,'
he narrated the events that followed the battle of Pavia, the decisive defeat
of French ambitions in Italy, and he probably intended to carry his story
to the sack of Rome. Clearly this was a history of very great importance,
but more than that it was one which he had seen at first hand and for
whose tragedies he had to carry some responsibility.

It has been conjectured, because of a conversation reported by his contemporary Nardi, that he intended a 'Commentary' after the manner of
Caesar. Guicciardini, of course, was no Caesar, nor even a Medici, and if
Caesar was his model, he was a distant one indeed. Certainly he does not
give his own actions any larger a place in this 'Commentary' than he later
did in his history. And that he saw himself, even at this stage, as writing
history is clear from those prescriptive remarks on the value of 'true history' which we have already examined.[7] But given the nature of his subject,
the events of 1525 to 1527, there can be little doubt that powerful personal motives underlay Guicciardini's projected history of his own times.
We cannot say how he would have dealt with his personal share of the disastrous events of 1527 because the 'Commentary' remains a fragment. If
he intended the 'Commentary' as an apology, however, it is not evident in
those pages he had completed on the aftermath of Pavia, nor in the corresponding chapters of the *Storia d'Italia* itself. The two texts differ very little in style and tone, and this is a clear indication that he had already
achieved a maturity sufficient for the greater challenge of full scale history.
But at some point which we cannot fix, he came to see the insufficiency of
his original chronological (and hence conceptual) framework, and recognized the unity of the history of Italy since the death of Lorenzo. His own
actions, those of his Medici masters, the struggle at Pavia and its aftermath
at Rome – all these would be understood only if these more recent calamities were retraced to their origins. Only when a comprehensive explanation
had been constructed for the breakdown of the Italian state system would

6 See Ridolfi, *Genesi.*
7 See above, chapter IV.

the present hegemony of Spain and impotence of the Italians be understood. This new plan represented a tremendous growth in intellectual power and historiographical ambition; to give a whole explanation meant that he would now have to tell the whole story.

Two things had come together in Guicciardini's mind, a combination of private impulse and historical distance. The 'Commentary,' despite its objectivity, can be taken to stand for the original subjective urge to write history, for the personal passion with which Guicciardini pursued his objectivity. The relationship of this fragment to the final work might be compared to that of the *Memorie di famiglia* to the *Storie fiorentine*. The smaller work, more private in conception if not in expression, stands closer to the historian's reticent self, and reveals the root of his preoccupation. At the same time, Guicciardini had acquired a kind of distance, a pessimistic acceptance of the vast dimensions of the thing, which is responsible for the loftiness of the *Storia d'Italia*. Form itself confers a kind of ease, and storytelling satisfies by promising an ending.[8] The very vastness of the *Storia* must also have given comfort to the historian, allowing him to lose himself in a universe which he, in some sense, controlled. Perhaps, too, this explains the extraordinary rate at which Guicciardini was able to write. All Guicciardini's histories (like most Florentine histories) are unfinished, but the creation of this one that was to be so much broader and more complex than the rest was accomplished swiftly. The bulk of the work was done in the last three years of Guicciardini's life, and most of it went through several revisions. Only crippling disease, not (as before) loss of interest, prevented its completion. And when the time came for him to write again about the aftermath of Pavia, the 'Commentary' was easily slipped into the larger work, where it forms the sixteenth and part of the seventeenth books. Obviously, he had made a good beginning.

Guicciardini's impulse to write the history of his times was certainly more than literary, though literary fame attracted him too. In the 'Commentary' he made his beginning not where later as a historian he would clearly recognize a beginning, but where as a participant the story touched him most closely. But it is not only in its genesis that the *Storia d'Italia* shows signs of Guicciardini's personal stake in the events he chronicles. On two occasions he had played a key role in a political or military crisis, first in Parma and later in Florence. Here, where his two roles converge, it should be possible to learn something about the relationship between the history which Guicciardini lived and the history he wrote.

8 See Frank Kermode, *The Sense of an Ending: Studies in the Theory of Fiction* (N.Y.: Oxford 1967).

The first of the two passages concerns his defense of Parma.[9] Guicciardini is serving as Governor of Modena and becomes Commissioner in Parma as well. The death of his patron, Pope Leo, however, disturbs both his personal position and the security of the area. He soon finds himself facing a far superior force of French and Venetians with only a small army and the youth of Parma available for the protection of the city. His crucial concern is whether the enemy have artillery with them; if they do, Parma is indefensible, but if they do not, the city can be defended with his meagre forces. One thing is essential, though. He must have the support of the townspeople, both to take part in the defence and to pay the troops their arrears and so prevent a mutiny.

Our text begins with a report of the cold and frank discussion of the interests of the 'Governor' as Guicciardini calls himself, without of course violating decorum by indicating that he is also the author of the history. Having little hope of further employment in the Church now that his patron is dead (indeed it is hinted that he might have reasons for wanting to see the Church humbled) and having no family or other personal stake in Parma, it seems reasonable that *il governatore* should choose to abandon the city rather than personally run the risks of siege. Addressing himself to the townspeople, the Governor argues that his own willingness to stay and fight proves his conviction that the enemy lack the necessary artillery. The burghers are uncertain and are inclined to avoid sack by surrender, but the Governor keeps them from doing so until it is too late and they are forced to defend their city. Thus the town is saved and Guicciardini can congratulate himself on having willingly exposed himself to dangers which brought him no hope of profit and which he could have escaped without any dishonour whatsoever.[10]

Despite this apparent victory of honour over interest, the narrative is told consistently in terms of utility and self-interest, for it is by appeal to these qualities that the Governor manages to sway the citizens and buy enough time. Having better information than the burghers, he is convinced that the enemy have no siege guns, despite rumours to the contrary. If the situation were different, he tells the town's notables, he himself would be the first to leave. Thus the Governor is able to win out by using rational arguments that appeal to utility, his own as well as Parma's. Among his winning qualities it is his *costanza* that is praised, not his *virtù*. He succeeds

9 *Storia d'Italia*, IV, pp. 134-9.
10 *Storia d'Italia*, IV, p. 139: 'piú presto, senza alcuna speranza di profitto, esporsi al pericolo che cercare di salvarsi, potendo farlo senza suo disonore o infamia alcuna.'

because he knows what he is doing, has better intelligence than the others, and has a crafty sense of their psychology – and fundamentally because his is the stronger position. He is not, it is emphasized, a soldier. Though the word is not used, it is *prudenza* that creates his success, a political rather than a military virtue. He is able to recognize that the true threat to Parma is not the *impeto* of the soldiers but the fearfulness of the townsfolk. And in the end, the Governor's appeal to his own self-interest wins him reputation and honour. In the *Ricordi* it was said that honour and reputation have a powerful utility, and now we see the converse – that an appeal to utility can also bring reputation. The fortunate man, Guicciardini had written in those maxims, is he whose honour and self-interest are the same.

The second major piece of self-description in the *Storia d'Italia* discloses more of Guicciardini's self-image. This time the occasion is an abortive coup in Florence attempted by a group of young nobles, an event which came just before the sack of Rome and hinted at the weakness of the Medici regime in Florence.[11] The young men managed to occupy the town hall, but they could not raise the city to arms as they had hoped. The Cardinal of Cortona, who acted for Clement VII as governor of Florence, prepared to defeat the rebellion with the aid of French soldiers in camp nearby. But Cortona gave no thought to what an armed clash might cost the vulnerable city:

> *Thus preparations were being made for the dangerous contest, for the palace could not be captured without the death of almost all the nobility within it, and also there was the peril that once having set their hand to arms and killing, the victorious soldiers would sack the city. Thus the Florentines prepared for many bitter and unhappy days. However the Lieutenant General [Guicciardini] swiftly cut this most difficult knot ...*[12]

Between these two events Guicciardini has been promoted and now appears as the 'Lieutenant,' though once again he is not identified as the author of the history. Here, in his own city, his quick action prevents a possibly disastrous clash of arms. Having noticed Federigo da Bozzole

11 *Storia d'Italia*, V, pp. 131-4.
12 Trans. Alexander, *History of Italy*, p. 377: 'Donde preparandosi pericolosa contesa, perché lo espugnare il palazzo non poteva succedere senza la morte di quasi tutta la nobiltà che vi era dentro, e anche era pericolo che, cominciandosi a mettere mano all'armi e all'uccisioni, i soldati vincitori non saccheggiassino tutto il resto della città, si preparava dì molto acerbo e infelice per i fiorentini; se il luogotenente con presentissimo consiglio non avesse espeditio questo nodo molto difficile ...' *Storia d'Italia*, V, p. 132.

come out of the palazzo after a fruitless negotiation with the rebels, the *luogotenente* intercepted Federigo before he could tell the Cardinal of the weakness of the rebels' position. The Lieutenant suppressed this information (which would have provoked the soldiers to attack immediately) and, going to the palazzo himself, was able to persuade the youths to give up their revolt.

> *Thus the tumult was put down and things returned as before. And nevertheless (as ingratitude and calumny are more present than remuneration and praise for good works), although everyone greatly commended the Lieutenant General at that time, nevertheless the Cardinal of Cortona complained a little later that he was more concerned about the safety of the citizens than the grandeur of the Medici and had acted cunningly, and that this had been the reason why Medici rule had not been established permanently on that day by arms and the blood of citizens. And the multitude also blamed him afterwards, because when he went to the palace presenting the dangers to be greater than they were, he had induced them unnecessarily to give up for the benefit of the Medici.*[13]

Guicciardini's 'self-complacency' in this passage has been remarked on.[14] Certainly he is not habitually modest, but bitterness not satisfaction is the hallmark of the text. The description of the actions of the *luogotenente*

13 Trans. Alexander, *History of Italy*, p. 378. 'Così, posato il tumulto, tornorono le cose allo essere di prima. E nondimeno (come è piú presente la ingratitudine e la calunnia che la rimunerazione e la laude alle buone opere) se bene allore ne fusse il luogotenente celebrato con somme laudi da tutti, nondimeno e il cardinale di Cortona si lamentò, poco poi, che egli, amando piú la salute de' cittadini che la grandezza de' Medici, procedendo artificiosamente, fusse stato cagione che in quel dì non si fusse stabilito in perpetuo, con l'armi e col sangue de' cittadini, lo stato alla famiglia de' Medici; e la moltitudine poi lo calunniò che, dimostrando, quando andò in palagio, i pericoli maggiori che non erano, gli avesse indotti, per beneficio de' Medici, a cedere senza necessità.' *Storia d'Italia*, V, pp. 133-4.

14 Sidney Alexander, the usually sensitive translator of the *Storia*, writes: 'Although Guicciardini writes objectively about his role in this affair a certain amount of self-complacency is visible through the ice.' (See *History of Italy*, p. 378n.) But had Guicciardini's history for some reason remained anonymous I do not believe that either of the two passages that I have cited would stand out. In tone and treatment there is nothing to distinguish these two incidents from thousands of others in the history. This judgement is confirmed in a sense by Alexander's own omission of the siege of Parma from his abridged translation. For a commentary on Guicciardini's version of these events and the claims of others to have had an important role, see the appendix to Cecil Roth's *The Last Florentine Republic* (New York: Russell & Russell 1968).

follows closely the lines already indicated at Parma. Prudence, quick-witted-ness, a clear understanding of his own mind, and insight into the position of others, these qualities rather than boldness or valour are his essential in-struments. But the revolt at Florence adds something missing at the siege of Parma. In Florence the *luogotenente* is a citizen not an administrator, and his actions are directed toward the public good defined in rather dif-ferent terms. True, he is once again concerned to prevent the plunder of civilians by soldiers. More than that, however, he now acts in the interests of order and what he would have defined as *buon governo*. And predictably he is attacked from the left and right for having done so. The autocrats have lost a golden chance to harden the absolutism of the regime, while their enemies have lost (for the moment) their opportunity to overthrow the Medici. Guicciardini's political stance here is a defense of the middle path in government and he acts as a protector of the people against the rapacity of their rulers. This seems consistent with his later actions at the time of the succession of Cosimo.

Guicciardini quite clearly was sure of the rightness of his actions, but there was hardly any room for complacency. This revolt that he had helped to defuse was quickly followed by a successful coup. Only a short time afterwards the news of the disaster at Rome would sweep the Medici once more out of Florence and replace them with a revived republic. We have already reviewed the course of Guicciardini's relations with this new re-publican regime, which ended three years later in a heroic but futile de-fense and succeeded only in re-establishing the Medici autocracy on a firmer footing. It seems to me obvious that Guicciardini could only be bit-ter about this incident. Not only was he personally reviled, as he says, for his *buone opere*, but he surely recognized that these violent oscillations in Florentine politics had steadily eroded the middle ground on which patri-cian regimes once stood. He was bitter, but not surprised; by now the cyni-cal conclusion was habitual with him: 'come è più presente la ingratitudine e la calunnia ...'

1 / The 'Imprudence of Princes': Chronology and Explanation of the Decline of Italy

When Guicciardini put aside his commentaries on his lieutenancy and began to recast the same material as a full scale history of Italy in his times, he had not buried the nagging question of his own failures but had chosen to see them as a small part of the general failure of Italian statesmanship. One fact dominates the *Storia d'Italia* because it dominated the history of Guicciardini's generation – the collapse of Italian independence. From the polished rhetoric of the first pages to the sketchy outlines and still unassimilated documents of the last, Guicciardini's history is a comprehensive investigation in narrative form of this collapse. The entire work responds to the challenge of Italian weakness and every page constitutes part of its explanation.

On the first page of the history Guicciardini announces the two chief didactic themes of the work. They are the domination of human affairs by change and the destructive cupidity of rulers:

> *Thus numerous examples will make it plainly evident how mutable are human affairs, not unlike a sea whipped by winds; and how pernicious, almost always to themselves but always to the people, are those ill-advised measures of rulers ...* [1]

Guicciardini's preoccupation with change will be the subject of the next chapter; in this one our concern is with the chronology and causes of the

1 Trans. Alexander, *History of Italy*, p. 3. 'Onde per innumerabili esempli evidentemente apparirà quanta instabilità nè altrimenti che uno mare concitato da' venti, siano sottoposte le cose umane; quanto siano perniciosi, quasi sempre a se stessi ma sempre a' popoli, i consigli male misurati di coloro che dominano ...' *Storia d'Italia*, I, p. 1.

loss of independence which the disastrous policies of the Italian princes brought about. We begin with the chronology of the invasions for two reasons. First it must be recognized that for a historian, especially one as rigorously concerned with narrative as Guicciardini, narrative is itself a major form of explanation. Our understanding of Italy's collapse thus must begin, as Guicciardini's did, with the sequence of events itself before moving to more abstract explanations. Secondly, it is important to see that the long tragic history which follows the first incursion of the French armies is neither uninterrupted nor inexorable. Too often we take 1494, the year of the French invasion, as a simple dividing line between good times and bad and ignore Guicciardini's clear perception that what happened was the more tragic because it was not inevitable. If 1494 did become a dividing line it was because of a persistent misuse of power and misunderstanding of politics on the part of the Italian rulers. Thus the Italian peoples were led, through several stages of worsening crisis, into complete subjugation to foreign powers. To take the long view, this was the end of the Renaissance and the beginning of the Italy derisively described by Stendhal when he writes that 'since they had become "loyal subjects" their great occupation was the printing of sonnets upon handkerchiefs of rose-colored taffeta ...'

In a famous passage marking the day that the French armies crossed the Alps, Guicciardini describes the full consequences of the invasions:

> *Charles entered Asti on the ninth day of September of the year 1494,*
> *bringing with him into Italy the seeds of innumerable calamities, of*
> *most horrible events and changes in almost the entire state of affairs.*
> *For his passage into Italy not only gave rise to changes of dominions,*
> *subversion of kingdoms, desolation of countries, destruction of cities*
> *and the cruelest massacres, but also new fashions, new customs, new*
> *and bloody ways of waging warfare, and diseases which had been un-*
> *known up to that time.*[2]

But it is only in retrospect that such rhetoric justifies itself. If disaster is coming there are scarce signs of it yet. Certainly regimes and kings will fall,

2 Trans. Alexander, *History of Italy*, p. 48. 'Entrò in Asti il dì nono di settembre dell'anno mille quattrocento novantaquattro, conducendo seco in Italia i semi di innumerabili calamità, di orribilissimi accidenti, e variazione di quasi tutte le cose: perché dalla passata sua non solo ebbono principio mutazioni di stati, sovversioni di regni, desolazioni di paesi, eccidi di città, crudelissime uccisioni, ma eziandio nuovi abiti, nuovi costumi, nuovi e sanguinosi modi di guerreggiare, infermità insino a quel dì non conosciute.' *Storia d'Italia*, I, p. 67.

but in the short run the only real victims are Piero de' Medici and Alfonso of Naples. Naples will soon be regained, though not for Alfonso himself, and the young Medici was little lamented, least of all by Guicciardini.

Guicciardini treats the first invasion with irony, and none of the participants is made to seem worthy of the great things which have been set in motion. By means of a grotesque physical description and an unflattering comparison with Hannibal, a far greater invader of Italy, Guicciardini deliberately emphasizes the defects of the French king.[3] But his aim is not to ridicule the French as much as it is to underscore the weakness of the Italians by emphasizing the unworthiness of their conqueror. The half-heartedness and duplicity of the Italians, not the strength of enemy, seem decisive in this mock campaign. Guicciardini comments ironically on the behaviour of the Italian prince who, though bound himself by *condotta* to fight for the Neapolitan side, hedged his bets by giving his son as a *condottiere* to the enemy. The French were amazed, he remarks gravely, not being accustomed to the subtlety of the Italians.[4] But the unheroic spirit of the campaign is best expressed by Guicciardini's ironic celebration of Charles VIII at the end of his bloodless romp to Naples. The king had had the unheard-of happiness, says Guicciardini, beyond even the example of Caesar, to have conquered before he saw.[5]

Horrible calamities and wholesale changes in the customs of peoples do not come from stage shows like this. And by the end of the second book the French king has recrossed the Alps more like the conquered than the conqueror, despite the victories he had won. The future importance of this period in the Italian wars is not in anything as tangible as the overthrow of states or the radical change of customs; it is the legacy left by the ending of the peninsula's long isolation and the disruption of her balance of power. This split between the real and the apparent effects of this first campaign gives the taste of irony to the first two books. Though the events in themselves seem negligible, each casts a shadow. Of all the future calamities announced on the 9 September 1494, only one has really manifested itself, the destruction of the instruments of peace ('e si disordinorono di maniera gli instrumenti della quieta e concordia italiana ...').

3 *Storia d'Italia*, I, p. 68. 'Perché certo è che Carlo, insino da puerizia, fu di complessione molto debole e di corpo non sano, di statura piccolo, di aspetto, se tu gli levi il vigore e la degnità degli occhi, bruttissimo, e l'altre membra proporzionate in modo che e' pareva quasi piú simile a mostro che a uomo ...'
4 *Storia d'Italia*, I, p. 99.
5 *Storia d'Italia*, I, p. 113: 'avendo con maraviglioso corso di inaudita felicità, sopra l'esempio ancora di Giulio Cesare, prima vinto che veduto ...'

The beginning of Book 3 is the first occasion when a common pattern of events begins to become recognizable. The narrative seems to have circled and we are back again in peaceful Italy as the bulk of the French troop home. Only a part of Naples is still in French hands, but it does not seem that they can hold out very long. Italy rings with the praises of the Duke of Milan and the Venetian senate for having saved 'so famous a part of the world' from servitude. But with peace free choice is also re-established. If war is now resumed, and on a far more serious scale, this is not predetermined. Guicciardini is neither positivist nor determinist and the reader must accept the reality of this chance for peace and independence or he will miss the tragedy of what follows. If the Duke of Milan and the Venetians, blinded by selfish greed, had not corrupted the good of all, there is no doubt that Italy would have been restored to her pristine splendour by their counsels and forces, and so would have been safe for many years from the attacks of foreign nations.[6]

Unfortunately, writes Guicciardini, ambition would not permit either Milan or Venice to stay content within their customary limits, and new disturbances quickly arose. Given this restlessness, this desire to profit from the turmoil in Italy, this refusal to join forces and counsel, this regard for particular interests before universal ones, given in other words an unwillingness to go back to Laurentian policies, a particular occasion for conflict must soon present itself. Both Milan and Venice were anxious to fill the vacuum left by the expulsion of the Florentines from Pisa and to prevent Florence herself from recovering the port city, the most important of her lost possessions. Guicciardini shows us the debate over Pisa in the Venetian Senate where the wisest senators warn their fellow citizens to avoid any conflict now that the ultramontanes have been taught the road to Italy.[7] But despite the timely advice ambition wins out and the Venetians intervene in Pisa as a step toward hegemony in Italy. The warning of the wise senators that from now on the vanquished side in any Italian dispute would always have recourse to superior foreign forces proves to be entirely true. The wars that commence, or recommence, with these events see the entrance of other European nations into the Italian theater. The Spanish and the French struggle over Naples; the Swiss fight for Milan and the best price; the German Emperor has his price too but proves an ineffective *con-*

6 *Storia d'Italia*, I, p. 207: 'i quali se, acciecati dalle cupidità particolari, non avessino, eziandio con danno e infamia propria, corrotto il bene universale, non si dubita che Italia, reintegrata co' consigli e le forze loro nel pristino splendore, sarebbe stata per molti anni sicura dall' impeto delle nazioni oltramontane.'
7 *Storia d'Italia*, I, p. 226.

dottiere. Florence remains a republic, and, though racked by internal struggles exemplified by the career of Savonarola, carries on a long, exhausting
(to the city and the reader alike) and self-destructive war against Pisa. At
crucial moments this bitter and dragging conflict over Pisa keeps the flames
of war alight in Italy, destroying hopes of peace. And Lodovico Sforza, the
first instigator and prime villain of the invasions, whose thoughts and
ambitions all Italy was once too small to contain, lives out his last decade
in a narrow French prison cell, a fine symbol of Italian fortunes.[8]

As we are led through these endless wars, we begin to perceive their pattern. Guicciardini divided his narrative into twenty books and, typically,
he opens each one with renewed hopes for peace which are too soon dissolved by the resumption of war. As the weight of a destructive history
builds up against them, these hopes appear increasingly desperate and the
prophetic list of changes that accompanied the narration of the first
French invasion begins to be fulfilled.

But the decline of Italy is not uniform. If we look carefully and do not
allow the sheer bulk of the work to overwhelm us, we find that the stages
are clearly marked. Thus the opening of Book 8 stands as the next important signpost, one which brings us near the midpoint of the journey. To
take an analogy from Dante, having passed through Limbo and then the
sins of incontinence, we now descend into the circles of violence. The pattern of ceasefire with hopes for peace leading only to further and more destructive war repeats itself here with a vengeance. Though Italy had already
suffered fourteen years of war, Guicciardini tells us, and many changes,
the killing had been mostly among the barbarians themselves and the peoples of Italy had suffered less than their princes. But this period, begun
with the second French invasion that opened Book 3, is now over. The
next years will bring new strife to all Italy and suffering for the Italians
themselves.[9] The new wars, says Guicciardini, will be characterized by a
military licentiousness equally pernicious to friends and to enemies, and
by the violation of religion and sacred things. Speaking generally, he says,
the origins of these troubles was, as is almost always true, the ambition
and cupidity of princes.[10] And in this particular case it was the rashness of
the Venetian senate that was to blame.

These opening remarks from Book 8 become thematic. The parasitic
nature of all soldiers, no matter whose banners they fight under, is a motif

8 *Storia d'Italia*, I, p. 393: 'rinchiudendosi in una angusta carcere i pensieri e l'ambizione di colui che prima appena capivano i termini di tutta Italia.'
9 *Storia d'Italia*, II, p. 245: 'per tutta Italia, e contro agli italiani medesimi ...'
10 *Storia d'Italia*, II, p. 246: 'se tu la consideri generalmente, fu come quasi sempre
l'ambizione e la cupidità de' principi.'

that is often repeated and is a principal explanation for the spreading circles of violence that devastate the lands and cities alike. Let one example stand for many:

> *And at the same time they looted and destroyed the whole area, from which all the inhabitants had fled. Not content with great looting of animals and furnishings, they wickedly destroyed the walls. With great cruelty they burned Mestri, Marghera and Leccia Fucina and all the towns and villages of the area, and especially all the finer and more beautiful houses.*[11]

The incident is typical; only a note of cultural nationalism and a very rare aesthetic concern distinguish Guicciardini's comments here from a hundred other texts. The impiety of the soldiers of the pope, the Venetians, and other Italians was not less than that of the foreigners. In fact, he laments, their guilt was that much greater since it was more damnable for them than for the 'barbarians' to devastate the monuments and beauties of their common homeland.

In one sense, as I have said, indications of chronology, such as the notice at the beginning of Book 8 that we are entering a new and more destructive age, are simply signposts. But like any imposition of order on the events of history, these chronological divisions also represent a kind of historical judgement. This fact becomes particularly clear when Guicciardini uses his chronological markers as a standard against which to measure the actions of his characters. In the first two periods of the Italian wars, when the destruction was limited and the most frequent victims were the imprudent princes or invading foreigners themselves, the unspoken need was for an Italian champion, a new Lorenzo who could pacify the peninsula. This man, of course, never appeared and Milan and Naples were permanently lost to Italian sovereignty. But in 1511 an unlikely sort of champion seated on an unwarlike throne begins to bid for the role. The aged and tempestuous Pope Julius II, so often in this history a 'fatal instrument,' proclaims a holy war and a league to match. His war cry is the famous 'Fuori i barbari!' ('Out with the Barbarians!'). Guicciardini indicates opposite but not entirely equal reactions to Julius' league.[12] Some were enthusiastic, he writes,

---

11 (My trans.) 'E nel tempo medesimo predavano e guastavano tutto il paese, del quale erano fuggiti tutti gli abitatori; facendo iniquissimamente la guerra contro alle mura, perché, non contenti della preda grandissima degli animali e delle cose mobili, abbruciavano con somma crudeltà Mestri, Marghera e Leccia Fucina e tutte le terre e ville del paese, e oltre a quelle tutte le case che aveano più di ordinaria bellezza o apparenza.' *Storia d'Italia*, III, p. 291.

12 *Storia d'Italia*, III, pp. 129-30.

carried away by the magnificence of the titles and slogans. Others, considering the league and its ramifications more closely, were opposed. It is
clear that Guicciardini stands with the latter group, but what is interesting
is that his response is directly tied to his periodization. He reviews for the
readers his general position. It would have been desirable, he says, that the
imprudence and discord of our princes had not opened the way for foreign
arms and led to the subjugation of Naples and Milan. However, given the
loss of two of the most noble members of the body of Italy – the organic
metaphor is time-honoured and quite useful in view of the politically frag-
mented state of Italy – it must be counted a lesser calamity that they remain so until such time as divine pity and fortune offer a better opportunity. In the meantime the *contrapeso* (counterbalance) of the Spanish
against the French is essential to defend the liberty of those Italians who
remain free. Under these circumstances new wars can only bring bitter
affliction to the parts of Italy as yet intact. And in the end the victor in
the renewed struggle between the foreign powers will inflict on everyone a
more dreadful servitude. The ironic result, not understood by the tempestuous pope so naively taken with his historical mission, is that wars begun
with the intention of liberating Italy will damage her more than those begun expressly to subjugate her.[13]

The fulfillment of this warning of worse to come is the substance of the
next phase of the wars, which begins with the fourteenth book. Once more
we slip into the spiraling pattern of decline, bringing us to still deeper crisis.
The beginning of the year 1521 finds Italy at rest. She has in fact enjoyed
three years of troubled sleep, but now it seems that her fate ('il cielo, il
fato proprio, e la fortuna') would not leave her so. The authors of the new
disturbances, destined to be longer and more dangerous than ever, are
those who, obliged more than others to conserve the peace, more often use
all their energy and authority to disturb it.[14] This, of course, is the familiar
theme of the ambition of princes, and on this occasion the foremost among
the princely villains is the pope himself, though by his office, his strategic
situation, and his character, he should have been the last to stir up new
troubles.

What caused Pope Leo to act so foolishly will be discussed below in a
slightly different context; for the moment our interest lies in the beginnings of a new and more terrible cycle of conflicts. The underlying cause

13 *Storia d'Italia* III, 129-30: This was the fear of those who opposed Julius' plans: te-
    mevano che le guerre che si cominciavano con intenzione di liberare Italia da' bar-
    bari nocerebbono molto più agli spiriti vitali di questo corpo che non aveano nociuto
    le comminciate con manifesta professione e certissima intenzione di soggiogarla.'
14 *Storia d'Italia*, IV, p. 77.

of this aggravation of an already grave situation in Italy is an all-out struggle between the kings of France and Spain, a struggle in which each will
exercise every effort to conquer Italy ('tutta la sua potenza e tutti gli
sdegni in Italia'). We begin now the march to the great battle at Pavia, the
decisive defeat of French ambitions in the peninsula and the beginning of
centuries of Spanish hegemony. Equally the signs now point towards the
sack of Rome, the greatest shock of the age and a disastrous moment in
the historian's own career. There, finally, all the prophetic rhetoric which
accompanied the first invasion will completely justify itself. The sack of
cities, the suffering of peoples, the violation of sacred things with even less
scruple than the profane, all these gather to a dreadful consummation in
Rome in 1527. And at the same time we remember the warnings of those
who opposed Julius' war of liberation. Renewed warfare, as they had pre-
dicted, had not liberated Italy. On the contrary, by destroying the balance
between the Spanish and the French, the 'war of liberation' had led to a
more thorough subjugation of all Italians to Hapsburg power.

All this, though it cannot be completely explicit at the beginning of this
final period (Book 14), is fully confirmed by the ending. Book 20, the
final book, unfinished and something of an epilogue, begins as always with
the outbreak of peace. But peace for the first time in close to four decades
is not the prelude to more bitter wars because, with Spain fully triumphant, it is the peace of death for Italian independence. Only the heroic
but quixotic Florentine republic holds out for a time against the anaesthe-
sia settling permanently over Italy. The second wind of republicanism in
Florence proved surprisingly (to Guicciardini) vigorous, but besieged by
both the pope and emperor the Florentines could not hold out for long.

> The aforesaid treaty of peace and confederation had put an end to the
> long and grave wars which had continued for more than eight years
> [i.e. 1521-1529] with no many horrible occurrences, and now Italy
> remained entirely free of tumults and dangers of arms, with the excep-
> tion of the city of Florence. For its war had served to maintain peace
> among the others, but peace among the others aggravated its war.[15]

This is how it all ends for Guicciardini, in quiet. Guicciardini's path,
like Dante's, begins in Limbo, then passes through circles of hypocrisy (of

15 Trans. Alexander, *History of Italy*, p. 425. 'Posto, per la pace e confederazione
   predetta, fine a sì lunghe e gravi guerre, continuate più di otto anni [i.e. 1521-
   1529] con accidenti tanto orribili, restò Italia tutta libera da' tumulti e da' pericoli delle armi, eccetto la città di Firenze; la guerra della quale aveva giovato alla
   pace degli altri, ma la pace degli altri aggravava la guerra loro.' *Storia d'Italia*, V,
   p. 289.

princes) and violence (against peoples), ending in a sort of frozen silence. Felix Gilbert sums it up: 'As the first consequence of foreign invasion, governments were overthrown, later the people suffered, and finally artistic treasures were destroyed, morals and customs were changed; and the Italy which had existed before 1494 was no longer.'[16]

In the *Ricordi* Guicciardini had written that things universally desired almost never happen. Power is in the hands of the few and the interests of the few are almost always opposed to the wishes of the many. The story of Italian history from 1492 to 1534 as Guicciardini writes it reads like an exemplification of this dictum. Peace is the condition universally desired in the *Storia d'Italia*, but the interests of the princes always seem to be served better by war. Princes usually have private interests, frequently the advancement of their families, which lead them to trample on the common good of their people. Most of all, princes are by the nature of their office and education ambitious and immoderate, totally given over to private pleasures and unwilling to take good counsel when it is offered – presumably by men like Guicciardini.

From the very first page, as we have seen, Guicciardini blames ambitious and imprudent rulers for the disasters he is about to chronicle. Greedy and ambitious, blinded by error and cupidity ('o errori vani o le cupidità presenti') they do not remember the instability of fortune. Converting to the detriment of others the power which was given them for the common good, either because of too little prudence or too much ambition, they make themselves authors of new disturbances. Echoes of this condemnation reverberate throughout the history. Almost every potentate exemplifies the type and every hope of peace is their victim. The blackest prince-villain must be Alexander VI, the Borgia pope, and the description of his death is probably the most purple passage in the history. But the archetype, the original ambitious meddler, is Lodovico Sforza. To him goes the credit for first calling in the French and in the *Ricordi* Guicciardini confesses (something he would never do in the history) to being unable to comprehend that God's justice would allow Lodovico's sons to inherit Milan, which their father had acquired wickedly and in doing so 'was the cause of the ruin of the world.'

Sforza spent his last decade as a prisoner of his former allies, the French. But if we look back for a moment to the beginning of Book 3 we are presented with a picture of a prince at the height of his power – and arrogance. There Sforza presides magnificently over an Italy still apparently intact, though a huge French army has come and gone, both times seemingly at

16 Gilbert, *Machiavelli and Guicciardini*, p. 287.

Lodovico's command. Or so, at least, the duke himself sees it, and the
Milanese appear to agree. The city rang day and night with his praises, all
celebrating the wonderful wisdom of Lodovico on which peace or war in
Italy depended. The duke himself is described in all his puffed up splendor,
glorying perversely in his nickname 'the Moor.' He measures the future,
always a dangerous pretense in Guicciardini's view, with the rule of his
own grandeur and judges his own 'prudenza e ingegno' as so far superior to
that of anyone else that he can direct the affairs of Italy by his own will.[17]

It is easy enough to see all this as the work of a traditional moralist
prating that pride goeth before a fall; but Guicciardini, though intensely
moralistic at times, is not given to kitchen wisdom. Lodovico's pride is of
that specific strain endemic to princes. Like most of his kind he is blinded
by error and cupidity. He lacks prudence and forgets the frequent varia-
tions of fortune. By extension we may say that like Pope Julius after him,
Sforza is betrayed by a shallow sense of history and fails to comprehend
the profound changes created by the invasions. But the Moor is not alone
in his error and Guicciardini carefully arches his description of the duke
against a similar picture of the Venetian senate. They too lack the prudence to recognize the altered conditions that prevail now that, as their
wiser senators say, the ultramontanes have been taught the road to Italy.
The paired speeches in the senate reveal republican overconfidence as
surely as the celebrations in Milan are a display of princely egotism. Taken
together these juxtaposed passages form a portrait of ambition and misused power which prepares and explains the resumption of war. As we
noted in our review of chronology, Milan and Venice quarrel over the lord-
ship of Pisa rather than joining their forces and counsel. Later, after the
French have begun their preparations for a second invasion, Lodovico
would recognize the danger he was in, being not only the usurping ruler of
a duchy to which the French have some geneological claim but also geographically the first in the line of fire. By then, however, it is too late for
the duke to extricate himself from his ambitious designs. Mutual distrust
and mutual offense push him further towards the war he does not want.
The passage is worth quoting for the taste it gives of Guicciardini's complex style, snakelike but precise.

> The Duke might easily have acceded to the King's requests if he had
> not been held back by the fear, knowing how much he had offended
> him and how much distrust these injuries had provoked on both sides,
> that it was easier to come to an agreement about their differences than

17 *Storia d'Italia*, I, p. 231.

*to find a means of guarantee for both of them. For neither was willing
to trust the other where the other refused to trust him, when it came to
subtracting from the one what had been agreed as assurances for the
other. So with necessity obliging him to adopt the course he least liked,
Sforza tried at least to put off the dangers as long as possible and continued the same subterfuges with Rigault that he had used up to now.*[18]

Thus what princely ambition began, princely fear allowed to continue, and
war recommenced. Guicciardini's twisting construction here only mimes
the intricacy of the Moor's too-crafty diplomacy, though it must be ad-
mitted that the duke is not alone in occasionally ensnaring himself in his
own complexities.

Today we are accustomed to look for broader explanations for great
events, and for that reason we may be inclined to see the princes as the
scapegoats rather than the true culprits of this history. But Guicciardini's
historical understanding is distilled from his sense of the particulars, especially of personalities. Psychology and self-interest guide the flow of events
in the *Storia*. For Guicciardini, then, princely cupidity is a perfectly serious
explanation and it is backed up by a clear picture of the psychology of rulers. He is not far from Acton in his appreciation of the licentiousness of
power, as we have already observed in reading the 'Considerazioni.' In the
Storia d'Italia, however, the best summary of the psychology of power is
not spoken by the narrator but comes in a speech to the Venetian senate
put in the mouth of a senator. By an odd coincidence he begins with one
of Guicciardini's favourite maxims. Few men are wise, he says, so if you
have to judge another man's action it is better to consider realistically
what such a man, given his own nature, is likely to do rather than assuming
that he will do the wisest thing.[19] Thus, continues the Venetian, if you
wish to understand the possible actions of the King of France, do not con-

18 Cecil Grayson, trans. in Guicciardini, *History of Italy* and *History of Florence*, ed.
John Hale (New York: Washington Square Press 1964), p. 314. 'Si sarebbe facilmente accomodato alle richieste del re se non l'avesse ritenuto il sospetto, per la
coscienza dell'offese fattegli, per le quali era generata da ogni parte tale diffidenza,
che e' fusse piú difficile trovare mezzo di sicurtà per ciascuno che convenire negli
articoli delle differenze; perché togliendosi alla sicurezza dell'uno quel che si con-
sentisse per assicurare l'altro, niuno voleva rimettere nella fede di altri quel che
l'altro recusava di rimettere nella sua. Così stringendolo la necessità a prendere
quel consiglio che gli era piú molesto, per cercare almeno d' allungare i pericoli,
continuò con Rigault l'arti medesime che aveva usate insino allora.' *Storia d'Italia*,
I, p. 242.
19 *Storia d'Italia*, II, p. 221: 'non tanto quello che verisimilmente farebbe uno savio
quanto quale sia il cervello e la natura di chi ha a deliberare.'

sider so much what might be prudent as the fact that the French are changeable ('inquieti e leggieri'). Then you must consider the nature of great princes, which is not like our own. They do not resist their appetites as private men do. They are used to being adored in their own kingdoms, understood and obeyed at a mere hint. Thus they are not only arrogant ('elati e insolenti') but they cannot tolerate being denied whatever seems to them just. And whatever it is they want, the senator adds, they consider just. They persuade themselves that with just a word they can remove all obstacles and overcome all situations ('la natura delle cose'). Moreover, they consider it shameful to draw back from what they desire merely because of difficulties. Measuring great things and small by the same rule, they proceed not by reason and with prudence but with willfulness and pride. These vices are common to all princes, the Venetian says, returning to the specific subject of his speech, including the French king.

As a citizen of a famous republic, the Venetian is free to name the sins of princes; Guicciardini himself would certainly have added that the Venetian senate had also experienced the corruptions of power. We cannot, then, naively equate the voice of the Venetian with the point of view of the author. Still the summary is apt and a speech of this type is not a bad place to look for political wisdom. In a history that holds so rigorously to narration, the speech is a perfectly functional device. It crystallizes analysis and motivation into an event, the one form in which they can be strictly integrated into a narrative. Nor would Guicciardini have lightly thrown away one of his favourite maxims so carefully polished in the *Ricordi* if he did not think these speeches a fit place to display his political wisdom.

The imprudent ambition of princes is a necessary but not a sufficient explanation of the Italian decline. After all, there had been ambitious princes before 1492, the year of Lorenzo's death and the beginning of hints of trouble. Yet Italy had not then suffered such calamities and had reached, according to Guicciardini, her highest point of prosperity since the decline of Rome. The answer must lie, then, in the lifting of some previous restraint on princes. They had always been ambitious but perhaps they had not always been allowed to be so imprudent. This is confirmed by the important passage, so often referred to here, that marks the entry of the first invading army into Asti in September 1494. Beyond the cruel deaths, the new methods of warfare, new customs and unknown diseases, beyond the destruction of the peace itself, a less definite but possibly darker threat is indicated:

> ... and the instruments of peace and harmony in Italy were thrown into such confusion that they have never since been able to be reconstituted,

so that other foreign nations and barbarian armies have been able to
devastate and trample wretchedly upon her. [20]

Not only had a plague broken out, though its seriousness was not yet fully
apparent, but the traditional remedies had somehow become useless. Before 1494 and not thereafter some agency had kept the instability of fortune and the ambitions of princes under control. The repeated outbreaks
of war are, therefore, not merely the signal that fresh provocation to violence had occurred but that the normal political restraints had failed or
even disappeared. It is at least partly for this reason that our chronology of
the wars consisted of recurrent opportunities for peace that never bore
fruit.

Guicciardini gives us in this passage a powerful and yet elliptical explanation for future instability. Guicciardini is characteristically a reticent
author, but we can be reasonably sure that he is referring here to the idea
of the balance of power. The first pages of the *Storia d'Italia* describe the
state of Italy when the instruments of peace were still intact, consciously
setting off the chaos that follows. Many things, says the historian, combined to conserve the happy condition of Italy in those days, but the virtue of Lorenzo the Magnificent was perhaps the most important. Knowing
that for himself and for the Florentine republic it would be dangerous if
any one of the major Italian states amplified its power, he tried with every
means to insure that Italian affairs remained balanced. But Lorenzo's (or
Guicciardini's) concept of the balance of power differs in one sense from
the modern one. Whereas we would be likely to say that you preserve the
balance to promote peace, Guicciardini says that Lorenzo preserved the
peace in order to keep the balance. [21] Thus, once the balance had disappeared with the introduction of foreign armies, it follows that for some
at least there would be little incentive to preserve the peace.

Of all the Italian powers Venice alone was in a position to profit from
disequilibrium, which is a clue to Guicciardini's typically negative attitude
towards the famous republic. Other rulers would seek temporary or personal advantage – as when the Borgia pope sponsored his son's efforts to
carve a new principality out of the disorder of the Papal States. But only

20 Trans. Grayson, *History of Italy*, pp. 148-9. 'Si disordinorono di maniera gli instrumenti della quiete e concordia italiana che, non si essendo mai poi potuta
   riordinare, hanno avuto facoltà altre nazioni straniere e eserciti barbari di concul-
   carla miserabilmente e devastarla.' *Storia d'Italia*, I, pp. 67-8.
21 *Storia d'Italia*, I, p. 3: '... procurava con ogni studio che le cose d'Italia in modo
   bilanciate si mantenessino che più in una che in un' altra parte non pendessino: il
   che, senza la conservazione della pace e senza vegghiare con somma diligenza ogni
   accidente benché minimo, succedere non poteva.'

Venice could match the power and ambition of the ultramontanes and hope to emerge from the struggle with a permanent hegemony in Italy.[22] The first disruption of the balance of power, however, came from another quarter, and the chapters that follow the death of Lorenzo are devoted to chronicling this breakdown. The first fault lay with the young Piero de' Medici and Alfonso of Aragon, both of them rash sons of wiser fathers. Evidence of an alliance between these two led Lodovico Sforza, whose insecurity originated in his usurpation of the Duchy of Milan from his nephew, to fear encirclement by Milan's former allies, Naples and Florence. And Lodovico's fears were not groundless since the displaced (and dimwitted) legitimate Duke of Milan was Alfonso's son-in-law. Lodovico's reaction was excessive, however, and by calling in the French he not only ensured his own downfall but the permanent disruption of the peninsular balance of power.

But even before the coming of the French, an incident reveals how difficult it is to re-establish equilibrium in a system already tending to imbalance. Lodovico had become alarmed by the sale of some castles to Virginio Orsini, a feudatory of the Aragonese rulers of Naples. The old Neapolitan king, Ferdinand, formerly one of the protectors of the balance of power, sensed his mistake in angering Lodovico and made a genuine attempt to compose the differences that had arisen over the castles. He persuaded himself, says Guicciardini, that with the reason for the disturbances removed, Italy would easily, even automatically, return to her former condition. Unfortunately the solution was not to be so simple. Removing the causes, comments Guicciardini, will not always remove the effects.[23]

Once the closed circle of the Italian state system had been broken into by a superior foreign power, it would never again be possible for the Italians to establish a balance of power by their own means. The obvious solution, of course, was to redress the imbalance by involving another European

---

22 The league between Florence, Milan, and Naples, which kept Italy at peace was designed to curb Venice: 'avendo per fine principalmente di non lasciare diventare piú potenti i viniziani; i quali, maggiori senza dubbio di ciascuna de' confederati ma molto minori di tutti insieme, procedevano con consigli separati da' consigli comuni, e aspettando di crescere della altrui disunione e travagli, stavano attenti e preparati a valersi di ogni accidente che potesse aprire loro la via allo imperio di tutta Italia.' Such was the state of things, Guicciardini continues below, 'tali erano i fondamenti della tranquillità d'Italia, disposti e contrapesati in modo che non solo di alterazione presente non si temeva ma né si poteva facilmente congetturare da quali consigli o per quali casi o con quali armi s'avesse a muovere tanta quiete.' Storia, I, pp. 4-5.

23 Storia d'Italia, I, 17: 'Ma non sempre per il rimuovere delle cagioni si rimuovono gli effetti i quali da quelle hanno avuto la prima origine.'

power, the Hapsburgs, and so Italy was absorbed into a continental system with an equilibrium of its own. The testing of French and Spanish dynastic ambitions on Italian soil proved disastrous for the Italians; but even when there was peace between the foreigners, Italy might still see renewed turmoil because of weaknesses internal to her political system. This is the situation we meet at the beginning of Book 13:

> *Thus not without reason it was thought that peace and harmony between two such great princes must extinguish all seeds of war and discord in Italy. And nonetheless, either because of the unhappiness of our Fate, or* because the division of Italy into so many states and principates, each with its own desires and interests, *made it almost impossible that she would not be subject to continual disturbances. Thus, the Emperor and the Venetians had hardly laid down their arms when the beginnings of a new turmoil appeared, caused by Francesco Maria della Rovere.* [24]

Characteristically, the rare general observation is at the same time a specific comment on the historical role of men like the Della Rovere, petty despots who still filled the crannies of Italy's complicated political geography. In the present case, the inflammatory possibilities of the smaller states are linked to the combustibility of bands of idle soldiers. Francesco Maria, for reasons of his own, stirred up the Spanish troops who had been left hanging at the end of the fighting. And this was easy to do, explains Guicciardini, because for the soldiers, used to war, sack, and rapine, nothing was more unwelcome than the peace to which they saw the state of Italy was disposed. Thus a formidable army of freebooters came into existence to be manipulated by petty princelings, and the cycle of destruction was renewed.

Guicciardini's recognition here of the importance of the fragmentation of Italy as a source of instability adds a third major explanation of the long wars of Italy. This completes a triangle of related explanations whose other sides are the ambitious self-interest of rulers and the breakdown of the Laurentian system of the balance of power. The discovery that politi-

24 (My trans.) 'Dunque, non senza giusta cagione si giudicava che la concordia e la pace tra i principi tanto potenti avesse a spegnere tutti i semi delle discordie e delle guerre italiane. E nondimeno, o per la infelicità del fato nostro *o perché, per essere Italia divisa in tanti principi e in tanti stati,* fusse quasi impossibile, *per le varie volontà e interessi di quegli che l'avevano in mano,* che ella non stesse sottoposta a continui travagli, ecco che appena deposte l'armi tra Cesare e i Viniziani ... si scopersono principi di nuovi tumulti, causati da Francesco Maria della Rovere.' *Storia d'Italia,* IV, pp. 1-2.

cal division builds instability into the state-system is clearly an aspect of Guicciardini's preoccupation with change and impermanence. From another angle, it is also a recapitulation of the ambitious princes theme, seen now from a more institutional perspective. And yet at the same time we should not forget the argument he had made against Machiavelli that this fragmentation had also allowed for a fuller development of Italian potential, for the growth of a number of rich and independent cities against the domination of a single capital. Thus Guicciardini recognized that both the greatness and the collapse of Italy had the same source.

Two general points should be made about these three connected explanations of the Italian collapse. The first is Guicciardini's complete italo-centrism. It might seem more natural for him to have laid the blame as far as possible on the invaders. And certainly Guicciardini has no great love for any of the 'barbarian' nations, though he has respect for the Spanish whom he knew best from early diplomatic experience. But the aggressiveness of the foreigners with respect to an Italy both richer and more cultivated seems to be taken for granted, and full responsibility is borne by those Italians who, as he says, taught the foreigner the road to Italy. The first fact we are told about the initial invasion was that the French came on invitation ('chiamate da' nostri principi medesimi'). And afterwards there would always be an Italian power willing to lend a hand to the Spanish, Germans, or Swiss.

Guicciardini's ethnocentrism may be counted a weakness in that he failed to see that the consolidation of the European powers in this period was an important precondition of protracted warfare in Italy. By seeing the contest entirely in terms of Italian weakness and not ultramontane strength, he obviously distorts the picture and may therefore have exaggerated the weakness of Italian arms, the chicanery of her princes, the fickleness of her peoples.[25] On the other hand, his perspective led him, on a course parallel to Machiavelli's, to examine the weaknesses of Italian institutions. In this sense the *Storia d'Italia* is a post-mortem on the Italian Renaissance; only in his fervent hope of a resurrection does Machiavelli go further. The example of Rome may also have been influential because her decline was attributed to the corruption of her ancient virtues.[26] In any event, the Italian wars are not shown as the onslaught of one people against another. Instead we see the failure of Italian policies, safeguards,

25 On this point see Piero Pieri, *Il Rinascimento e la crisi militare italiana.* (Turin: Einaudi 1952)
26 *Storia d'Italia*, I, p. 2: 'Lo imperio romano, indebolito principalmente per la mutazione degli antichi costumi, cominciò, già sono più di mille anni, di quella grandezza a declinare ...'

and prudence. Despite his obvious interest in the dramatic possibilities of
pitched battles, Guicciardini takes as his fundamental subject the progressive disintegration of a political system, revealed step by step through the
discovery of the weaknesses of its guardians and the ineffectiveness of its
institutions.

The second point to emphasize about Guicciardini's explanations of
Italian collapse is the apparent freedom of choice of the participants. By
now it should be clear that Guicciardini did not see the people of Italy,
and more especially their rulers, as being locked into an unalterable sequence of events. In retrospect, of course, any series will probably appear
logical and may even appear necessary, and Guicciardini's fatalism sometimes makes this freedom of choice seem more apparent than real. But the
fate of Italy is not governed by anything so rational as cause and effect;
rather the destiny of Italy, as Guicciardini sees it, works itself out in the
irrational realms of fortune and psychology. The free will of men is real
enough, but men are not rational and they live in a world subject to the
caprice of Fortune. Thus their choices are most often imprudent, unhappy,
and unsuccessful. If the fortune of Italy were not so consistently unhappy,
if human affairs were not by nature so unstable, if princes could control
their irrational greed by rational prudence, the sickness of Italy might have
been cured. But clearly once the initial stages of the disease had passed,
the odds were against a cure.

I use the word 'sickness' advisedly because it comes closest to Guicciardini's own sense of Italy's condition and the way in which he explains it.
Guicciardini consistently draws on natural images to describe historical
change. Not in this sense an imaginative writer, he constantly repeats medi-
cal metaphors of disease and cure. Equally frequent are similar references
to seeds, roots, and fires. Book 7, for example, opens with the typical pattern of new hopes of peace and the 'semi non piccoli di futuri incendi,' the
germ of future conflagrations. Here Guicciardini has rather confused his
stock metaphors, but the organic images point to a sense of historical
change based on an idea of growth and decay, of sequence in nature. The
Storia d'Italia is a world in which human freedom to choose is consistently
misused; taking our cue from Guicciardini's language, we might think of it
as a vast and increasingly parched forest inhabited by a tribe of particularly
careless smokers.

In making our chronological survey we noted the pivotal significance
of the year 1521, the beginning of longer and more dangerous conflicts
than in the past. The crucial development in the period that begins here is
the second breakdown of the balance of power in Italy, a balance no longer
of Italian but of foreign powers. Book 14 begins with a stalemate between

France and Spain. Despite their aggressive intentions neither king had immediate cause for renewing the war, and their forces were so balanced in
Italy that neither could proceed without the help of one of the Italian
princes. The logical guarantor of the peace was the pope, both by virtue of
his spiritual office and his comparative strength among Italian states. After
the elimination of Naples and Milan as independent states and the long de-
fensive wars of Venice, Rome became increasingly the representative Italian
power, the centre of Italian diplomacy and of Guicciardini's history – indeed it seems reasonable to think that it was his connection with Rome
that made Guicciardini an Italian rather than a Florentine historian. For
Florentines Rome's pivotal importance was particularly apparent during
the pontificates of the two Medici popes, when Florence was tied to Rome
and frequently paid heavily to further papal ambitions.

Thus the papacy had the most to lose from any easing of the deadlock
between France and the emperor, and both by temperament and personal
inclination Pope Leo seemed well disposed to enjoy the ease of peace. By
nature, writes Guicciardini disapprovingly, Leo was disinclined to activity.
Rather, he was dedicated to music, farces, and other 'shameful pleasures'
('che si godevano con grande infamia'). In short it seemed certain Leo
would be completely opposed to war. And, as if these reasons were not
sufficient, Guicciardini gives several others, which need not be reproduced
here, against Leo's acting as the instigator of fresh troubles.[27]

All this is easily recognized as a build-up to new hostilities, which we
have already been told will be worse than any before, as well as another
instance of Guicciardini's condemnation of princes. Even so, after such a
wealth of arguments has been given against the pope's following an aggressive policy, Leo's irrationality had better be well explained. In fact, Guicciardini rather overdoes it. In the first place, he observes that prosperity
can be the worst enemy of men, 'because it makes them unable to control
themselves, licentious, eager for bad things, and so greedy for novelty that
they disturb their own well-being.'[28] This is more than a mere truism;
Guicciardini offers it as a genuine explanation of the pope's psychology as
well as of his character. But having made his psychological (and moral)
point on a general level, Guicciardini goes on to offer us no less than five
possible specific motives for Leo's actions, including matters of personal or
family pride, of political objectives, and of strategic considerations. Finally,
to cap it all, Guicciardini offers us free choice of all the possible permuta-

27 *Storia d'Italia*, IV, pp. 77-80.
28 (My trans.) 'Perchè gli fa impotenti di se medesimi, licenziosi e arditi al male e
   cupidi di turbare il bene proprio con cose nuove.' *Storia d'Italia*, IV, p. 79.

tions: whichever of these reasons moved Leo, the historian says, either
singly or all together, Leo turned all his thoughts to war.

What then is Guicciardini's explanation of the events of 1521? Evidently
it is not possible to talk about a single explanation. From the point of view
of the reader, it must be doubted that the extraordinary profusion of motivation offered is much help at all. Certainly the apparent corollary throm-
bosis suffered by the historian must weaken the reader's confidence in the
strength of his guide, though it could also be argued that Guicciardini is
only reproducing the confusion of motives felt by Leo himself.

In this case, Guicciardini has helped himself to too much of a good
thing, and the exaggerated example cited above was chosen deliberately. It
is important to see, however, that the exaggeration is also characteristic.
Multiplicity of explanation is present in another, more fundamental sense
in this text and is an essential feature of Guicciardini's habitual description
of events. If we look back over the text, we find that three distinct levels
of description are employed in order to explain the resumption of warfare
in 1521. The first is the will of superhuman forces, 'il cielo, il fato proprio
e la fortuna,' which appear to be envious of Italy's quiet or afraid that she
might return to her former prosperity. The second element is (as expected)
the ambition of princes. Those who more than any are entrusted with
keeping the peace, says Guicciardini, more frequently than others disturb
it. Guicciardini is aiming specifically at the pope in this case and the explanation that prosperity made Leo lose control of himself ('impotenti di
se medesimi') is a psychological elaboration of this theme. Finally, on the
most concrete level, there is the description of specific personal and public ambitions harboured by Leo. The simultaneous presentation of these
three types of explanation is characteristic of the *Storia d'Italia*; it is only
the elaboration or overelaboration in detail that is unusual, and that is a
reflection of the importance of the occasion.

Undoubtedly most modern readers are happy enough to pass over the
first two levels of description as literary trimming or vague psychological
and moralistic generalization and save their attention for the 'real' explanation that follows. It is characteristic of Guicciardini, the pragmatic diplomat with great faith in the importance of particulars, that the 'real'
explanation is always there. And the very detail and authority with which
Guicciardini describes specific personalities and their policies may encour-
age us to follow only this strand in the narrative. Yet, as we have seen in
the present example, even that single strand has a disconcerting tendency
to unravel, leaving us with a free choice of motives; and always there is the
accompaniment of psychology and fortune. This multiplicity in the description of single events vastly complicates any attempt to create fixed

and purely secular sequences of causation. In a swirling mass of influences, some general and psychological, some particular and political, some not human at all, how can we identify cause and effect?

Guicciardini's characters are always making choices, though it is not always individual choice that is decisive in determining events. Individuals choose within the framework of general psychologically established patterns. And both their choices and the consequences of their choices are subjected to quite arbitrary influences of fate and fortune. But Guicciardini tells us nothing about the priority of these influences or how they affect each other. And yet for the historical individual real alternatives exist and to his own knowledge he acts freely. The act of choosing and the consequences of choice make up the materials of the story, and both are observed with Guicciardini's customary exactness. The full background, both in terms of character and situation, is established and any external pressures influencing the decision are drawn in. Most importantly, we are told what the range of alternatives is, and so we follow the actual choice with empathy.

All these things the historian can be quite precise about because they are exterior. Thus Guicciardini puts a real man, Leo X, into a concrete situation and describes in great detail the alternatives that man faced and the choices he eventually made. When we slip below the surface of the action into the realm of motivation, we seem at first to have entered an area of still more exacting observation. The range of motivations offered more than matches the range of possible actions. Perhaps our compliments go out to the historian because he has drawn us into the story by demanding that the final interpretation be made by us. This should not, however, obscure the fact that the historian himself has failed to choose. Implicitly he is putting severe limitations on his (or anyone else's) ability to judge the interior motive from the external fact, no matter how exactly the latter is observed. Although Guicciardini is deeply concerned with motivation as well as with behaviour, he cannot honestly make the tight, rational links between the two which he would like to make. In this realm he must admit a good deal of indeterminacy. And this indeterminacy is quickly multiplied when we leave behind the comparatively simple problem of the individual action and examine a whole event or a sequence of events. How can the historian say, to take up a former example, whether the resumption of war in Book 13 is finally explained by the influence of fate, the division of Italy, the ambition of princes, the actions of Francesco Maria della Rovere, or the troublemaking of restless soldiers?

By working on multiple levels, and by providing ad hoc answers in each, the historian recognizes his ultimate inability to create firm explanations while emphasizing his need and ability to provide exacting description. Perhaps this is the reason that we come back so willingly to the concrete attractions of narrative, to events in a sequence that is always in Guicciardini meaningful and swift. The clusters of explanation that surround each action take their significance from the event and not vice versa. The historian's narrative skill and the authority of his powerful intelligence carry us willingly from event to event. In the end Guicciardini offers us the explanatory force of narrative itself, and the explanation of the Italian collapse is the *Storia d'Italia*.

2 / 'A Sea Tossed by the Winds': Change and the Structure of the Narrative

In Guicciardini's times unprecedented events seemed to have become almost ordinary. Most were heavy with disaster but there were some happy departures too. The discovery of the New World, for instance, proved that in one way at least modern man had surpassed the ancients. But these optimistic signs were few, and without doubt the burden of change was depressing indeed. As an Italian, Guicciardini had no reason to look on the changes that came with the collapse of Italian independence with anything but despair. As a Florentine conservative and a patrician, he naturally resented the political fluctuations that gave power in Florence alternatively to democrats and autocrats and finally ended in the consolidation of the Medici Grand Duchy. And perhaps most importantly, writing in the late 1530s, Guicciardini had no way of knowing what new order, if indeed any order at all, would come out of more than a generation of chaos. Change seemed independent and uncontrollable. The future of Italy lay in the least reliable hands, those of her princes and of Fortune.

As a political conservative, Guicciardini resented and resisted change, but as a historian he analysed it in unsurpassed detail and accommodated all his labours to its unwelcome force. We have already noted that of the two principal themes announced on the opening page of the history the first is the overwhelming instability of human affairs, which Guicciardini compares to a wind-tossed sea, 'né altrimenti che un mare concitato de'venti.' The image of the sea points to a picture of change as continual flux, a back-and-forth motion without point or effect except the destruction of the unskilled sailor. This image of mutability is probably the most common and certainly the most conventional of Guicciardini's understandings of the meaning of change. It is a concept that links the whole generation of post-humanist Italian historians. But what is remarkable about this initial thematic passage is not the isolated statement of instability but how rapidly the conventional opening is pulled into a vortex of causation, guilt, error, and Fortune. The changefulness of all human affairs and the imprudence of princes, Guicciardini's twin themes, are quickly spun together in a single strand. Princes forget how variable Fortune is and they therefore do great harm to themselves and their peoples.

The invocation of Fortune is not unexpected but still important. At times Fortune seems to be a kind of uncertainty principle which confounds any attempt by men to predict the outcome of events. Elsewhere Fortune is given feminine form and manner and is seen as deliberately derailing the best laid plans simply in order to resist the encroachment of human reasoning or control.[1] In either case, flux is Fortune's godchild; and nowhere more than in military affairs is the unpredictable so predictable: 'But (as everyone knows) the power of fortune is most great in all human affairs, even more in military matters than any others, but inestimable, immense and infinite in actual warfare ...'[2] In a sense, of course, Fortune is simply a shorthand for other more complex and specific explanations of the uncertainty of battle. And, too, it may be an explanation of last resort, an explanation of the inexplicable. But Fortune is clearly more than a symbol of accident and human error, though these provide the materials with which she works. Fortune is wilful as well as random. And, as an explanation, Fortune is invoked as a parallel motivation of events for which the most meticulous explanations have been given. To call one kind of explanation instrumental and the other ornamental is, I believe, to impose an artificial clarity on a mind disturbed by uncertainties on this question.

Fortune is a great leveller. It ensures a sort of rough justice by giving all men the same long odds. When a man dies in Guicciardini's history the occasion is marked not by a biography so much as by an assessment of his fortunes. When the balance is struck for the last time the question is not the biographical 'what has he done?' – because that is already in the history – but 'how has Fortune dealt with him?' Here no rule can be applied. Prudence, ability, ambition: these can give a man a place in history, but they do not ensure his ultimate success, as Guicciardini points out in dis-

1 See *ricordo* 20. On the concepts of Fortune in Guicciardini see Palmarocchi, 'Il concetto di fortuna nel Guicciardini' in *Studi Guicciardiniani* (Città di Castello, 1947), and more generally on Fortune in the early sixteenth century, see Mario Santoro, *Fortuna, ragione, e prudenza nella civiltà letteraria del Cinquecento* (Napoli: Liguori 1967).
2 Trans. Alexander, *History of Italy*, pp. 101-2. 'Ma è grandissima (come ognuno sa) in tutte l'azioni umane la potestà della fortuna, maggiore nelle cose militari che in qualunque altra, ma inestimabile immensa infinita ne' fatti d'arme ...' *Storia d'Italia*, I, p. 168.

cussing the opposite fates of such exemplary villains as Alexander Borgia and Lodovico Sforza.

The rise or fall of such spectacular scoundrels takes up a good deal of the *Storia d'Italia*, but there is time as well for a more purposive idea of change. To use Guicciardini's own image, the meaningless, defeating waves of the sea are accompanied by more consistent tides and currents which can be charted. This kind of change has direction as well as speed and, though Guicciardini never makes a consistent distinction, we would be more likely to call it fate than Fortune. What the fate of Italy is we already know from having followed the chronology of the dying spiral of Italian independence. But, as is so often true, the *Storia* is not as explicit on this question of directed change as are the *Ricordi*. Number 140 of the B text reads:

> *The things of this world do not stay fixed. In fact, they always progress along the road on which they should, according to their nature, come to their end. But they move more slowly than we believe. We measure them by our lives, which are brief, and not according to their own time, which is long. But their movements are slower than ours - so slow, by their very nature, that although they move we do not notice it. And for that reason, the judgements we make concerning them are often wrong.*[3]

As in the opening page of the history, we are told that change is an inseparable part of human affairs; but against the capriciousness signified by that often quoted simile to the sea, in this passage Guicciardini writes of a change that is directed by some teleological principle inherent in things themselves. Where in the *Storia* human affairs are subjected (*sottoposte*) to pervasive instability, here change is seen in the guise of 'progress' towards an end, a progress which is not imposed on the changing thing but is *per sua natura*. For this reason, Guicciardini can speak of the reasonableness of the change ('a che *ragionevolmente* per sua natura'). As usual, however, his intention is to caution us. Though the fact of change is sure, the rate of change is easily misjudged. The pace of events may, in fact, be so slow that we are not even aware of the motion. Change so slow as to be unrecognizable was not likely to be a major problem in post-invasion Italy, but Guic-

---

3 *Maxims*, pp. 129-30. 'Le cose del mondo non stanno ferme, anzi hanno sempre progresso al cammino a che ragionevolmente per sua natura hanno a andare e finire; ma tardano più che non è la opinione nostra, perché noi le misuriamo secondo la vita nostra che è breve e non secondo el tempo loro che è lungo; e però sono e passi suoi più tardi che non sono e nostri, e sì tardi per sua natura che, ancora che si muovino, non ci accorgiamo spesso de' suoi moti: e per questo sono spesso falsi e giudici che noi facciamo.' *Ricordi*, p. 82.

ciardini's historical sense is always broader than the immediate past. Most importantly, his understanding that the movements of history can proceed with glacial slowness is part of his remarkable recognition that individual life and historical life may be regulated by different calendars. Thus, errors arise from measuring events according to the brevity of our lives rather than 'secondo el tempo loro che è lungo.'

The final version of this *ricordo* is built along the same lines but incorporates some important alterations:

> *If you see a city beginning to decline, a government changing, a new empire expanding, or any such phenomenon – and these things are sometimes quite clearly visible to us – be careful not to misjudge the time they will take. By their very nature, and because of various obstacles, such movements are much slower than most men imagine. And to be mistaken in it is a step on which people often stumble. The same is true even of private and personal affairs; but much more so of public and general matters, for these, because of their bulk, move much more slowly and are subject to many more accidents.*[4]

Here the cautionary note is even stronger, being introduced from the beginning, and the explanation for the slow movement of history somewhat different. Guicciardini now abandons the biological metaphor for change he used earlier ('la vita nostra ... el tempo loro') in favour of one drawn from physics. Public events move more slowly than private ones because they have more mass or weight ('maggiore mole'). At the same time the new text takes into account both kinds of change that we have been discussing, random and purposive, in explaining the slow pace of events. Thus, the movement of things is slowed by their nature and various obstacles; and public affairs move more slowly than private ones because, aside from their greater weight, they are subject to many more accidents ('sottoposte a piú accidenti').

4 *Maxims*, pp. 59-60. 'Se vedete andare a cammino la declinazione di una città, la mutazione di uno governo, lo augumento di uno imperio nuovo e altre cose simili – che qualche volta si veggono innanzi quasi certe – avvertite a non vi ingannare ne' tempi: perché e moti delle cose sono per sua natura e per diversi impedimenti molto più tardi che gli uomini non si immaginano, e lo ingannarti in questo ti può fare grandissimo danno: avvertiteci bene, ché è uno passo dove spesso si inciam pa. Interviene anche el medesimo nelle cose private e particulari, ma molto più in queste publiche e universali, perché hanno, per essere maggiore mole, el moto suo più lento, e anche sono sottoposte a più accidenti.' *Ricordi*, 71, p. 82.

This last phrase takes us back to the opening page of the *Storia*: 'a quanta instabilità ... siano sottoposte le cose umane.' And there is an equally clear bridge to the history contained in the opening lines of the *ricordo*. In the earlier version of this text Guicciardini had spoken in an abstract way, taking 'the things of this world' as his subject. Now he particularizes and historicizes this general statement, filling in the abstract category with the particular kinds of changes and events he has in mind: the decline of a city, the mutation of a government, the augmentation of a new empire, and so on. How similar this is to the recitation of plagues that accompanies the French entry into Asti: 'changes of dominions, subversion of kingdoms, desolation of countries, destruction of cities and the cruelest massacres ...' The correspondence between the words of the *ricordo* and these from the *Storia* only underlines what is in any case clear in a hundred places and was already implied in our investigation of the chronology of defeat: that Guicciardini saw his story as a description of pervasive change and general decline.

Over and over Guicciardini announces his subject in terms of a series of changes or compares things as they were to what they are about to become. Just as we can take the list of changes, mostly deplorable, that enter into Italy with the armies of Charles VIII as thematic for the entire history, so we can find many more limited versions of this grand opening which introduces smaller episodes. The major thematic introduction has a weight and urgency that comes from being at the heart of something, but just for that reason the repetition of quieter, smaller examples may tell us more. Often we find declarations that new changes are about to occur at the beginnings or endings of chapters. These chapters are an invention of the modern editors and an aid to the modern reader who is unused to reading long unarticulated texts. No one would want to argue with this service to the reader, but the point is that Guicciardini's text was already well articulated by a host of directional signs. These provide points of departure for the author, and also position one event among a series, or reorient the reader's attention from one series and one locale to another. And rhetorical emphasis can also be given to a forthcoming narration. Thus at the beginning of Chapter 9 in Book I, all signs point to greater and more frequent changes, to events stranger and more horrible than have been seen in the world for many centuries.[5] Chapter 7 in Book V begins rather differently:

These things were happening in Tuscany and the unexpected things which were about to occur were not yet apparent. But greater and

5 *Storia d'Italia*, I, p. 63.

*more dangerous movements from which would proceed very important
effects were beginning to materialize in the kingdom in Naples.*[6]

Elsewhere the people of Naples are characterized by their fickleness and
special eagerness for novelty.[7]

Many more examples could be cited, but very shortly we shall be examining one book in detail and it should then be clear how frequent is
Guicciardini's use of this device. We shall see also that these passages reflect
a structural pattern in the *Storia d'Italia* which is related to the needs of a
narrative built around the fact of change. For the moment I have wanted
simply to underline the fact that Guicciardini's themes are dynamic and
tend to announce themselves as a series of changes.

One final piece of evidence should be added here: Guicciardini's frequent use of the small-scale history. These miniatures, as we shall see in a
particular instance, are constructed on the same lines as the major narrative, and they are usually employed to fill in the background to an important situation. A famous example is the brief history of the papacy in
Book IV. Like the thematic statements we have been examining, these
small-scale histories indicate the historian's rejection of static means of
presenting his story. Even elements brought in from outside the major
narrative are introduced as the end products of another historical sequence and not simply accepted as given. Change, whether it is understood
as flux or progression, as merely destructive or determined, is clearly a
major motif, almost oppressive in its ubiquity. The conclusion seems to be
that 'it is certainly not wasted effort or without reward to consider how
times and things change.'[8] But as so often, Guicciardini stops short of ex-
tracting any prescription from his study of change. Though he is willing to
affirm the value of contemplating change, he will not indicate explicitly
what lessons we are meant to learn. We are left, presumably, to contemplate his history and draw our own prudent conclusions.

Not only is change a theme around which narratives are organized, but
it is also an important characteristic of the way they are organized. Broad
aspects of the narrative form reflect an implicit idea of change and meet
the needs of a history in which change is a predominant fact. Thus our

6 (My trans.) 'Queste cose si moveano in Toscana, non apparendo ancora quel che
   fuori dell'espettazione degli uomini aveano a partorire. Ma maggiore e molto più
   pericolosi movimenti, e da' quali avevano a procedere importantissimi effetti,
   cominciavano a scoprirsi nel reame di Napoli ...' *Storia d'Italia*, II, p. 33.
7 *Storia d'Italia*, I, p. 142.
8 (My trans.) 'non è certo opera perduta o senza premio il considerare la varietà de'
   tempi e delle cose del mondo.' *Storia d'Italia*, I, p. 29.

contemplation of the mutability of history must extend beyond the explicit logic of the *Storia d'Italia* and comprehend its language and texture.

The *Storia d'Italia* is an extraordinary technical achievement. It is well known that Guicciardini tapped archival and documentary sources in an unprecedented way. For example, he was able to take home with him the entire archive of the Dieci, the important committee which handled Florence's foreign affairs.[9] Equally remarkable, and less often recognized, is the skilfulness with which he drew together the endless detail of his researches into a lucid narrative. This second aspect of his mastery must be called an artistic achievement and is harder to demonstrate concretely than the accuracy of his researches. This is especially so given the positivist assumptions of most modern historiography, which, even longer than the history of science, has clung to a notion of scholarship which is progressive and continuous. Thus positivist scholarship has downgraded the image of the historian as literary artist while stressing his function as a researcher.

Guicciardini's clarity and care are obvious at first reading. His concern for detail is extraordinary, perhaps obsessive. Yet the lucidity and energy of the narration are seldom marred. The reader feels that he is sitting in on the telling of a great and universal tale, and like the devotee of Proust or Thomas Mann, he regrets its brevity not its length. All this one feels. But the technical and literary mastery of the author hides a difficult problem. Guicciardini's understanding of the breadth of the events of his day led him to establish an extraordinarily wide scope for his history, a range that includes every corner of Italy and frequently the rest of the continent as well. But his experiences as a diplomat and the intellectual struggles of the *Ricordi* and the *Cose fiorentine* had convinced him that history must be a detailed, exhaustive search. Only a thorough mastery of the processes of history, atom by atom, could satisfy the historical scepticism of the author of the *Considerazioni*. These two requirements, detail and scope, are not incompatible, but they are certainly in tension. In our own day it is usually assumed that a broader field automatically implies less intimate detail; but

9   Guicciardini's use of sources has never been thoroughly documented, but such a study has now been promised by the latest editor of the *Storia d'Italia*, Silvana Seidel Menchi. And the notes to her edition offer some help on this subject (*Storia d'Italia* [Turin: Einaudi 1971]). In the meantime there is the brief discussion by Antonio Gherardi in his introduction to the first critical edition of the *Storia* (Florence 1919), Vol. I, pp. xlv-lix. Roberto Ridolfi's catalogue of the Guicciardini archives is also informative (*L'Archivio della famiglia Guicciardini* [Florence: Olschki, 1931]). The older work by Pasquale Villari, which refutes Ranke's attack on Guicciardini's reliability, is also important (*Niccolò Machiavelli e i suoi tempi* [Florence: Le Monnier, 1877-82] Vol. III, pp. 488-96).

no one complains that the *Storia* is too general or too vague. And when one recalls that Guicciardini was his own chronicler for much of his history, the intellectual effort involved in collecting and organizing so much unformed material becomes more astonishing still.

Guicciardini's resolution of the contrary tensions of depth and scope was to compromise neither but to combine both in a new narrative order. It is a solution that makes great demands on the reader, but rewards him well. Sharp detailed pictures are the indispensible core of the history, and no one who considers Guicciardini's economy in recounting individual incidents could make the customary accusation of prolixity. One picture succeeds another rapidly. We cannot quite settle into a customarily Florentine view of affairs because too soon we are in Naples with the French. We cannot follow Lodovico Sforza directly from intrigue to intrigue; there are too many others trying to pre-empt the Moor as the magus of Italian diplomacy, and we must observe them all. There is not even enough uninterrupted space for the systematic exposition of the author's own views; like the other characters in this vast story, Guicciardini himself appears occasionally, commenting on the death of Borgia, or the humiliation of the Roman women, or omens marking a new year.

This technique can be compared to modern cinema. The whole is made up of the suggestion of many parts. The camera constantly focusses on particulars. No one angle is allowed to dominate and identify itself with the true perspective. The viewer is consequently asked to be more supple, more energetic, because he must follow the rapid editing. There are no long tableaux in which one can relax and only half listen. And yet this constant movement from place to place builds up a sense of the whole. The author seldom needs to refer us to the larger perspective because we are never more than a few pages away from the other elements in his story. Soon we are habitués of the court in Milan or France or Naples. We have heard many speeches in the Venetian senate, marched with many armies, and felt the shock of political clashes in Florence.

Narrative technique is not something that can be isolated from other elements of the history. It does not appear in the first sentence of each paragraph and disappear from the others. Nor does the writer provide us with a concise statement about how he feels stories should be told, and even if he did we would not necessarily be any wiser. We must make our own way. In order to have some tangible grasp of this difficult subject I have performed a rough and rather mechanical analysis of the frequency of changes of scene in a single book. By counting place names, each one the locus of an event described in the narrative, we arrive at a kind of index of the pace of the narrative.[10] The number of these place names, it turns out, is remarkable: fifty-one in ninety pages. Though one could quibble over individual entries, the magnitude is not in doubt. And these places cover the entire peninsula as well as France, Spain, and Germany. The rapidity and repetition of the visits may take us by surprise: six times in Milan and near it several more, six times in Pisa, and seven in Florence. Within a single 'chapter' we even visit one city twice, and there is great geographical versatility to all our comings and goings.

Our analysis gives us a picture of movement that is almost unseemly – a major relocation less than every two pages. And yet a normal reading of the text has none of this hurry; rather it impresses us with its coolness, lucidity, and strict control. Some have even attributed to Guicciardini the stylistic and emotional composure, the aloofness of an Olympian.[11] Both impressions are correct, but one concerns style and the other structure. In the *Storia*, I believe, a controlled, rational, even ponderous, formal manner operates over a strained and complex narrative structure. Each contributes to the final effect. The alert reader feels an excitement and dynamism in the narrative which must be traced back to the extraordinary rapidity of Guicciardini's stride. He also feels a sureness which can only be the measure of the historian's great intelligence. The product is tension and dynamic balance.

10 I chose Book III for this purpose, but any other would do as well. This book does have one special feature, as I explained in the previous chapter. In it the narrative has returned to the point of departure. The French have left and Italy returns seemingly to the status quo ante, only to resume warfare on a far more serious basis. Thus in this book we have passed through the preliminaries of the first campaign and enter into the main body of the history of the Italian wars. So as to limit the possibilities of special pleading, I have taken this list of places as much as possible from the summary headnotes in the standard edition. However, I did fill out the notes when they refer to an event without fixing it geographically. On the other hand I have limited the loci by using the names of the territorial states of France and Naples as inclusive of any specific towns within the kingdoms; otherwise the list would at certain points have been considerably longer. Certainly there can be no claim for exactness, but the general position must be clear. The sign // indicates the modern chapter divisions. The significant loci are as follows: Italy – Milan – Pisa // Florence – Perugia – Umbria // Naples – France // Pisa – Venice – Milan – Sarzana // Naples // France – Italy // Naples – France // Milan – Florence – Pisa // Florence –Pisa – Genoa – Milan // Livorno – Pisa – Pavia – Como – Germany // Naples – Genoa – Papal States // Lombardy – Genoa – Spain – France – Pisa – Florence // Milan – Florence – Rome – Florence // Naples – France – Spain – Genoa – France – Milan – Venice // France – Florence.

11 This is a major point in the analysis given by Rafaello Ramat in his *Guicciardini e la tragedia d'Italia* (Florence: Olschki 1953).

Let us keep this structure in mind and return to the text of the third book. It is not difficult to find explicit expression of the underlying lattice, especially if we look at the beginnings of the chapters that the modern editors have cut into the continuous narrative. As I have already remarked, Guicciardini, precisely because his history lacked chapters, needed to channel and periodically to reorient his narrative. Chapter divisions are only a mechanical way of marking these points of transition. Chapter 2 begins: 'While such action was being awaited, there was no lack of new and dangerous troubles for the Florentines in other directions ...'[12] We almost see the narrative, hot in pursuit, suddenly dig in its heels and go chasing off after new developments. Similarly, Chapter 6 begins: 'While all was thus in suspense, the King of France was taking steps to relieve his people.'[13] Guicciardini was clearly aware of the dramatic possibilities of his kind of quick-moving narration. Here he leaves two armies on the point of battle in suspended animation. He will come back, but only after a tour of France to investigate why French aid was not forthcoming in time to help their soldiers in Naples. And so the next chapter begins: 'Affairs in the Kingdom of Naples could not however wait for these slow remedies.'[14]

The chapter following opens with a similar resumption of a suspended argument: 'We said above that, fearing the preparations of the French, negotiations had been begun – more to please Lodovico Sforza than the Venetians – to have Maximilian enter Italy.'[15] This strand was left off twelve pages earlier. Most often the chapter begins with a shift of scene which also includes a comparative reference: 'A situation of greater danger now arose in Lombardy because of the movements of the French, freed for the time being from the threat of the Spanish.'[16] Often the introductory phrase refers to the annual divisions of the narrative, themselves not

12 Trans. Grayson, *History of Italy*, p. 286. 'Le quali mentre che s'aspettano, non mancavano da altre parti a' fiorentini nuovi e pericolosi travagli ...' *Storia d'Italia*, I, p. 213.
13 Trans. Grayson, *History of Italy*, p. 311. 'Nella quale incertitudine mentre che si sta, il re di Francia, da altra parte, trattava delle provisioni di soccorrere i suoi.' *Storia d'Italia*, I, p. 239.
14 Trans. Grayson, *History of Italy*, p. 318. 'Ma non potevano le cose del reame di Napoli aspettare la tardità di questi rimedi.' *Storia d'Italia*, I, p. 245.
15 Trans. Grayson, *History of Italy*, p. 327. 'È detto di sopra che, per paura degli apparati franzesi, si era cominciato, piú per sodisfazione di Lodovico Sforza che de' viniziani, a trattare di fare passare Massimiliano Cesare in Italia ...' *Storia d'Italia*, I, p. 255.
16 Trans. Grayson, *History of Italy*, p. 348. 'Maggiori pericoli si dimostravano in questo tempo in Lombardia per i movimenti de' franzesi, assicurati per allora da' minacci degli spagnuoli.' *Storia d'Italia*, I, p. 276.

overly important structurally but obviously a useful way of keeping a general uniformity and control over chronology. 'In the same year,' writes Guicciardini, 'King Federigo obtained the investiture of his kingdom from the Pope ...'[17] Finally, the last chapter of Book 3 begins with a change that results from the intrusion of the unexpected and accidental: 'While these discussions were proceeding among the allies with unconcealed disagreement, an event occurred which had unexpected results. On the night of April 7th King Charles died at Amboise ...'[18]

Restlessness seems to be the dominant characteristic of Guicciardini's narrative, at least in regard to geography. Restlessness is in turn very close to our theme, which is change. And there is an intimate connection. A story-telling style like this one, flexible and fast-paced, is ideal for close description of change. And, hard though it is to be precise about such effects, this dynamic structure must contribute mimetically to our sense of change, as the metrical clacking of the rails under the wheels of a fast train becomes identified in the mind of the passenger with the intimate rhythm of the landscape around him.

Compared to such pervasive but subtle rhythms, the formal convention of the annual narrative has very little significance. Great fuss has been made over the loyalty of Renaissance historians to such 'archaic' practices by those whose own loyalty is strictly and unthinkingly to whatever is modern. But given the decision to present a detailed chronology of events over a relatively short period, the annalistic scheme seems almost inevitable. It is certainly the simplest method of maintaining some uniformity of pacing and unity in a narrative that in most respects is extremely complex. This is the first point; the second is the very slight structural importance attached to these annual divisions. Like the faint blue lines of a graph, the change of years remains unaccented except where it corresponds to a significant event or, on the contrary, if there is no event at all that could provide a convenient stopping point. Never is the annual change itself made into an event, and only occasionally does it coincide with the opening and closing of the twenty books of the history. These books are the chief formal convention giving internal organization to the narrative, and most often they correspond to phases in the long wars of Italy, as a glance

17 Trans. Grayson, *History of Italy*, p. 359. 'In questo anno medesimo Federigo re di Napoli, ottenuta la investitura del regno dal pontefice ...' *Storia d'Italia*, I, p. 288.
18 Trans. Grayson, *History of Italy*, p. 365. 'Le quali cose mentre che con aperta disunione si trattano tra i collegati, nuovo accidente che sopravenne partorì effetti molto diversi da' pensieri degli uomini; perché la notte innanzi al'ottavo dì d'aprile morì il re Carlo in Ambuosa ...' *Storia d'Italia*, I, p. 294.

back to the chapter on chronology will show. Most often the break in the continuity of the narrative occurs when there is a corresponding break in the seemingly continuous wars. The first time the annual division corresponds to the change of books comes at the end of Book VI and the beginning of Book VII. Guicciardini narrates a bizarre episode in which the rivalry of two brothers for the love of a woman leads to one, a cardinal of the house of Este, having the other's eyes put out. 'Thus,' concludes Guicciardini, 'ended the year 1505.' This, of course, is nonsense; the year did not end this way at all, but in the absence of any really significant event a trivial, if revolting, incident and the end of the year are the best materials at hand with which the historian can bring the book to a close. Reciprocally, by placing the incident here Guicciardini emphasizes the importance of the story and the feeling it conveys of moral breakdown. Though Book VII begins on the same note, it is the thematic statement that follows which is really significant: 'These things happened in the year 1505; which year had given hope that the peace of Italy would continue since the wars over the Kingdom of Naples were finished; nonetheless elsewhere there appeared the not unimportant germs of future conflagrations.'[19] The significant point here clearly is not the mundane fact that the year 1505 has become the year 1506 but that once again the false peace of Italy is about to be shattered.

Book XII represents something of a departure, but one which is not followed up. Here the annual division is again marked at the end of the preceding book, but in this case Guicciardini uses the beginning of a book not to open the new year but to narrate ultramontane events. Thus it is essentially a geographical and not a chronological shift which is emphasized by the organization of the text. In Book XIV there is again the conjunction of the annual change and the shattering of a fragile peace; the new book announces events which mark a new phase in the progressive worsening of the Italian wars. These events lead to the great battle of Pavia, and a battle such as this provides its own chronology, irrespective of annual divisions. And so Book XVI begins with a review of the Italian situation on the morrow of Pavia.

Enough has been said to show that Guicciardini uses the annual chronology as a kind of unaccented graph against which to plot the rise and fall of events. The events themselves articulate the narrative, given always the

19 (My trans.) 'Queste cose erano succedute l'anno mille cinquecento cinque; il quale benché avesse lasciato speranza che la pace d'Italia, dappoi che erano estinte le guerre nate per cagione del regno di Napoli, s'avesse a continuare, nondimeno apparivano da altra parte semi non piccoli di futuri incendi.' *Storia d'Italia*, II, p. 167.

need to provide the reader with an occasional break and the obvious desirability of building the story out of chapters of roughly equal length. In sum, each New Year gets the attention it deserves and not even a new decade is especially marked: the year 1510, for example, slips quietly in a half a dozen pages before the end of the eighth book.

To this point, we have been concerned with the gross structure of the *Storia d'Italia*, the way in which Guicciardini carries his reader and his researches from event to event. The construction of the narrative on a smaller scale is equally important, and in some ways is a more difficult subject to approach. It is certainly impossible to be comprehensive because that would mean reproducing the details of whole books. The best that we can do is to find an example which concentrates some typical characteristics into a manageable space, and Chapter 13 of Book II serves this purpose well. It is as self-contained as any other 'chapter,' but it is only one page long:

After having narrated so many other things, it seems to me not unworthy of note that those very times when it seemed destined that the woes of Italy should have begun with the passage of the French (or at any rate were attributed to them), was the same period when there first appeared that malady which the French called the Neapolitan disease and the Italians commonly called either boils or the French disease. The reason was that it manifested itself among the French when they were in Naples and then, as they marched back to France, they spread it all over Italy. This disease, which was altogether new or at least unknown up to that time in our hemisphere, if not in its most remote and out of the way parts, was for many years especially so horrible that it deserves to be mentioned as one of the gravest calamities. For it showed itself either in the form of the most ugly boils which often became incurable ulcers, or very intense pains at the joints and nerves all over the body. And since the physicians were not experienced in dealing with such a disease, they applied remedies which were not appropriate, indeed often actually harmful, frequently inflaming the infection. Thus, this disease killed many men and women of all ages, and many became terribly deformed and were rendered useless, suffering almost continuous torments; indeed, most of those who seemed to have been cured, relapsed in a short time into the same miserable state. But after the course of so many years (either because the celestial influence which had produced so virulent a plague, had mitigated, or from long experience, suitable remedies were eventually found to cure it) the disease became much less malignant; also because it transformed itself into other kinds of ill-

ness diverse from its original form. This calamity is certainly one which men of our time might justly complain about, if it had been transmitted to them through no fault of their own; but all those who have diligently observed the nature of this illness agree that never, or very rarely, can anyone acquire it except by contagion during coitus. But it would be just to absolve the French from this ignominy because it is obvious that this malady had been carried to Naples from Spain; nor was it really a product of that nation either, for it had been brought there from those islands which (as we shall discuss more pertinently elsewhere) began to be known in our hemisphere almost during those same years as a result of the voyage of Christopher Columbus, the Genoese. In those islands, however, beneficent nature provides a very quick remedy for this disease, for the natives are very easily cured simply by drinking the juice of a wood which grows there, highly valued because of its great medicinal qualities.[20]

20 Trans. Alexander, *History of Italy*, pp. 108-9. 'Nè pare, dopo la narrazione dell'-altre cose, indegno di memoria che, essendo in questo tempo fatale a Italia che le calamità sue avessino origine dalla passata de'franzesi, o almeno a loro fussino attribuite, che allora ebbe principio quella infermità che, chiamata da' franzesi il male di Napoli, fu detta comunemente dagli italiani le bolle o il male franzese; perché, pervenuta in essi mentre erano a Napoli, fu da loro, nel ritornarsene in Francia, diffusa per tutta Italia: la quale infermità o del tutto nuova o incognita insino a questa età nel nostro emisperio, se non nelle sue remotissime e ultime parti, fu massime per molti anni tanto orribile che, come di gravissima calamità, merita se ne faccia menzione. Perché scoprendosi o con bolle bruttissime, le quali spesse volte diventavano piaghe incurabili, o con dolori intensissimi nelle giunture e ne' nervi per tutto il corpo, né usandosi per i medici, inesperti di tale infermità, rimedi appropriati ma spesso remedi direttamente contrari e che molto la facevano inacerbire, privò della vita molti uomini di ciascuno sesso e età, molti diventati d'aspetto deformissimi restorono inutili e sottoposti a cruciati quasi perpetui; anzi la maggiore parte di coloro che pareva si liberassino ritornavano in breve spazio di tempo nella medesima miseria; benché, dopo il corso di molti anni, o mitigato lo influsso celeste che l'aveva prodotta così acerba, o essendosi per la lunga esperienza imparati i rimedi opportuni a curarla, sia diventata molto manco maligna; essendosi anche per se stessa trasmutata in più specie diverse dalla prima. Calamità della quale certamente gli uomini della nostra età si potrebbono più giustamente querelare se pervenisse in essi senza colpa propria: perché è approvato, per consentimento di tutti quegli che hanno diligentemente osservata la proprietà di questo male, che o non mai o molto difficilmente perviene in alcuno se non per contagione del coito. Ma è conveniente rimuovere questa ignominia dal nome franzese, perché si manifestò poi che tale infermità era stata traportata di Spagna a Napoli, né propria di quella nazione ma condotta quivi di quelle isole le quali, come in altro luogo più opportunamente si dirà, cominciorono, per la navigazione di Cristofano Colombo genovese, a manifestarsi, quasi in questi anni medesimi, al

On a reduced scale this passage exhibits the same organizational characteristics that we have observed before in the *Storia* as a whole. To a large
degree, of course, this is predetermined by the selection itself, since we
could equally have chosen a page in which very little happens at all. But
the page quoted above demonstrates in concentrated form the swiftness,
power, and efficiency of Guicciardini's narrative art. And, as mentioned
before, there are a number of such capsule histories enfolded in the *Storia
d'Italia*.

Guicciardini begins by telling us how the miniature fits into the larger
history – it follows it as a sort of coda. And yet syphilis is related to the
other calamities narrated in the *Storia* because, like so many disastrous
changes, it seems to have originated with the coming of the French. 'Seems'
is an important word here because in fact, despite popular belief, the
disease did not really have its beginnings in the invasion. Thus in two sentences he has positioned his little history, and from the beginning we are
alerted to the complexity of his attitude towards the event he is to describe.

Guicciardini begins not with the origins but with the incidence of the
disease. To put it another way, he begins with its impact on history. And
he describes it in the context of Italy's other ills. Like so many features of
contemporary Italy, it had no precedent before the wars. Then he describes
the symptoms, still concentrating on the reality of the event. He finds time
to castigate the doctors, members of a profession for which generally he
has little use. Ignorantly they aggravate rather than alleviate the disease;
and in this respect they might be compared to the princes of Italy who
similarly bring disaster on their peoples. The analogy is not explicit, of
course, but this kind of failure of rationalism or *prudenza* on the part of
doctors, princes, astrologers, and others is very important to Guicciardini.

The middle section essentially deals with change. The disease becomes
less virulent and has produced of its own accord several variant strains.
Characteristically, Guicciardini gives two explanations for the falling off
of the plague. It happened either because of the influence of the stars or
because of the actions of men, and as in all such simultaneous explanations
in Guicciardini the question is left hanging. But men, and particularly Italian men, are culpable in one sense. Though in general man is not responsible for the plague, the infection of an individual results from his having

nostro emisperio. Nelle quali isole, nondimeno, questo male ha prontissimo, per
benignità della natura, il rimedio; perché beendo solamente del succo d'un legno
nobilissimo per molte doti memorabili, che quivi nasce, facilissimamente se ne
liberano.' *Storia d'Italia*, I, pp. 204-5.

had coitus, obviously an act deserving punishment in the eyes of our cen-
sorious author. It may also be significant that the plague was brought to
Italy as a result of the voyages of Christopher Columbus, himself an Italian.
Thus at the end the miniature history returns to its point of departure: the
French who 'seemed' responsible for the disease are absolved. Instead
Guicciardini has accurately traced it back to America and thus put it into
another historical context altogether. Finally, he ends on a note of characteristic (albeit rare) idealistic naiveté, with the picture of the fortunate
islands where the natives have merely to drink the sap of a tree to be cured.
As he promises, Guicciardini will return to idyllic America later in the history where he re-establishes the same tone.

There is much in this short history of syphilis that is characteristic of
Guicciardini's ideas as well as methods. In fact in so concentrated a pack-
age the two are impossible to separate. His desire for completeness, surprising in so narrow a compass, for judiciousness, for an explanation that leaves
no part unexamined and yet makes no final judgement, all are marvellously
joined here with his typical quickness. Characteristic also is his ironic enjoyment of the confusing, and accusing, names for the disease, called by
the French the Neapolitan disease and commonly known to the Italians as
the French sickness. The similarity of the structure to what we have seen
before is striking. Here in miniature we have explicit concern for change,
and change is implicit too in the tracing of an event back to its source.
Typically we are given a multiple explanation which provides a freer and
more flexible scheme of analysis. Even the shifting geography so characteristic of Guicciardini's gross narrative technique is present. Most of all,
the same sense of movement and rhythm underlies the confident narration.
But although the event is described and defined with the greatest economy,
the impression (typical of textbooks, for example) that we are merely
reading a précis of a more elaborate text is completely absent. Here all the
essential elements seem to be present and to be original.[21]

21 The history and characteristics were, of course, already well known in Italy
   through the long poem *Syphilidis* by the physician Fracastoro.

3 / Two Studies:
The Portrait and *Impeto*

Ever since Boccalini invented the story of the criminal who chose to serve in the galleys rather than read Guicciardini's account of the Pisan wars, readers faced with the less arduous choice between a good story and a great history have chosen the easy way out. Even a serious reader, however, may be daunted by the great length of the *Storia d'Italia* and will need to focus his reading on key passages or problems. The two studies which follow are an attempt to exemplify the themes of this essay on the more concrete level that a narrower focus allows.

1 THE PORTRAIT

The clearest way of seeing the qualities of the *Storia d'Italia* is often to go back to the early *Storie fiorentine*. There we find seeds of future developments but, more dramatically, some striking contrasts to the final achievement. The portrait of Lorenzo the Magnificent is often singled out as the finest piece of writing in Guicciardini's early history. Certainly it is the most polished and sustained character description in the early works, a kind of set-piece exercise that he never returned to in the mature history. If one accepts it for what it is, static and somewhat externally conceived, this portrait is a fine thing, and it constitutes ample proof of the young historian's ability to master aspects of the inherited historiographical style. In ten pages of smoothly drawn description Guicciardini lays before our eyes a balanced and polished picture of an enlightened despot, a man whose one real vice in Guicciardini's eyes was to have deprived his city of its republican freedom.

The type of the portrait is set from the opening sentence:

Lorenzo was a man of many outstanding virtues. He also had several vices, some of them natural, some the products of necessity. He had so

much authority that the city, one might say, was not free in his time;
and yet it abounded in all the glories and happiness there can possibly
be in a city that is free in name, but in fact tyrannized by one of its
citizens ... [1]

This balance of virtues and vices, of glory and unfreedom, is never disturbed, disputed, or developed in the ten full pages of Lorenzo's portrait.
The subsequent text adds to the already precise formulation only through
example. The portrait of Lorenzo is consistent throughout: he is a tyrant,
but the best possible tyrant.

Guicciardini's procedure would have been completely familiar to a liter-
ate humanist Florentine audience. Character is described as an accumula-
tion of virtues and vices, laid out side by side, and not as the growth of experience, acquired layer by layer. So preconceived is the portrait that it
begins not with one of the many virtues Lorenzo possessed, but with the
one he lacked – military fame. This must be excused him, says the young
historian, as the fault of the times and not of the man. The existence of
this empty category and the explicit reference to the ancients ('che recono
tanto fama negli antichi') indicate clearly that behind the individual description of this man lies a generic prescription of what a great man should be
and what a portrait is. Further character description proceeds in terms of
categories of virtue and vice that are not always or even predominantly of
a particularly political nature. The assumption seems to be that the greatness of a man like Lorenzo lies in his amplification of common humanity
rather than in some more specifically political monopolization of heroic
qualities. Furthermore, moral values are assumed to be self-evident and unambiguous. If Lorenzo spends much time womanizing this is clearly a bad
thing, not because there is any sign that he has been distracted from his
public duties or that the woman has had an influence on policy, but simply because it is undignified in a man of Lorenzo's age and position to
carry on in this way. On the other hand, Guicciardini's linking of certain
virtues and vices creates a kind of shading. Thus Lorenzo's need to excel
in all things leads him to both good and bad actions, and there is a clear
connection between his liberality and his need to take from the public
purse. Even so, these complexities are already implied in the initial outline
('furono in lui alcuni vizi, parte naturali, parte necessari') and are reprised
even more clearly in the summing up:

1 *History of Florence*, pp. 70-1. 'Furono in Lorenzo molte e preclarissime virtù;
   furono ancora in lui alcuni vizi, parte naturali, parte necessari. Fu in lui tanta autorità, che si può dire la città, non fussi a suo tempo libera, benché abondantissima
   di tutte quelle glorie e felicità che possono essere in una citta, libera in nome, in
   fatto ed in verità tiranneggiata da uno suo cittadino.' *Storie fiorentine*, pp. 73-4.

In fact, we must conclude that under him the city was not free, even
though it could not have had a better tyrant or a more pleasant one. His
natural inclinations and goodness gave birth to an infinite number of
good results; the exigencies of tyranny brought with them several evils,
but these were moderate and never exceeded the limits of necessity.[2]

Guicciardini's description of Lorenzo as a tyrant but the best possible tyrant is as precise a formula as one could ask for. It is also a complex one.
Lorenzo's character itself is not particularly complicated; he is seen in
fairly straightforward terms of libido, liberality, urge to excel, great intelligence but lesser discretion, pride and so on. Nor does the shadow of vice
behind Lorenzo's virtues unduly complicate the picture, for it is standard
humanist procedure to sum up character as a balance of good and bad
qualities. But what is complex, to the point of ambivalence, is Guicciardini's attitude towards a man who, more than displaying these virtues and
those vices, possessed an illegitimate hegemony over the city. The young
historian's attitude toward the Medici tyrant was necessarily qualified by
loyalty to his own class, men whose aims and values were not fundamentally different from those of the Medici, but who for that very reason resented the exaltation of one of their number above all the rest, and who
complained bitterly (as Guicciardini does here) that the rise of the tyrant
brought with it the rise of many men of lower station. On the other hand,
taken in the context of recent history, Lorenzo assumed symbolic value as
a figure from a prelapsarian age. Seen from the distance of only a few years
but nonetheless across an already frightening gulf, Lorenzo represented to
the next generation the seemingly lost magic of order, peace, and balance.
Thus Lorenzo assumed sunset colours and came to symbolize Italian cultural superiority and diplomatic skill in an age now lost, when, as Guicciardini says, politics were still made in the study.[3]

The ambivalence of the portrait reflects a double focus. The depiction
of the historical Lorenzo is only half the effort, the other half of which is
the presentation of the author's moral/political verdict. This second intention appears most clearly in the comparison between Lorenzo and his
grandfather Cosimo, which is the culmination of the description. Such a
comparison has no narrative purpose. Like the apology for Lorenzo's lack
of military fame that began the study, the comparison lifts the portrait out

2 *History of Florence*, p. 76. 'Ed insomma bisogna conchiudere che sotto lui la città
   non fussi in libertà, nondimeno che sarebbe impossibile avessi avuto un tiranno
   migliore e più piacevole; dal quale uscirono per inclinazione e bontà naturale
   infiniti beni, per necessità della tirannide alcuni mali ma moderati e limitati tanto
   quanto la necessità sforzava.' *Storie fiorentine*, p. 80.
3 Cf. Gilbert, *Machiavelli and Guicciardini*, p. 116.

of its historical context, by implication placing the portrait in a gallery of pictures of famous men. The portrait exists, then, not to further the narrative but to invite judgement. This purpose is implicit in the humanistic method itself which abstracts the event from its context in history in order to examine it in terms of pre-existing categories. Ambivalence enters in this case because there is a strong tension between the moral/political judgement (that Lorenzo is a tyrant) and the historical context, in which he is seen to be the preserver of the peace.

Guicciardini's method in his early history invites the participation of his audience on a moral level. At the same time, he limits that participation severely by providing the final verdict at the outset. The two halves of his formula, that Lorenzo was a tyrant and that he was the best of tyrants, effectively stabilize the ambivalence Guicciardini feels towards his panglossian 'tyrant.' This formula itself is set out in pages of even prose free of tensions or surprises whose function is not to advance the historical action but to decorate it. Only a narrative which is itself statically conceived could accept such an ornament with grace.

When we turn from the early history to the *Storia d'Italia*, we find a changed image of Lorenzo presented by a different means. In his essay on the changing evaluation of Lorenzo in Florentine writings, Felix Gilbert suggests that Guicciardini's favourable portrayal of Lorenzo in the *Storia* should be seen in terms of a reassessment of the moral basis of politics which takes place in the political dialogues.[4] In Gilbert's view, Guicciardini's ambivalence towards Lorenzo disappears when he recognizes that all politics is based on force and all power is a form of usurpation. Thus the question of whether Lorenzo was a tyrant becomes a non-political one and is no longer asked. While this analysis may be true for the political writings, it does not provide the best starting point for looking at Lorenzo in the *Storia*; here historiographical considerations should come first. And Gilbert goes some way towards putting them first when he writes:

> *This portrait of Lorenzo has been called 'a transfiguration' [by De Caprariis] for here Lorenzo assumed almost superhuman proportions. The enlargement of the figure of the Magnificent resulted from the perspective into which he had been placed. The stage on which he acted was no longer Florence, but the whole of Italy. The function which he fulfilled was no longer that of governing a city-state but of maintaining peace in Italy.*[5]

4 Felix Gilbert, 'Guicciardini, Machiavelli, Valori on Lorenzo Magnifico,' *Renaissance News*, XI (1958). His argument in the article is incorporated into his book, *Machiavelli and Guicciardini*, pp. 106-22.
5 *Machiavelli and Guicciardini*, p. 121.

It is clear that Lorenzo appears in a more positive light in the later history than he did in the earlier, but there is also a change in the method of presentation itself. Indeed, given the contrast in scope between the two works, it would be very surprising if Lorenzo were handled the same way both times. The characters of a history, like the characters of fiction, must serve the purpose of the author and the design of his story. The way in which character is modelled is an element in the full design.

To begin with, the word 'portrait' itself is misapplied. Lorenzo does not become the object of special study in the *Storia*, and the reader who expects the extended, individualized description of the *Storie fiorentine* will be disappointed. Lorenzo this time is left almost uncharacterized and without individuality. There are two occasions when he enters the story significantly, and both times he is seen as a member of a group. In the early pages of the first book Lorenzo keeps company with Pope Innocent and Ferdinand of Naples and the three leaders seem almost interchangeable. Together they symbolize a generation of prudent statesmen now waning. They stand like the columns of a portal through which the reader steps into the world of experience and history. Later, when the Medici family is expelled from Florence, Lorenzo is recalled to mind again. This time the context is his family, as earlier it was his generation. Once again the figure of Lorenzo is flattened and generalized, but now his symbolic value is made explicit. Lorenzo was greatly admired, writes Guicciardini, 'And after his death his reputation became a memory of great renown, for it seemed that with his life the peace and happiness of Italy had come to an end.'[6] This is less a matter of nostalgia than of Guicciardini's self-consciousness about the specific role he had assigned Lorenzo in his history (and the key word is *parendo*, 'it seemed'). In the *Storie fiorentine*, too, Guicciardini had made clear his recognition of the mythic element in Lorenzo, but Lorenzo as the symbol of peace and Lorenzo the tyrant lived uneasily together. In the *Storia d'Italia* Guicciardini is only interested in the symbol; an extended personality sketch is avoided and the character of Lorenzo is left magnificent but appropriately vague.

This Lorenzo, then, is even more static than the earlier one, and to say that he acts at all seems an exaggeration. Guicciardini has not so much put Lorenzo into perspective as he has used him to create perspective. Lorenzo frames the action, providing an entry into the work and a fixed point that measures the deepening spaces behind. Such foreshortening leaves time only for symbolic or two-dimensional figures, not for historically true character. After only five pages of the *Storia*, we come to the hinge of the work, the one fixed point:

6   Trans. Grayson, *History of Italy*, p. 169. 'In grande estimazione ... la quale dopo la morte si convertì in memoria molto chiara, parendo che insieme con la sua vita la concordia e la felicità d'Italia fussino mancate.' *Storia d'Italia*, I, p. 88.

*Such, therefore, was the state of affairs, such were the foundations of
the tranquility of Italy, disposed and counterposed in such a way that
not only was there no fear of any present change, but neither could
anyone easily conceive of any policies or situations or wars that might
disrupt such peace.*[7]

The description is, of course, deliberately – dramatically – naive. And then
in the next sentence with a quick breath we step across the balance point,
and for the rest of the history we never stop plunging: 'When, in the month
of April in the year 1492 the death of Lorenzo de' Medici occurred ...'
Here, with the first of so many changes, the narrative truly begins. But unlike the *Storie fiorentine* in which the portrait of Lorenzo interrupted the
story with a heavy caesura, the brief symbolic description of Lorenzo in
the late history perfectly suits its function. All beginnings and endings in
literature are artificial;[8] enlarged though he may be, Lorenzo is only a
marker at the beginning of the road.

Evidently we must look further for something to match the early
Lorenzo portrait, but such a comparison is not hard to find. The most remarkable piece of character study in the *Storia d'Italia* again deals with the
Medici, this time with Popes Leo and Clement, and it appears to negate
every quality of the earlier writing.[9] A structure that was flat and evenly
distributed and a style that was lacking in tension or self-consciousness
now become wilful and dynamic. The tendency to diffuseness in both
style and content is replaced by a new concentration carried by sentences
that are structured complexly. Most of all, a traditional set-piece designed
to ornament the narrative is transformed into a tight coil within the narrative which, far from allowing the story to lose pace, brings new energy to
the events.

Let us begin with the last of these points. Unlike the first portrait, which
was presented on its subject's death, the study of Clement is part of a
concrete investigation into the factors affecting an important diplomatic
decision, and it is perfectly integrated into the narrative. Briefly, Rome
was faced with a perplexing choice between joining or opposing a league
against the emperor. The pros and cons of the decision have already been

7 Trans. Alexander, *History of Italy*, pp. 8-9. 'Tale era lo stato delle cose, tali erano
   i fondamenti della tranquillità d'Italia, disposti e contrapesati in modo che non
   solo di alterazione presente non si temeva ma né si poteva facilmente congetturare
   da quali consigli o per quali casi o con quali armi s'avesse a muovere tanta quiete.'
   Storia d'Italia, I, p. 5.
8 Cf. Frank Kermode, *The Sense of an Ending* (New York: Oxford University Press,
   1967).
9 *Storia d'Italia*, IV, pp. 327-31.

discussed in such a way as to emphasize the difficulties of either path; and to Clement's natural irresolution, the bickering of his advisors adds further confusion. With this as its starting point, the portrait aims not so much at explaining Clement's eventual choice of joining the League as at indicating the futility of any policy so much the child of weakness and indecision.

Guicciardini's purpose takes him well beyond an isolated analysis of Pope Clement's character. The promise, false as it turns out, that Clement showed when still a cardinal is introduced as the essential background to his failure as a pope. This in turn requires some description of his cousin Leo, the pope whom Clement earlier assisted so brilliantly. The web of indecision then widens further to include Clement's two principal advisors, who serve him as badly as he once served Leo well. Accordingly, the counterpointing of the two Medici, in which the virtues of each ironically bring into relief the weaknesses of the other, is followed by the simpler contrast of the two unworthy counsellors. Had one expected here a set-piece portrait in the manner of the *Storie fiorentine*, the presence of these two minor figures would be an intrusion, a falling off from the decorum of the portrait. But the humanist conventions of the earlier portrait no longer serve Guicciardini's purpose, which is now to analyse the interaction of characters as an explanation of events. And, aside from his long delay at arriving at any decision, the concrete evidence of Clement's weakness is his reliance on advisors who do not have his best interests at heart and aggravate his difficulties by their quarrelling.

All these pieces are essential elements of the puzzle of Clement's inactivity. There is no discontinuity in theme because Clement's earlier relationship to Leo is ultimately revealed to have been that of a counsellor, not – as first believed – the real power behind St Peter's throne. Clement was only the executor of Leo's ideas ('esecutore e ministro de' suoi disegni'), Guicciardini writes. Ironically, Clement's former excellence in the role of advisor thus becomes the standard against which we measure the failings of his own two self-serving ministers, and of the weak-willed pope who employs them. No wonder then that when Clement finally comes to a decision in favour of the League it is 'more because it was necessary to decide something than because of a firm judgement or resolution, especially because he found himself in a position where even indecision became a kind of decision ...'[10] This is the end of the character study, and here, at exactly the point where we left it only a short space before, the main narrative resumes, but with added clarity.

10 (My trans.) 'Più perché era necessario deliberare qualche cosa che per risoluzione e giudicio fermo, trovandosi massime in termine che anche il non deliberare era specie di deliberare.' *Storia d'Italia*, IV, p. 331.

This strict integration of the portrait with the narrative reflects Guicciardini's subordination of character to action. He probes Clement's performance in office, specifically the decision on the League that has been too long left hanging, while assuming that the underlying traits of Clement's personality are more or less constant. Thus attention is focused on how the same characteristics led to success as a cardinal and now bring failure as a pope. This procedure is consistent with a favourite maxim of Guicciardini's, one which sums up his final view of Clement on his death and brings the *Storia* to a close. 'For most true and deserving,' declares the historian solemnly, 'is that proverb which says that the office brings forth the worth of the person exercising it.'[11] Guicciardini's intention, then, is not so much to sum up Clement's character as to reveal those of his qualities which become apparent in office. Character is not independent of the context of action and cannot, therefore, be summed up all at once. Thus the passage we have been discussing, though elaborate, is only a part of the continuing study of Clement's use of power. This subordination of character to action gives character an important and continuous role in the determination of events and, paradoxically, increases its explanatory value. At the same time, characterization necessarily loses some of its roundedness. If it is to serve the political narrative, a description of personality must focus narrowly on the political life and omit a wider humanistic appreciation of a man's virtues and vices. The portrait of Clement is far more limited than that of Lorenzo, but it is this fact that allows the concentration which makes it effective.

The portrait of Lorenzo was conceived somewhat abstractly in terms of inherited categories that were morally unambiguous and universal. These categories exist independently of the individual and allow the historian to make trans-historical comparisons such as the one Guicciardini draws between Lorenzo and his grandfather Cosimo. This exercise seems strikingly unhistorical and inorganic when contrasted with the comparison on which Guicciardini builds his analysis of Clement. Here there is no question of juxtaposing two abstractions in order to reward each on a standard, if heroic, scale. On the contrary, Guicciardini's first task is to separate the two intertwined personalities in order to understand the separate characteristics of each. Thus the major point of the dual portrait is to show how much each needed the other; sometimes, says Guicciardini, the combination of two opposites works very well ('convenga bene insieme la mistura

11 Trans. Alexander, *History of Italy*, p. 442. 'Perché è verissimo e degno di somma laude quel proverbio, che il magistrato fa manifesto il valore di chi lo esercita.' *Storia d'Italia*, V, p. 318.

di due contrari'). By separating the two he reveals the weaknesses of each without the other. While Leo lived, Clement took most of the credit away from his lazy, pleasure-seeking cousin; when Clement himself becomes pope, the memory of Leo's strengths is recalled to accent Clement's failure. Neither one comes out ahead in this ironic comparison.

The clear moral categories of the Lorenzo portrait survive in the later one only in ironic and distorted forms that cannot accommodate the historian's pointed observations. Thus, like Lorenzo, Leo is described as 'a man of very great liberality,' but with the ironic qualification: 'if such be the proper name for excessive and boundless spending.'[12] Further, Leo is said to have a truly regal spirit which would have been marvellous *even* in one who was descended from a long line of kings and emperors. If the ironic attack is not already sufficiently clear, Guicciardini goes on to say that with this magnificence he debased the spiritual authority of the papacy and disordered the style of the court. And by spending too much he made it necessary to be always seeking money by extraordinary means – an echo of the major disaster of Leo's pontificate, the indulgences affair. Heavily sarcastic now, Guicciardini declares that dissimulation made Leo seem a wonderful prince: 'I don't speak of apostolic goodness, for according to our own corrupt customs the goodness of a pope is praised when it does not exceed the malignancy of other men.'[13] Thus Guicciardini plays with traditional moral categories, seemingly inapplicable to his present subject, and allows the humanist pattern to survive in his mature style only as an ironic echo.

Guicciardini's exploration of Clement's character is also ironic in a different sense. As I have already said, the underlying traits of Clement's personality remain more or less constant, yet his strengths as a cardinal turn out to be his weaknesses as a pope. But in the text we have been discussing Guicciardini withholds this realization from us and plays on the natural expectation that a great cardinal will make a still greater pope. Condensing and rehearsing again for the reader decades of fluctuating fortunes, Guicciardini builds up our faith in Clement's promise by playing him off against Leo, for whose successes he seems to deserve the credit, only to explode our

12 Trans. Alexander, *History of Italy*, p. 361. 'uomo di somma liberalità; se però si conviene questo nome a quello spendere eccessivo che passa ogni misura.' *Storia d'Italia*, IV, p. 328. In the case of Lorenzo it was recognized that his virtue of *liberalità* also had something to do with his vice of occasionally borrowing from the public purse. Nonetheless *liberalità* itself remains unambiguously a good thing.
13 Trans. Alexander, *History of Italy*, p. 361. 'Non dico di bontà apostolica, perché ne' nostri corrotti costumi è laudata la bontà del pontefice quando non trapassa la malignità degli altri uomini.' *Storia d'Italia*, IV, p. 328.

misconceptions and Clement's false reputation when Leo is dead and Clement himself is pope. Leo, who at the beginning of the passage is diminished in order to make him a foil for Clement's rising reputation, appears in the end as the larger man. Of course, Guicciardini's real point is not to measure one against the other but to show that together they had an adequacy for office that neither possessed alone.

Thus, says Guicciardini, Clement enters the pontificate with the expectation in everyone's mind that he will do greater things than had ever been done before:

> But soon it was known how vain were the judgements made about Leo and him. [Leo was by far more capable than good, but] Giulio had many characteristics different from those which had previously been believed: he did not possess either that desire for change, or grandeur, or tendency of mind for generous and magnanimous ends that had previously been supposed, and had been rather Leo's executor and minister of his plans far more than the director and initiator of his councils and of his will. And although he had a most capable intelligence and marvelous knowledge of world affairs, yet he lacked the corresponding resolution and execution.[14]

Only in the course of description is reality released from the cloak of appearance. By carefully restricting and then expanding the reader's understanding, Guicciardini arrives at a final judgement in an atmosphere not so much of surprise as of certainty, and the reader, feeling that he too has pierced illusion, is compelled to agree.

Guicciardini's new style of characterization seems to require a new relationship to his reader. The universal values and uncomplicated harmonious lines of the early portrait would pose no problem for an audience accustomed to humanist conventions. In the description of Lorenzo special concessions to time or place were not needed because both the historian and his public drew on an inherited and seemingly universal idea of man; and this despite the fact that the young Guicciardini wrote out of a parochial,

14 Trans. Alexander, *History of Italy*, p. 363. 'Ma si conobbe presto quanto erano stati vani i giudizi fatti di Lione e di lui. Perché in Lione fu di grande lunga più sufficienza che bontà, ma Giulio ebbe molte condizioni diverse da quello che prima era stato creduto di lui: con ciò sia che e' non vi fusse né quella cupidità di cose nuove né quella grandezza e inclinazione di animo a fini generosi e magnanimi che prima era stata l'opinione, e fusse stato più presto appresso a Lione esecutore e ministro de' suoi disegni che indirizzatore e introduttore de' suoi consigli e delle sue volontà. E ancora che avesse lo intelletto capacissimo e notizia maravigliosa di tutte le cose del mondo, nondimeno non corrispondeva nella risoluzione ed esecuzione.' *Storia d'Italia*, IV, pp. 329-30.

class-bound patriotism. But now, when only vestiges of humanism remain, Guicciardini concentrates his attention on his reader in a way that he never did before. He manipulates his reader's access to information, building and destroying his expectations through several stages of understanding. These stages, unlike the moral categories of the first portrait, are organized dramatically to give conviction to the final insight. The conventional audience of the *Storie fiorentine* is clearly not suited to this less universal and more concretely political analysis of character. A more private work than its predecessors, teaching less public truths, the *Storia d'Italia* in a sense requires a reader rather than an audience.

The conventional audience does not entirely disappear, however, but is internalized within the text as public opinion. As was stressed above, it is the reputation, not the personality of Clement that changes; and reputation requires a reflector. The false expectation of men about what Clement will accomplish is as important to Guicciardini's design as the reality of what he actually accomplishes. Public opinion, here as elsewhere in the history, is called upon to establish the conventional and superficial view. The historian, of course, knows the truth all along, but his intended reader must first be taken in by and then released from the naiveté of public opinion: 'But soon it was known how vain were the judgements made about Leo and him.'

The quality of these changes can be made more graphic by calling on a close analogue: the change in architectural space between the Early and High Renaissance. The portrait of Lorenzo, like a Quattrocento Florentine palazzo, is linear, with harmonious and clear lines and even accents adding up to a static balance. The Quattrocento palazzo is best set off by a broad street or piazza. The flat walls with their shallow decoration define the line of the street exactly and from any spot on the thoroughfare the frontality of the building is unchanged. By contrast, Guicciardini's presentation of character in the *Storia d'Italia* seems to parallel the new perspective and sense of movement Michelangelo creates in the Campidoglio. Like Michelangelo, Guicciardini builds on the traditional structures but diverges from them to create a new dynamism through the use of more muscular, accented, and unclassical forms – the ambivalent virtues, particularized observations, and intertwining of several figures (contrary to decorum) we encountered in the late portrait. And, as we have seen, there is now a new sense of movement, the result of the historian's awareness of his reader and manipulation of his expectation and understanding. Similarly, Michelangelo, it goes almost without saying, created new and unclassical forms of great power. The vocabulary of his buildings is much more sculptural: niches, blind windows, open porticoes create new space and unprecedented

tension between architectural elements. And an analysis of the new quality
of movement bears a remarkable resemblance to the reader's experience in
the *Storia*:

> *The offer of alternative routes imposes an unclassical ambivalence:*
> *while the visitor enters the piazza, and later the Senators' palace, on*
> *axis, his direct progress is barred first by the statue, and then by the*
> *entrances to the double-ramped stairway. He is not only forced to*
> *choose between two equally efficient routes, but is distracted by an*
> *emphatic stellate pavement that suggests movement of a different sort,*
> *along curvilinear paths towards and away from the centre. He thereby*
> *becomes intensely involved in the architectural setting to a degree never*
> *demanded by earlier Renaissance planning. By forcing the observer into*
> *a* personal solution *[my emphasis]* of this paradox, *Michaelangelo en-*
> *dowed movement which usually is just a way of getting from one place*
> *to another, with aesthetic overtones.*[15]

The radiating lines of Michelangelo's square provide a magnificent setting
for the central statue, but help to disguise the unorthodox shape of this
piazza set on the top of a hill. And for the viewer who has made his way
up the many steps of the Capitoline these lines, like the patterned side-
walks of Rio, now cut across his path rather than indicating the direction
he should take. By contrast the straight lines of the ideal Quattrocento
piazzo, like the grid of virtues and vices of the Lorenzo portrait, measure
out an easily understood and consistent space. Michelangelo's viewer, like
Guicciardini's reader, is presented with a series of partial views, and tra-
verses an irregular space organized less by geometry than by drama.

2 IMPETO

An author's preoccupations are often revealed by a recurrent word or
phrase. Guicciardini's concern with change, which we have seen reflected
in the narrative structure of the *Storia d'Italia*, is manifested once again in
his repeated and persistent use of the word *impeto* or 'impetus.' Its appli-
cations are diverse but characteristic. It is applied to individuals, nations,
and groups, to Fortune, historical forces, military machines, and even emo-
tions. Yet it is applied to each of these selectively and purposefully. Most
of all, though *impeto* is often contrasted to much-valued active virtues like
prudence, it has a great deal to do with success – the elusive idol of Floren-

15 James Ackerman, *The Architecture of Michelangelo* (Harmondsworth, Middlesex:
   Penguin 1969), p. 156.

tine political thought. In sum, *impeto* crystallizes around itself some significant elements of the history, and not least of these the element of change.

Impeto acquires many connotations in the *Storia*, but its core meaning is the same as the English word *impetus*. In medieval physics the idea of impetus held an important place in the theory of motion. According to this theory, the movement of a projectile is accounted for by its impetus, and this impetus was itself acquired by the simple fact of being in motion. Impetus, then, is an energy contained within a body in motion, an idea which helped to solve the problem of why a moving body did not stop immediately that the original moving force was withdrawn. It is obvious that these ideas would find a place in the discussion of ballistics. And from there it is not hard to imagine that *impeto* should pass into the vocabulary of an observer of military affairs like Guicciardini. Guicciardini finds new uses for this word beyond the stricter definitions of physics, but even in the world of history *impeto* never loses its core meaning of a kind of energy contained in bodies – or in men.[16]

The word enters the history with the invading French and, with a few significant exceptions, it remains associated with them through the first book. We meet the word, for example, in a description of the young, less than lustrous French king: 'He was only twenty-two, little gifted by nature with understanding of human affairs, and carried away by a burning desire for conquest and the appetite for glory, based more on whim and *impulse* (impeto) than on mature thought.'[17] This same negative sense of *impeto* is repeated only a few pages later when many in Italy, having heard of the French preparations, dismiss the danger lightly because the expedition seems to derive from youthful impulse ('impeto giovanile') rather than considered advice ('fondato consiglio').[18] Thus far *impeto* seems strictly an individual characteristic and a rather lightweight one, but a few pages later it appears more formidably as a national characteristic of the French. King Charles has asked for Florentine support, but the Florentine ambassadors, despite their reasonable arguments for delay, 'were forced by French *impetuosity* [impeto] – being threatened otherwise with the closing down of

16 On the theory of impetus, see Herbert Butterfield, *The Origins of Modern Science* (New York: Free Press 1957), pp. 13-28.
17 Trans. Grayson, *History of Italy*, p. 110. 'Giovane d'anni ventidue, e per natura poco intelligente delle azioni umane, era traportato da ardente cupidità di dominare e da appetito di gloria, fondato più tosto in leggiera volontà e quasi *impeto* che in maturità di consiglio.' *Storia d'Italia*, I, p. 27.
18 *Storia d'Italia*, I, p. 31.

Florentine trade …'[19] The French use the powerful threat of an expropria-
tion of Florentine commerce, yet it seems that as much as commercial
blackmail, for which the Florentines must have been prepared, it is some
less tangible quality in the French that frightens the ambassadors into surrender.

Impeto is particularly associated with military events and machines.
Artillery, especially, possesses *impeto*, and this is an aspect of its terrifying
novelty. Guicciardini gives us a short history of artillery in the first book
in which he describes how the 'terrible noise and astonishing *violence*' [*impeto*][20] of these guns makes the weapons of the ancients seem ridiculous.
This assertion of the 'superiority' of the moderns over the ancients, taken
up again, and again conventionally, in the brief history of the exploration
of the New World, is interesting in itself; but what concerns us here is the
obvious sense that the menace of the guns is greater than the simple destructive impact of the cannonballs. The more limited military sense seems
clearer, however, shortly afterwards when Guicciardini refers to the rapidity and *impeto* with which the French were able to fire their more advanced guns. Like artillery, mines also have great *impeto*, presumably because of their explosive force. Soldiers, however, are only rarely described
as having *impeto*. A reference to the 'impeto de' soldati' is illuminating because it is exceptional; it refers to an incident in which a private soldier
menaces a powerful cardinal.[21] Armies as a whole, mobs, powerful individuals, the tides of battle, prosperity, Fortune, all can be characterized as
having *impeto*. Thus, neither the season nor any other difficulty can restrain the *impeto* of King Charles, here more a personal or psychological
characteristic than a force.[22] But a few pages later it is said that the Florentines were ill-prepared to defend themselves 'da tanto impeto,' and Florence is occupied by the French.[23] *Impeto* is on the Italian side for the first
time in the famous incident of Capponi's bold challenge to the occupying
French army. Florence was saved from great difficulties, says Guicciardini,
by Capponi's *virtù*. With impetuous gestures ('gesti impetuosi') Capponi
angrily challenged the French, saying: 'You sound your trumpets and we

19 Trans. Grayson, *History of Italy*, p. 122. 'Nondimeno erano con *impeto* franzese
   stretti a prometterlo, minacciando altrimenti di privargli del commercio.' *Storia
   d'Italia*, I, p. 40.
20 Trans. Grayson, *History of Italy*, p. 152. 'sì orribile tuono e *impeto* stupendo'
   Storia d'Italia, I, p. 72.
21 *Storia d'Italia*, I, p. 157.
22 *Storia d'Italia*, I, p. 77.
23 *Storia d'Italia*, I, p. 83.

will ring our bells.' And with the same *impeto* with which he had delivered this challenge, he and his companions rushed out of the negotiating chamber.[24] This display of impetuosity and heroics won back for the Florentines some of the respect that Piero de' Medici's cowardice had lost them.

In this incident arms were not involved directly but only as a threat, since the clanging bells would have roused an armed citizenry. This potential for violence is always present in the populace. Thus it is explained that the French lack good infantry because, fearing the *impeto* of the people, they have kept the people disarmed.[25] Of course, it is not always possible to repress this violence. The young King Ferdinand of Naples, the only Italian in the first book besides Capponi and the future Pope Julius II who demonstrates heroic and impetuous qualities, decides that it is impossible to save his throne against the 'sudden *thrust* [*impeto*] of fortune.'[26] He becomes so angry, however, on hearing of the sack of his stables, that he goes out to challenge the mob; and the royal name proves sufficient to halt the *impeto* of the people. On the next page, *impeto* is back on Ferdinand's side as he proves his *virtù* by taking back a castle from an insubordinate castellan. The man had demanded that the young king enter alone, but when Ferdinand entered he fell on the impudent official with such *force* ('con tanto *impeto*') that his ferocity and the memory of royal authority won back for him his castle. Here personal bravery and traditional authority give Ferdinand an *impeto* that is much like charisma. Despite these minor heroics, however, *impeto* remains largely a French monopoly; with Ferdinand parted from Naples, the rest of his kingdom gives in to the French as to a *raging* torrent, 'uno *impetuosissimo* torrente.'[27]

The most impetuous character in the history, the most colourful and stubborn, the most paradoxically successful, and ultimately the most damaging to the Italian cause is Pope Julius. His impetuosity is dramatized from the very beginning, long before he becomes pope or takes on a major role in the *Storia*. Guicciardini paraphrases in the first book a speech delivered by Julius to the French, and then to add realism to the paraphrase (a technique, it should be noted, that he often prefers to the more elaborate conventions of formal oratory) he adds a description of the speaker and his manner of oration. 'These things,' writes Guicciardini, 'which are the substance of what the cardinal said – although he conveyed according to his nature with direct statements and *impetuous* and fiery gestures rather

24 *Storia d'Italia*, I, pp. 94-5. 'e col medesimo *impeto*, andandogli dietro i compagni, si parti subito della camera.'
25 *Storia d'Italia*, I, p. 187.
26 *Storia d'Italia*, I, p. 109. '*impeto* tanto repentino della fortuna.'
27 *Storia d'Italia*, I, p. 112.

than ornate words ...'[28] Clearly the historian felt that there was a force in
the man that his words alone could not convey, and this impetuosity remains the keynote of Julius's character throughout this history. The most
notable instance, perhaps, is Julius's soldiering at the siege of Mirandola,
an action, says Guicciardini, unheard of through all the centuries. Since
the attack was not going well enough to suit him, Julius decided to bolster
the siege with his own presence. Putting his *impulse* and desire (*'L'impeto
e l'ardore dell'animo'*) before everything else, he would not be restrained
by the real danger to his own person or the bad name it would give to the
papacy. He criticized his captains with very *forceful* words (*'impetuosis-
sime parole'*) and with no less *impeto* did the office, in words and deeds,
of a military captain.[29]

Though for the sake of simplicity we have surveyed only the first book,
this list could be added to from all the books of the *Storia*; but this would
exaggerate the importance of the exercise. No doctrine should be constructed around Guicciardini's use of *impeto* as has been done round
Machiavelli's *virtù*, but the above analysis of it reveals several important
points. In the first place, *impeto* is a dynamic word, never far from force
and movement. Here, obviously, is the connection with the larger theme of
change. The simple repetition of *impeto* on so many pages of the *Storia*,
and not notably in Guicciardini's earlier histories or in those of his con-
temporaries, is suggestive of his preoccupation with turbulence. Secondly,
impeto is so often associated with success, particularly military but also
political. Usually it is instrumental in a successful action, as in the tide of
victory that sweeps an army on, or the horrifying *impeto* of the new artillery, which is terrifying as well as destructive. Often, too, success creates
its own impetus and can lead to difficulties, as when an army prematurely
flushed with victory cannot be restrained from sack, thus allowing the
enemy to escape a full defeat. And in the case of certain impetuous men,
Piero Capponi or Julius II, *impeto* seems in fact to substitute for more
conventional forces. For them *impeto* becomes a direct cause of success.
Finally, it is important to remember that the word never loses the negative
significance with which it was first introduced. *Impeto* is opposed in every
respect to *prudenza*, and yet both are keys to success. There is no doubt
that personally Guicciardini was committed to the path of prudence, but
impeto is often more crucial in the real politics of his history. Energy itself

28 Trans. Grayson, *History of Italy*, p. 148. 'Queste cose, dette in sostanza dal cardi-
    nale ma, secondo la sua natura, più con sensi efficaci e con gesti *impetuosi* e accesi
    che con ornato di parole ...' *Storia d'Italia*, I, p. 67.
29 *Storia d'Italia*, III, pp. 63-5.

creates its own successes and it does so in ill-defined, even mysterious ways. This recognition of the efficacy of sheer *impeto* is a kind of historical judgement; in an age of declining political and military force in Italy mere energy could win victories. That these victories were often sham or even ultimately disastrous only confirms the need for Guicciardini's type of political intelligence. Nonetheless, the only heroic moments, the most startling though short-lived victories, were created by impetuous 'fools' like Julius or the defenders of the last Florentine republic. Guicciardini's own lieutenancy, on the other hand, led to the sack of Rome.

The basic dichotomy had been drawn long before. When Guicciardini lamented in the *Storie fiorentine* the passing of an age when politics were still made in the study, he had already begun his lifelong recognition of the grimmer realities that followed on the French invasion – the horrible weaponry, the unrestrained greed, the victimization of civilian populations and destruction of cities, the profanation of sacred things, in sum, the long catalogue of plagues that circulated and multiplied in the bloodstream of Italy. But it was not until he wrote the *Storia d'Italia* that he found a word to oppose to the politics of the study, of Lorenzo, and of balance and reason. In the prescriptive pages of the *Ricordi, prudenza* is still central; in the descriptive pages of the *Storia* he gives us the politics of energy and unreason and the success of *impeto*.

4 / The Historian's Language

In the present century, when extended prose narrative is by far the dominant literary form, historians have largely abandoned their commitment to story-telling. In the sixteenth century, on the contrary, the art of prose narrative was still in its infancy, but historians were among its leading practitioners. The historian's craft is literary as well as analytic. Guicciardini's extraordinary intellectual achievement cannot be separated from the way in which his great book works upon the reader. The vast chronological scheme of the *Storia d'Italia*, its preoccupation with the decline and fall of Italy, its hesitations over the limits of historical understanding, all these are absorbed by the reader as part of the discipline, so to speak, imposed by the author. We respond to his style and tone, to his sense of decorum and of audience, and in so doing we learn to accept and comprehend the larger dimensions of his story.

Guicciardini's language is his signature. Complex, mannered, coldly impressive, it is uniquely his own and uniquely suited to his task. The reader who is familiar with the simpler diction and less elaborate periods of a contemporary historian like Nerli, or who comes to the *Storia d'Italia* from the more energetic rhythms of Machiavelli's prose is immediately struck by the elaborateness and complexity of Guicciardini's slower moving sentences. His style, says the most ambitious of his translators, is 'Jamesian, Proustian – that is to say, his basic meanings reside in his qualifications.'[1] Rather than arranging themselves, his sentences complicate themselves as they proceed, spinning a web of qualifying phrases as if to catch hold of those tiny distinctions the *Ricordi* so insist on. At times these sent-

1 Sidney Alexander, introduction to his translation of the *History of Italy*, p. xvii. On Guicciardini's style, see G. Getto, 'Note sulla prosa della *Storia d'Italia* di Francesco Guicciardini,' *Aevum*, XV, 1941, pp. 141-223.

ences stretch continuity and attention to the breaking point. But, unlike the prose of traditional stylists who also indulge in lengthy periods, Guicciardini's is not clarified to the ear by rhetorical conventions of symmetry and balance. The ear, in fact, seems to be ignored in favour of the silent eye. These slow sentences are the evidence of Guicciardini's strained effort to collect together in a single structure the many elements necessary to describe a single event. And as his descriptions are typically both exactingly precise and yet open-ended, in that he so often presents us with simultaneous motivations to choose among, so his sentences have to carry on a number of arguments at once. Thus, these structures do not close with the satisfying resolution (however long delayed for rhetorical effect) of the Ciceronian period. Their complexity is not resolved within the sentence, but is frequently carried across the formalities of punctuation so that Guicciardini seems to write in paragraphs rather than in sentences. Sometimes indeed a single sentence can be a paragraph in length, but more often sentences are strung together with conjunctions which make no more break between two sentences than between two phrases. Not until the whole complex of motives and events is assembled and examined can the interconnections of the prose be cut and work on a new assembly begun.

This style has been described as 'labyrinthine,' but that suggests confusion rather than control. On the contrary, for all its complexity, Guicciardini's prose sometimes has the airless clarity of bright days in winter:

Certainly nothing is more necessary when making difficult decisions than asking advice; on the other hand nothing is more dangerous. No doubt wise men are less in need of advice than fools; nevertheless the wise derive much more profit from taking it. Who is so universally wise that he can always know and judge everything on his own, and in conflicting arguments can always see the better cause? But what certainty has the man who seeks advice of being faithfully advised? The one who gives the advice, if he is not particularly fond of or faithful to the one who asks, is not only moved by considerable interest but for any small convenience of his own, for any slight satisfaction, will often give such advice as will bring about the result most profitable or pleasing to himself. As the one who asks advice is usually unaware of these purposes, he does not realize – if he is not very prudent – the unreliability of the advice. This is what happened to Piero de' Medici.[2]

2 Trans. Grayson, *History of Italy*, p. 174. 'Niuna cosa è certamente più necessaria nelle deliberazioni ardue, niuna da altra parte più pericolosa, che'l domandare consiglio; nè è dubbio che manco è necessario agli uomini prudenti il consiglio che agli imprudenti; e nondimeno, che molto più utilità riportano i savi del consigliarsi.

The elaboration here is less labyrinthine than Ptolemaic; and we recognize still the paradox-haunted (or paradox-loving?) author of the *Ricordi*.

Guicciardini's style is shaped by his task. Analytic often to the point of bloodlessness, it conveys no colours, paints no landscapes, and attempts very little physical characterization of any kind. His is a language that gathers and sifts. Corio can take seven pages off from his rambling history of Milan to describe Pope Alexander VI's elaborately colourful coronation.[3] Machiavelli, equally vivid but in a suitably grimmer vein, describes at length the furious mutilation of two men by a mob that tore, bit, and even tasted the flesh of its victims.[4] For nearly two thousand pages, however, Guicciardini goes directly at his task. I have noted only one aesthetic reference – praise for the beauty of the Certosa di Pavia – in all those pages. Nerli quotes verses and Corio quotes Latin, but for Guicciardini, and from him, there are no distractions. A few spare similies comparing events to fires, seeds, and diseases are unsparingly repeated. Even the colloquialism of the *Storie fiorentine* is gone. What is left is the unremitting intellectual pressure that we feel sentence by sentence and page by page. This is our reward in place of all the verses, metaphors, and colourful description of other narrators.

But I do not want to exaggerate; certainly along with intellectual pressure there is passion too. Perhaps the most notable eruption is the one which greets the death of Alexander VI, the Borgia pope. His body, poisoned by his own wine, is described as black, bloated, and ugly ('nero, enfiato e bruttissimo') and all the populace came to see him dead:

All Rome thronged with incredible rejoicing to see the dead body of Alexander in St. Peter's, unable to satiate their eyes enough with seeing

Perché chi è quello di prudenza tanto perfetta che consideri sempre e conosca ogni cosa da se stesso? E nelle ragioni contrarie discerna sempre la migliore parte? Ma che certezza ha chi domanda il consiglio d'essere fedelmente consigliato? Perché chi dà il consiglio, se non è molto fedele o affezionato a chi 'l domanda, non solo mosso da notabile interesse ma per ogni suo piccolo comodo, per ogni leggiera sodisfazione, dirizza spesso il consiglio a quel fine che più gli torna a proposito o di che più si compiace; e essendo questi fini il più delle volte incogniti a chi cerca d'essere consigliato, non s'accorge, se non è prudente, della infedeltà del consiglio. Così intervenne a Piero de' Medici.' *Storia d'Italia*, I, pp. 93-4.

3   Bernardino Corio, *Storia di Milano*, ed. E. De Magri (Milano, 1855), p. 464 ff.

4   See Machiavelli's account of the expulsion of the Duke of Athens from Florence in Chapter 37, Book II of the *Storie fiorentine*. Machiavelli's interest in physical characterization is discussed by Peter Bondanella in his recent *Machiavelli and the Renaissance Art of History* (Detroit: Wayne State University Press 1973). He fails to recognize, however, that this is not a new feature but a direct borrowing from Villani.

spent that serpent who in his boundless ambition and pestiferous per-
fidy, and with all his examples of horrible cruelty and monstrous sen-
suality and unheard-of avarice, selling without distinction sacred and
profane things, had envenomed the entire world. And nevertheless he
had been exalted by the most unusual and almost perpetual good for-
tune from early youth up to the last days of his life, always desiring the
greatest things and always obtaining more than he desired.[5]

Here the full force of Guicciardini's grand strain, usually reserved for mo-
mentous events, is directed at a single head; even so the historian is immediately drawn into a wider reflection on the illusoriness of men's opinions
and the paradox of earthly success:

A powerful example to confound the arrogance of those who, presum-
ing to discern with the weakness of human eyes the depth of divine
judgements, affirm that the prosperity or adversity of men proceeds
from their own merits or demerits: as if one may not see every day
many good men unjustly vexed and many depraved souls unworthily
exalted; or as if, interpreting it in another way, one were to derogate
from the justice and power of God, whose boundless might cannot be
contained within the narrow limits of the present, and who – at an-
other time and in another place – will recognize with a broad sweep,
with rewards and eternal punishments, the just from the unjust.[6]

The pope is all the more a monster for being, contrary to humanist pre-
cept, an *esempio* (example) of vice rewarded. And some of the passion

5 Trans. Alexander, *History of Italy*, p. 166. 'Concorse al corpo morto d'Alessandro
   in San Piero con incredibile allegrezza tutta Roma, non potendo saziarsi gli occhi
   d'alcuno di vedere spento un serpente che con la sua immoderata ambizione e
   pestifera perfidia, e con tutti gli esempli di orribile crudeltà di mostruosa libidine
   e di inaudita avarizia, vendendo senza distinzione le cose sacre and le profane,
   aveva attossicato tutto il mondo; e nondimeno era stato esaltato, con rarissima e
   quasi perpetua prosperità, dalla prima gioventù insino all'ultimo dì della vita sua,
   desiderando sempre cose grandissime e ottenendo più di quello desiderava.' *Storia
   d'Italia*, II, pp. 97-8.
6 Trans. Alexander, *History of Italy*, p. 166. 'Esempio potente a confondere l'arro-
   ganza di coloro i quali, presumendosi di scorgere con la debolezza degli occhi
   umani la profondità de' giudici divini, affermano ciò che di prospero o di avverso
   avviene agli uomini procedere o da' meriti o da' demeriti loro: come se tutto dì
   non apparisse molti buoni essere vessati ingiustamente e molti di pravo animo
   essere esaltati indebitamente; o come se, altrimenti interpretando, si derogasse alla
   giustizia e alla potenza di Dio; la amplitudine della quale, non ristretta a' termini
   brevi e presenti, in altro tempo e in altro luogo, con larga mano, con premi e con
   supplici sempiterni, riconosce i giusti dagli ingiusti.' *Storia d'Italia*, II, p. 98.

with which Alexander is condemned carries over into the denunciation of those who judge too simplistically. In the sweep and dignity of the final lines, however, any quality of personal anger is forgotten. Here, in language that is as unusually simple and bare as the condemnation of Alexander was uncharacteristically purple, we have a rare glimpse of Guicciardini moving to a higher moral vision of history. Momentarily at least, history becomes inviolate, an event occurring in the eye of God, and so not to be judged foolishly by childish notions of reward and punishment. In the name of a remoter God, Guicciardini dismisses the whole didactic tradition of Florentine historiography from Villani on.

Moments like this are crucial in a great book. They demonstrate the author's range and power and therefore help to establish his authority. Thus although it is far more typical of Guicciardini to tack against the wind than to run before it, the grand strain is still characteristic. And this passage is characteristic in another way. Seldom in the *Storia d'Italia* is the smooth flow of the narrative interrupted by an authorial presence. Even in this intervention, Guicciardini speaks with the objective majesty of history itself. Similarly, throughout the history the author remains impersonal and aloof. We might have expected just the opposite from the opening sentences of the book, which announce the author's intentions and begin with an emphatic 'I': 'I have decided to write about the events which have taken place in Italy within our memory ...' But it is as though once having taken the decision to set this world in motion the author feels it unnecessary to refer to himself again.[7] Occasionally the first line will find an echo in programmatic statements announcing that it is now necessary that we be told of the background to one situation or another, but these interruptions are few and impersonal. He never stops to chat as others do, never takes us aside for a confidence or addresses us rhetorically. The author does not identify himself with Florence, much less with the historical character Francesco Guicciardini, papal lieutenant. In this respect as in others Guicciardini reminds us of Thucydides, a historian equally involved in the events he narrates and equally absent from his own narrative. By contrast, Nardi slips (not quite noiselessly) between triple roles as author, witness, and actor, so that his history in places takes on added characteristics of chronicle or memoir.[8]

---

7 Even this opening is brief and 'objective' when compared to the apologies with which historians like Corio, Bembo, or Vettori preface their work. And one of the principal tendencies in the revisions of the 'Commentary' text is the suppression of the first person.

8 See Nardi, *Istorie della Città di Firenze* (Florence 1858), especially his account of his role in the 'Friday tumult' of 1527, an incident we have already looked at in

And yet Guicciardini's implicit presence is felt everywhere in the history. Neither his individual sentences nor the line of his narrative unfolds with the effortlessness or natural logic of more classical works. The wilfulness of his structures and of his style reveal his effort to control the elements of his analysis and to qualify and make as precise as possible the truth as he finds it. The author reveals his presence in this, even while he studiously effaces his personality. Guicciardini's order, then, is an imposed order that implicitly acknowledges the limits of reason and the fragmentary nature of experience.

Matching this veiled author, isolated in some cold tower of the imagination that appears to allow him equally clear sight of events in all corners of Italy, is an equally isolated reader. This stands in sharp contrast to the *campanilismo* of the *Storie fiorentine*, a loyalty which united the historian to his audience in implicit understanding. In that early work 'we,' 'us,' and 'our' came easily to Guicciardini in the unself-conscious intimacy of his identification with Florence. In the *Storia d'Italia*, however, the potential readership is enormously widened and the individual reader is so much more alone.[9] As noted earlier, this late history implies not so much an audience as a reader. Like the first person singular, the first person plural appears prominently in the opening lines of the book and then disappears.

terms of Guicciardini's self-description (*Istorie*, II, p. 116ff). The very rare occasions on which he reveals his identity are interesting. The first self-reference that I have found marks his appointment at a very young age as Florentine ambassador to Spain: '... imbasciadore Francesco Guicciardini, quello che scrisse questa istoria, dottore di legge, ancora tanto giovane che per l'età era, secondo le leggi della patria, inabile a esercitare qualunque magistrato ...' (*Storia*, III, 154-5). A quarter of a century later his pride at his youthful appointment was still uncontainable and spills over into this self-display, while his much larger historical role as papal governor and lieutenant is covered with suitable anonimity. Not modesty, of course, but decorum governs this decision. A second such intrusion, motivated by filial piety, is his identification of Piero Guicciardini as his father: 'gl'imbasciadori fiorentini, tra' quali fu Piero Guicciardini mio padre ...' (*Storia*, II, 134). In the sixteenth book he marvels over why Ieronimo Morone allowed himself to be taken in by the Marquis of Pescara and captured since he remembers well that Morone had told him that there was not a man in Italy more faithless or more evil than Pescara. Since these late books are not fully revised, however, it is likely that Guicciardini would have brought this observation into line with his usual practice.

9 One ironic indicator of this expanded readership is the way in which readers with local loyalties up and down the peninsula took offense with Guicciardini's views and rose to defend their cities. And to this category we might add the attacks of the Florentine exiles and the censorship of offensive passages by the Church. Apparently Guicciardini was able to offend everybody equally. For this literature, see V. Luciani, *Francesco Guicciardini and his European Reputation.*

The foreigners, says Guicciardini, have been brought in 'by our princes themselves' and thus from the start he identifies his readership with Italy rather than with Florence. But there can be no question of the wider identity fully substituting for the narrower. It would be centuries before such a reference could create bonds of sympathy between a writer and his unknown reader that could supplant the closed circle of city walls. Italy is still an unemotional abstraction, though the loss of independence had strengthened a sense of a common culture and a common fate. It is generally accepted that Guicciardini made a great leap when he abandoned the municipal horizons of earlier historical writing, but the implications of this 'progress' are not often examined. The extensiveness of his research, the complexity of his narrative, and not least the cold dispassionateness of his presence are all implied. Something is lost as well as won in Guicciardini's development from historian of Florence to historian of Italy.

Perhaps it is useful to see Guicciardini's use of classical conventions in the same light. If Guicciardini had projected himself to a great height in order to achieve an Italian perspective, he was able to support himself in that thinner atmosphere by borrowing two major conventions of classical historical writing. I have previously down-graded the discussion of rhetorical speeches and annalistic narrative because I do not regard the first as being disfunctional or the second as structurally very important. But there is another side to these classical borrowings that we should consider. By shaping nearby events with the canonical forms of a revered past, Guicciardini, like his humanist predecessors, gained a sense of perspective without which his narrative could not have been so vast and so measured. He could not always remain distant from the great changes of his lifetime, but in the lofty and serious tone of classicism he could find composure.

Gravity is the desired effect. Many of the characteristics we have observed amount to the search for a style that will lend dignity to the story. Guicciardini is impressed with the momentousness of the events he describes and through the formality and artificiality of his language he impresses us with the same idea. But if the dignity of the language is never lost, the same cannot be said of its decorum. Certainly there are times when we feel its presence strongly, as in the majestic rhetoric of the opening pages. There the grandeur of the theme dwarfs anything personal, ironic, or eccentric. But as we read further we observe the restless complexity of Guicciardini's narrative. There is nothing decorous in its rapidity, nor anything classical in its lack of straight lines. And this criss-cross geography also has its analytic and moral counterparts. In Bruni or even in Machiavelli events have definite causes and clear significance. In their histories there is a kind of narrative space which is rational and open. The motives behind an event, the event, and the significance of the event are carefully aligned on clear orthogonals that converge on a moral or political lesson as on a vanishing point. We saw that Guicciardini too used this technique in his early history. The story of the Pazzi plot was clearly told, and then its significance was elaborated, first for Florentine government and then for the politics of conspiracy in general. The straight lines of this progressive abstraction were equally evident in the portrait of Lorenzo, where good and bad characteristics could be defined easily because they were moral abstractions that did not depend on the specific historical context. These clear categories were then matched up with all the balance and care of an attentive hostess's seating arrangements.

We have already seen how the portraiture of the late history is transformed. The simple linearity of the early work is gone and with it a kind of ease and hopefulness. By comparison the new character study is a tangle in which radical changes of viewpoint are compressed into a few pages. Where clarity was the hallmark of the first, illusion and reality become the theme of the second, and irony its mood. That ease in which a single formula could define a man is lost, and now we are impressed by the difficulties of judgement, the illusiveness of expectation, and the incapacity of rulers. The writing is much more compressed and its scheme is more dynamic. The whole exercise depends on a kind of tension between the personalities of the two popes. And when Leo dies, Clement's single character is described in terms of internal contradictions which now replace the external ones. In its concreteness as well as in its complexities, the dual portrait distinguishes itself from its predecessor. Clement and Leo are not fitted into a pre-existing space which has been defined by universal standards of conduct. Rather they are judged by historical standards of success or failure which can only be clarified by the progress of the narrative itself. Hence we have the irony that the abstemious and intelligent Clement is revealed in time to be a failure in concrete historical terms, though abstractly he is certainly more virtuous than the lazy, pleasure-seeking Leo.

Similar observations can be made about the motivation and explanation of events. Here again we see a cluttering of narrative space. In Giovanni Villani's chronicle earthly events directly reflect divine providence and astrological influence. Thus even though his history lacks the lucidity the humanists would give to historical writing, it has a moral unambiguousness because there is always a direct and simple relationship between the event and the moral world which it reflects. The humanists bring to history a more sophisticated morality as well as more classical techniques of narrative. In a sense narrative was freed to respond to its own needs because human events no longer were required to mirror a non-historical world. Nonetheless, their didacticism was as strong as Villani's, and this very didacticism, located now within history rather than cutting across it, help to confer additional clarity on events. The moral and political lessons that humanist history teaches tie events together into well-understood units and give the reader a core of meaning to follow. But in Guicciardini the vestiges of didacticism have no such effect, and a multiplicity of overlapping explanations attaches to events. There are, of course, lessons in the *Storia d'Italia*, the wickedness of princes and the instability of human affairs being the most explicit. But the meaning of these 'salutiferi documenti' is meditative rather than didactic, passive rather than active. They enlighten the reader, but do not arm him. In this they are consistent with the prudential and paradoxical character of the *Ricordi*, many of which indeed show up as maxims in the history.

What are the consequences of our knowing these lessons? In the public sphere there can be none. Guicciardini offers us an understanding that is private to the political individual, though the subject is fully public. He alerts us to the complexity of history and politics, demanding prudence, foresight, rationality, humility in the face of Fortune. Himself a private man once again, he writes without a public commission. Addressing no single polity or recognizable collective group, Guicciardini speaks to a reader somewhat removed from the public forums of humanism, and unlike Bruni he neither makes a public celebration of the past nor prescribes for the future. As individual readers we are left to draw our own conclusions. History becomes a meditation.

In short, the *Storia d'Italia* lacks the public spirit, the composure, or the clarity that we expect from a work written in the classical spirit. There is grandeur but there is not simplicity. There are too many questions and too few lessons, too many objects and not enough space, too much irony and too little certainty, too much movement and too little repose, too much strain and very little ease. In all these respects Guicciardini has severely modified the traditions of humanism, though his continued dependency is equally obvious.

It is not fanciful to recognize in this some analogy to the anticlassical strain in the contemporary visual arts, usually called 'Mannerism.' New subjects call for experiment in form. Guicciardini broached a vast new subject and endowed history with a special kind of truthfulness. Just as Machiavelli helped to divorce politics from traditional moral codes, so Guicciardini simultaneously undermined both the moral and political uses of history which had been at the basis of the humanist historiography. Adopting Walter Friedlaender's description of classicism in his famous essay on the classical and anticlassical in sixteenth-century art, we can say that humanist historiography too was 'idealistically heightened and ethically stressed.'[10] It too sought an idealized space expressing 'a higher reality purified of everything accidental.' It too produced 'an unambiguous, constructed space in which equally unambiguous fixed figures move and act.' Of course, history can never purify itself of everything accidental in the sense that art can, but it can engage in a constant comparison of the accidental with the eternal, of the particular with the universal. The didacticism of the humanists provides that essential link between history as the study of particulars and a higher and normative world of ethical politics. Once that link is cut, as it is in Guicciardini, history is set free to pursue the particular *ad infinitum*, with not entirely happy results. Guicciardini's history has the 'freer and apparently more capricious rhythms' of Mannerist painting because it too has lost its obligation to the universal. His observation has an obsessive edge to it that comes from a tendency to equate particularily with truth. But his particulars are so concrete because his abstractions are so vague. Abstractions and higher forces remain, but they no longer constitute a unifying element. Ethics linger as ironies. Somewhere a remote God judges. Fortune enters history more frequently than ever, but only to complicate it. The most universal element in the history, it is the most inscrutable.

The humanist historian, and to a lesser degree the chronicler as well, had two functions, both of them public: his task was to commemorate and to teach. Guicciardini's lessons are few and negative, and the story he commemorates is a tragedy that never becomes heroic. More a modern than a Greek drama, it is filled with petty men and wasted opportunity. The grandeur of the history lies entirely in its vast scope, which is the historian's own contribution. Only he has been able to unify so many incidents into so large a story. And the creation is all the more personal as it corresponds to the boundaries of no recognized polity. To whom then would he commemorate these deeds? Not a historian by virtue of any public office or responsibility, he writes for posterity and to satisfy some private desire. And as he meditates on the vast story, he finds nothing in it that constitutes a public lesson except the mutability of history and the selfishness of power.

10 W.Friedlaender, *Mannerism and Anti-Mannerism in Italian Painting* (New York: Schocken 1965), pp. 6-8.

Appendix:

A Query on the Dating of the 'A' Text of the *Ricordi*

In the course of examining the *Ricordi* we paid special attention to that small group of maxims which appear in all four major stages of the work's development: the Q, A, B, and C texts. It is not difficult to see that these *ricordi*, which span almost two decades from 1512 to 1530, may be particularly significant as indicators of Guicciardini's development. But in examining one member of the group – the series Q 2, A 78, B 1, C 32 – we found a strange aberration from the expected development. If one judges by style and expression, it seems that the Q and B versions have affinities, as do the A and C versions, and thus either A or B is somehow out of sequence. And the particular series which we have examined is not unique. The sequences of *ricordi* associated with C 44, C 68, and C 134 show the same 'distorted' development as the series which culminates in C 32. Thus out of the eight *ricordi* which appear in all four versions, four belong to the type discussed, and I am also inclined to think that C 6 belongs in this class, though here the issue is less clear cut. In the remaining three out of eight, the differences between the A and B versions are marginal, as they are in most of the work. In short, in half of these eight cases the supposedly earlier A text seems clearly to be closer to the final C text than B is, and in no case is the reverse true.

On the face of it, it seems that B is strangely out of sequence. Emanuella Lugnani Scarano, the most recent critic of the *Ricordi*, has attempted to deal with this problem, though unfortunately without admitting that it is indeed a problem, by postulating a regression in Guicciardini's development as a result of the disastrous events of 1527. She sees a revived 'municipalism' and a polemical spirit in B, a falling off from the theoretical heights of A, that amounts to 'più che una stasi, una sorta di regressione di tono, uno chiaro scadimento di livello ...'[1]

1   E. Lugnani Scarano, 'Le redazioni dei *Ricordi*,' p. 231.

I find this explanation suspect. In general the notion of a regression seems of dubious value in intellectual history, and in particular, I cannot believe that by any process whatsoever, regressive or progressive, Guicciardini could have arrived in 1528 at the same thoughts and the same words as he had written in 1512, *if* he had in the meantime developed a more mature reflection on the same subject in 1525. Let us grant Lugnani Scarano first that Guicciardini's attention had been forced after 1527 to turn more exclusively to Florentine affairs than for many years past, and also that there was once again a republic in the city. Let us grant, if only for the sake of argument, that Guicciardini was in a polemical mood. (Though polemic is always a feature of the *Ricordi*: 'Chi disse uno popolo disse veramente uno animale pazzo, pieno di mille errorri, di mille confusione, sanza gusto, sanza deletto, sanza stabilità,' he remarks mildly.) But, on the other hand, it seems unlikely that Guicciardini's relations to the new republican regime could revive the optimism and determination of his youthful republican enthusiasm, nor could his return to his native city be expected under any circumstances to erase the breadth of experience and almost European perspective that he had acquired with many years of diplomatic service.[2]

Let us compare Guicciardini's situation in the two years, 1512 and 1528. In the first, he was a young man of great promise waiting in the wings of Florentine politics, setting his thoughts in order in the leisure hours of his first public office and dreaming of the reputation he would conquer on his return from Spain to his native city. In the latter year his leisure was of a different sort: forced retirement resulting from personal and public disaster and from his necessarily ambivalent relations to the new anti-Medicean regime in Florence. How could such a man recapture the optimism of his youthful writings? What could he see in those naively optimistic words that he wished still to put his name to? It was, after all, optimism that gave the early *ricordi* their special tone; the ambition he defends there is his own and the reputation he lauds is the one that he is determined to acquire. In 1528, though the recent crisis in Italy and in his own career might be expected to turn his thoughts in new directions or towards bitter self-criticism – witness the *Accusatoria*, *Defensoria*, and *Consolatoria* – it could hardly be reasonable to think that he would pull out of a drawer and dust off such old thoughts *if* in the meantime he had developed maturer reflections.

The fact that Guicciardini in his much altered situation of 1528 repeats his text of 1512 almost word for word can only mean that in idleness and

2 It is only fair to say, however, that the *Cose* does give evidence of strong republican feeling. Nonetheless, there is no hint in this second Florentine history of a revival of the language of the first.

some aimlessness he was recopying his earlier thoughts without much further reflection. In fact he is quite explicit on this point. He wrote in the notebook containing the B series that these were 'scritti innanzi al 1525 in altri quaderni che in questo, ma ridotti qui nel principio dell' anno 1528, nel grandissimo ozio che avevo, insieme con la più parte di quelli che sono indietro in questo quaderno.' Yet why not recopy A if, as is generally assumed, A is identical to that lost notebook of 1525? The *ricordi* of series B do not necessarily represent Guicciardini's thinking in 1528 unless it can be shown that he has made changes in the 1525 text. This is certainly the case if the identity of A with the 1525 text is accepted. Thus, it seems that there are only two possibilities: either Guicciardini changed his mind about this *ricordo* between 1525 and 1528 (and then changed it back in 1530); or the A text is not identical to the lost notebooks. If A is identical to the lost text, and identical in every detail, then the conclusion is forced on us that Guicciardini in this instance rejected a mature thought in favour of an immature one, only to reverse himself totally just two years later.

On the assumption of the uniform reliability of A, we are forced to regard B as somehow freakish or anachronistic, a startling hair-pin bend in Guicciardini's course. And this is exactly the choice Lugnani Scarano has made. The B text is, however, entirely reliable, as it exists in autograph; it is A that has been ingeniously reconstructed from later printed texts. Should we not consider the possibility that this reconstruction, ingenious though it is, may not be uniformly reliable? Let me cite the authority of Ridolfi here: 'For one may go on for ever developing theories,' he writes, 'but the accurate collation of all the manuscripts deriving from Piero Guicciardini's text can give us the perfect reconstruction of this text (and this is what Spongano has done admirably), but not the certainty of its complete authenticity and genuineness, still less of its derivation from a single autograph.' The possibility exists then, at least in Ridolfi's mind, that the present A text derives from more than one source and thus represents not one but several moments in the evolution of the *Ricordi.*[3]

If the A text represents anything, in whole or in part, other than the 1525 manuscript – a revision intermediate between B and C, for example, as logically in the present case it seems to be – then B 1 can have been written at any time between 1512 and 1528: and judging by its language and tone, as well as its numbering, it may well have been written quite early. This is certainly the conclusion suggested, though suggestion is the most one can expect, by my textual reading.

To recapitulate briefly, an anomaly exists in a particular group of *ricordi*, and it makes more sense to locate the difficulty, which is after all

3 Ridolfi, *Life*, p. 314, n.8.

only a problem of chronology not authenticity, in A, the hypothetical text, rather than in B, the dated and autograph text. If we insist on seeing the difficulty as being in B, we are forced into downgrading the value of an entire stage in the evolution of the work (and along with it the other writings that date from the same period), thus presenting a strange and unbelievable version of Guicciardini's intellectual biography. If the anomaly is in A, on the other hand, we are only forced to doubt the uniform (and I stress uniform) reliability of a hypothetical text reconstructed from later evidence. The choice is between authorial logic and editorial infallibility, and I would opt for the author.

Selected Bibliography

I / GUICCIARDINI'S WORKS

Guicciardini, Francesco. *Storia d'Italia*. Florence: printed by Lorenzo
  Torrentino, 1561.
- *Storia d'Italia*. Edited by Allessandro Gherardi, 4 Vols. Florence:
  Sansoni, 1919.
- *Storia d'Italia*. Edited by Costantino Panigada. *Opere*: Vols. I-V
  ('Scrittori d'Italia'). Bari: Laterza, 1929.
- *Storia d'Italia*. Edited by Silvana Seidel Menchi, 3 Vols. Turin:
  Einaudi, 1971.
- *Opere inedite*. Edited by Giuseppe Canestrini. 10 Vols. Florence, 1857-67.
- *Opere*. Edited by Emanuella Lugnani Scarano. Turin: Utet, 1970.
- *Storie fiorentine*. Edited by Roberto Palmarocchi. *Opere*: Vol. VI
  ('Scrittori d'Italia'). Bari: Laterza, 1931.
- *Dialogo e discorsi del reggimento di Firenze*. Edited by Roberto
  Palmarocchi. *Opere*: Vol. VII ('Scrittori d'Italia'). Bari: Laterza, 1932.
- *Scritti politici e ricordi*. Edited by Roberto Palmarocchi. *Opere*: Vol.
  VIII ('Scrittori d'Italia'). Bari: Laterza, 1933.
- *Ricordi: edizione critica*. Edited by Raffaele Spongano. ('Autori
  Classici e Documenti di Lingua Pubblicati dall' Accademia della
  Crusca'). Florence: Sansoni, 1951.
- *Cose fiorentine*. Edited by Roberto Ridolfi. Florence: Olschki, 1945.
- *Carteggi*. ('Fonti per la Storia d'Italia') 16 Vols. Vols. I-IV edited by
  Roberto Palmarocchi, and Vols. V-XVI edited by Pier Giorgio Ricci.
  Rome: Instituto Storico Italiano, 1938-1970.

II / GUICCIARDINI IN ENGLISH

Guicciardini, Francesco. *History of Italy and History of Florence*.
  Edited and abridged with an introduction by John R. Hale and
  translated by Cecil Grayson. New York: Washington Square Press, 1964.

- *The History of Italy*. Translated, edited, with notes and an Introduction
  by Sidney Alexander. New York: Macmillan, 1969.
- *Selected Writings*. Edited and introduced by Cecil Grayson and trans-
  lated by Margaret Grayson. London: © Oxford University Press, 1965,
  by permission of the Oxford University Press.
- *The History of Florence*. Translated by Mario Domandi. New York:
  Harper and Row, 1970.
- *Maxims and Reflections of a Renaissance Statesman ['Ricordi'].*
  Translated by Mario Domandi with an Introduction by Nicolai
  Rubinstein. New York: Harper and Row, 1965.

III / SECONDARY WORKS ON GUICCIARDINI

Albertini, Rudolph von. *Firenze dalla repubblica al principato: storia e
  coscienza politica*. Translated by C. Cristofolini. Turin: Einaudi, 1970.
Cantimori, Delio. 'Francesco Guicciardini,' *Storia della letteratura italiana*,
  vol. IV. Milano: Garzanti, 1966.
Cecchi, Emilio. *Ritratti e profili: saggi e note di letteratura italiana.*
  Milan: Garzanti, 1957.
Chabod, Federico. 'Francesco Guicciardini,' *Enciclopedia Italiana*,
  vol. XVIII.
De Caprariis, Vittorio. *Francesco Guicciardini: dalla politica alla storia.*
  Bari: Laterza, 1950.
De Sanctis, Francesco. *Storia della letteratura italiana.* Bari: Laterza, 1912.
- 'L'uomo del Guicciardini,' *Saggi critici*. Edited by L. Russo. Bari:
  Laterza, 1952.
Francesco Guicciardini nel IV centenario della morte (1540-1940)
  (Supplement No. 1 of *Rinascita.*) Florence: Centro Nazionale di Studi
  sul Rinascimento, 1940.
Fubini, Mario. 'Le quattro redazioni dei Ricordi del Guicciardini,' *Studi
  sulla letteratura del Rinascimento.* Florence: Sansoni, 1948.
Fueter, Eduard. *Histoire de l'historiographie moderne.* Paris: Alcan, 1914.
Garin, Eugenio. 'La storia nel pensiero del rinascimento,' *Medioevo e
  rinascimento: studi e ricerche.* Bari: Laterza, 1966.
Getto, Giovanni. 'Note sulla prosa della *Storia d'Italia* di Francesco
  Guicciardini,' *Aevum*, XV (1941).
Gilbert, Felix. 'Alcuni discorsi di uomini politici fiorentini,' *Archivio
  Storico Italiano*, XCIII (1935), 3-24.
- 'Guicciardini, Machiavelli, Valori on Lorenzo Magnifico,' *Renaissance
  News*, XI (1958), 107-14.

- *Machiavelli and Guicciardini: Politics and History in Sixteenth-Century Florence.* Princeton, N.J.: Princeton University Press, 1965.
- *Niccolò Machiavelli e la vita culturale del suo tempo.* Bologna: Il Mulino, 1964.
- 'The Venetian Constitution in Florentine Political Thought,' *Florentine Studies.* Edited by N. Rubinstein. London: Faber, 1968.
Goldthwaite, Richard A. *Private Wealth in Renaissance Florence: A Study of Four Families.* Princeton, N.J.: Princeton University Press, 1968.
Hale, John R. 'Introduction' to Francesco Guicciardini, *History of Italy and History of Florence.* Translated by Cecil Grayson. New York: Washington Square Press, 1964.
Ilardi, Vincent. 'Italianità among some Italian Intellectuals in the Early Sixteenth Century,' *Traditio,* XII (1956), 339-67.
Luciani, Vincent. *Francesco Guicciardini and His European Reputation.* New York: Karl Otto, 1936.
- 'Il Guicciardini e la Spagna,' *Papers of the Modern Language Association,* LVI (1941), 991-1006.
- 'Recent Guicciardini Studies (1945-48),' *Italica,* XXVII (1950), 109-27.
Lugnani Scarano, Emanuella. 'Le redazioni dei Ricordi e la storia del pensiero guicciardiniano dal 1512 al 1530,' *Giornale Storico della Letteratura Italiana,* CXLVII (1970), 183-259.
- *Guicciardini e la crisi del Rinascimento.* Bari: Laterza, 1973.
Lupo, Gentile, M. 'Studi sulla storiografia fiorentina alla corte di Cosimo I de' Medici,' *Annali della R. Scuola Normale Superiore di Pisa,* XIX (1906).
Malagoli, Luigi. *Francesco Guicciardini.* Florence: La Nuova Italia, 1939.
Mylonas, Alexander George. 'Francesco Guicciardini: A Study in the Transition of Florentine and Bolognese Politics, 1530-1534.' (Unpublished Ph.D. dissertation, Dept. of History, Harvard University, 1960).
Oietti, Ugo. 'La prosa del Guicciardini,' *Pegaso,* III, Pt. II (1931), 613-14.
Otetea, André. *François Guichardin, sa vie publique et sa pensée politique.* Paris: Librairie Picart, 1926.
Palmarocchi, Roberto. *Studi guicciardiniani.* Città di Castello: Lapi, 1947.
Ramat, Raffaele. *Il Guicciardini e la tragedia d'Italia.* Florence: Olschki, 1953.
Ridolfi, Roberto. *L'Archivio della famiglia Guicciardini.* (2nd ed.) Florence: Olschki, 1931.
- 'Francesco Guicciardini e Cosimo I,' *Archivio Storico Italiano,* CXXII (1964), 567-606.
- *Genesi della 'Storia d'Italia' guicciardiniana.* Florence: Olschki, 1939.

- 'L'itinerario storiografico del Guicciardini,' *Il Veltro*, V. fasc. 11-12 (1961), 5-16.
- *Opuscoli di storia letteraria e di erudizione.* Florence: Olschki, 1942.
- *The Life of Francesco Guicciardini.* Translated by Cecil Grayson. New York: Alfred A. Knopf, 1968.

Rossi, Paolo. *Guicciardini criminalista.* Milan: Fratelli Bocca, 1943.

Rubinstein, Nicolai. 'The "Storie Fiorentine" and the "Memorie di Famiglia" by Francesco Guicciardini,' *Rinascimento*, IV (1953), 171-225.

Santoro, Mario. *Fortuna, ragione, e prudenza nella civiltà letteraria del Cinquecento.* Naples: Liguori, 1967.

Sasso, Gennaro. 'Postilla guicciardiniana: i problemi del particulare,' *Studi in onore di Pietro Silva.* Firenze: 1957.

Spini, Giorgio. 'The Art of History in the Italian Counter-Reformation,' *The Late Italian Renaissance 1525-1630.* Edited by E. Cochrane. New York: Macmillan, 1970.

Spirito, Ugo. *Machiavelli e Guicciardini.* (rev. ed.) Florence: Sansoni, 1968.

Starn, Randolph. 'Francesco Guicciardini and His Brothers,' *Renaissance Studies in Honor of Hans Baron.* Edited by A. Molho and J.A. Tedeschi. De Kalb, Ill.: Northern Illinois University Press, 1971.

Tenenti, Alberto. 'La storiografia in Europa dal Quattro al Seicento,' *Nuove questioni di storia moderna.* Milan, Marzorati (1964).

Valeri, Nino. 'Sul *particulare* del Guicciardini,' *Belfagor* (V) 1950.

Villari, Pasquale. *Niccolo Machiavelli e i suoi tempi.* Florence: Le Monnier, 1877-82.

NOTE: For further bibliography on Guicciardini and related themes, the reader is referred to the series of bibliographical essays by Felix Gilbert in his *Machiavelli and Guicciardini.*

Index

UNIVERSITY OF TORONTO ROMANCE SERIES